▪ R O C K O N T H E ▪
▪ W I L D S I D E ▪

Gay Male Images in Popular
Music of the Rock Era

W A Y N E   S T U D E R

Leyland Publications
San Francisco

▪ ROCK ON THE WILD SIDE ▪

The Smiths in the mid-1980s, fronted by lead singer Morrissey. (Photo: Courtesy Sire Records.) See reviews on pp. 148, 221–223.

To the people who make music

for the fun and the freedom

and to George

for the love that makes it all worthwhile

Boy George. (Photo: Harry Goodwin. Michael Ochs Archives/Venice, CA.) See reviews on pp. 45–46, 65–67.

∎ T A B L E   O F   C O N T E N T S ∎

Photos: Front cover—David Bowie and Mick Ronson; back cover—Jobriath; page 2—The Smiths; p. 6—Boy George; p. 12—Wayne Studer (author); p. 36—David Bowie; p. 51—Bronski Beat; p. 77—Divine; p. 82—Erasure; p. 89—Flirtations; p. 112—Elton John; p. 121—Kinks; p. 127—Kitchens of Distinction; p. 137—Johnny Mathis; p. 141—Mickey Brewster; p. 149—Morrissey; p. 165—Pet Shop Boys; p. 180—Queen; p. 188—Lou Reed; p. 195—Tom Robinson; p. 199—Romanovsky & Phillips; p. 204—RuPaul; p. 218—Sister Double Happiness; p. 224—Soft Cell; p. 237—Sylvester; p. 251—Village People; p. 259—Tom Wilson Weinberg; p. 264—San Francisco Gay Men's Chorus.

Wayne Studer. (Photo: Barry.)

Wayne Studer (born 1955) is a lifelong fan of rock music—and nearly obsessive about it, too. He holds B.A. and M.A. degrees in English from the College of William and Mary and a Ph.D. in American Studies from the University of Minnesota. While at William and Mary he wrote record and concert reviews for the campus newspaper and served as one of its Associate Editors. As a Teaching Associate at the University of Minnesota he taught English Composition, Communications, and American Studies. Since 1983 he's made his living in the field of computer software, though continuing to write on the side. He lives in Minneapolis with his partner of more than thirteen years, George, and two terribly spoiled cats, Jeoffrey and Jasper.

Music filled our household when I was growing up. But unlike a lot of people who can say things like that, nobody in my family could play a musical instrument. Well, my brother was a late bloomer on the guitar. But we were all virtuosos on the record player and transistor radio. We loved to play music, whether it was my mother's recordings of church hymns, my father's Johnny Cash albums, my big brother's guitar rock, or my older sister's stack of 45's. I suspect I learned to sing along with music at the same time I was learning to talk.

As far as I can remember, however, the first record that really grabbed me—that I heard on the radio and realized that I personally loved and enjoyed without having been influenced by any other member of my family loving and enjoying it first—was Neil Sedaka's "Breaking Up Is Hard to Do." Not the treacly torch-song remake he crooned in the 1970s, but the hand-clapping uptempo doo-wop 1962 original with those urgent alto vocals of indeterminate gender. My lifelong love of pop music—particularly that branch known as "rock"—had begun.

Growing up gay, I received mixed messages from rock music. For one thing, before the 1970s, there was hardly any suggestion of gayness in rock at all—although, as you'll see, there were a few bits here and there. But as the seventies dawned and I entered my mid-teens, references to gay people began to appear with greater frequency in music, just as they did in the rest of our culture. Early on, the most notorious purveyor of "rock gayness" was David Bowie. Heaven help me, I didn't know what to think of *him* in 1972! Here I was, despite my love of rock music a good Southern Baptist teenager, active in my church youth group, trying desperately hard to repress my homosexuality—and I catch a glimpse of Bowie! I was shocked, horrified, almost sickened. I was sure that civilization as we knew it was coming to an end. Or maybe that the Second Coming was at hand. Surely this was a sign. I loudly disdained Bowie and his growing ranks of glam-rock ilk, detesting both them and their depraved music. A lot of my friends (probably totally secure heterosexuals to whom Bowie and his clones posed little psychosexual threat) laughed about it, insisting that it was all an act designed to get attention and increase record and ticket sales. How little I knew then the extent to which we were all correct. Yes, it *was* an act—a calculated commercial ploy—but it was also *more* than an act. Bowie and company, as we shall see, were both "gay" and "anti-gay," celebrants and exploiters, commentators and humorists, rubbing our collective noses in queerness with one hand and cashing our checks with the other.

The glitter faded during my college years. Bowie, for one, became Aladdin Sane during my freshman year and the Thin White Duke before graduation. But another powerful "gay angle" was emerging in popular music: disco. And with it emerged my awareness of how inescapably gay I was. I "came out" precisely at the peak of disco, when I discovered a whole new aspect of gayness in pop music. Like so many others of my generation, I set about dancing my reservations away—with an awful lot of postponed adolescence to catch up on. I had my year-and-a-half of wild abandon, got it out of my system, fell in love, and settled down. This happened to be right at the beginning of the AIDS crisis, which, while devastating, also forced a new openness and determination in the gay community.

And through it all I retained my intense interest in music.

The goal of this book is to examine the ways in which gay men have been described, depicted, or presented in pop music of the "rock era" (1955 to the present) and to demonstrate some ways in which gayness or "gay sensibilities" have influenced rock music. My goal is *not* to provide an exhaustive, comprehensive examination of every pop song in the rock era to deal with gayness in one way or another. Such a task would be virtually impossible since there's simply too much music and too many records. If I were to try such a thing, I'd surely miss quite a bit. No, I freely admit that my selection here is incomplete, skipping many items of which I'm aware and missing many, many more of which I'm surely unaware. I would welcome, however, any information that readers might be willing to share with me. If you know of any songs that you feel I have committed a cardinal sin by omitting, tell me about them and maybe I can deal with them in some future sequel or revised edition (knock on wood). You can contact me at P.O. Box 580187, Minneapolis, MN 55458-0187.

A number of performers have dealt with gayness in their music quite often, sometimes because they themselves are gay or bisexual. Rather than try to deal with every "gay" song those artists have recorded, I've generally chosen only a few—say, from one to three tracks—to focus on as examples of their work. In some cases, however, such as David Bowie, Elton John, and Queen, there were some things I just *had* to say about a larger number of their songs. In those cases I hope you will indulge me.

A great many people may wonder why I haven't also focused on lesbians in rock music. In fact, earlier drafts of my manuscript did so. But I discovered that lesbians aren't referred to in mainstream pop music of the rock era nearly as often as gay men are. Of more than 200 mainstream songs that I covered in an early version of this book, only about 10% dealt with depictions of lesbians. This fact is surely the result of sexism. From the perspective of our deeply sexist culture, lesbians are considered less interesting, noteworthy, and significant than gay men because, presumably, men are more interesting, noteworthy, and significant than women. In our society in general, gay men tend to be more visible than lesbians—and perhaps even to some extent more widely despised—because our culture tends to attach more importance to things that men do than to any parallel things that women do. In addition, the chief subject of rock music has always been sex, and rock music has always been dominated by men. Some of these men have exploited gayness or bisexuality as one aspect of the general sexual titillation and provocation that have been at the root of rock 'n' roll from the start. In these contexts, it's not surprising that male homosexuality should play a larger, far more visible role in rock music than female homosexuality.

Of course, if I had delved into the very large and vital "women's music scene"—which includes such superb artists as Holly Near, Meg Christian, Cris Williamson, and Teresa Trull, among many others—I would have greatly increased my pool of songs dealing with lesbians. But when I began to do this, I ran into another problem: my own lack of expertise. I'm thoroughly well versed in mainstream pop music, and can write about depictions of lesbians therein quite capably. And as a gay man, I'm well qualified to discuss the non-mainstream "gay male music scene." But my knowledge of non-mainstream "women's music" is limited, and I'm surely more attuned to the nuances regarding male homosexuality in music than to those of female homosexuality. I can better examine and comment on things that I know more about. While I could have conducted a "crash course" for myself on women's music, it would have taken a great deal of time—after which I probably *still* couldn't write about it as well as a similarly qualified lesbian could. So I decided to limit the focus of this book to images of gay men in popular music. I hope my readers will understand.

Even now, however, I'm continuing to educate myself about women's music, and perhaps before long I'll be ready to write a companion volume to this book, or maybe an expanded edition, in which depictions of lesbians in pop music receive their full share of attention. On the other hand, perhaps an enterprising lesbian music critic will beat me to the punch and do it first—and probably do a better job of it than I could. I'll be glad to share the data and insights I've already accumulated about images of lesbians in mainstream pop music with anyone who wishes to contact me about it. Knowledge grows by sharing it, not by hoarding it. In the meantime, I direct readers' attention to the Beatles' "Polythene Pam" (John Lennon's ignorant portrayal of a lesbian), Joan Baez's "Stephanie's Room," Sandra Bernhard's hilarious "The Women of Rock 'n' Roll," the Eurythmics' "Who's That Girl" (catch the video), Janis Ian's "Miracle Row/Maria," k.d. lang's "Bopalena" (currently available only on video or Canadian import), Laura Nyro's "Emmie," Michelle Shocked's "Sleep Keeps Me Awake," Patti Smith's remake of "Gloria," anything whatsoever by Phranc, and other songs too numerous to mention here.

One other thing along these lines: you'll notice that occasionally I *do* discuss songs that deal directly with lesbians, such as Elton John's infamous "All the Girls Love Alice." When I do this, it's for one of two reasons: either the reference to lesbians goes hand-in-hand with a reference to gay men,

15

so that the two inform each other, or the reference to lesbians is made under such circumstances that it provides valuable insight into the performer's or society's opinions about gay men. Let me assure you that this certainly does *not* mean that songs concerning lesbians are of interest or value only insofar as they relate to gay men. It simply means that those particular songs about lesbians are of special interest within the context and constraints of this book.

To summarize, here's what I've set out to do: to compile a selective list of pop songs from the rock era that are either about gay men, make reference to them in some way, or are of special interest to them, and to describe and critically analyze these songs, telling what they mean to me and trying as best I can to understand what the artists are saying to their listeners. I try to approach this task with humor and some irreverence, but I'm very serious about what I say, too. If I were a betting man, I'd wager that everyone who reads this book will find lots to disagree with. Perhaps even much to get angry over. Terrific. Listen to the music. Think about it. Form opinions. Love it or hate it. And take this book for what it is: the product of one flawed, opinionated devotee, a gay man in love with rock.

An earlier draft of this book contained far many more direct quotations from the songs I discuss. Because I was going beyond the confines of "fair use" in providing these lengthy excerpts, I went about trying to obtain formal permission from the various music publishing companies involved. Of the many publishing companies that I contacted, requesting permission to quote lyrics, *only two of them* provided that permission. Some simply ignored my letters, while others forthrightly denied me permission, generally offering no reason for their refusal. But it doesn't take much imagination to figure out why most if not all of them denied my requests. Often I was denied permission to quote lyrics that I had seen quoted in other books, apparently with the publishers' blessing. As far as I could tell, the chief difference between my book and these others was that I was dealing directly with the issue of gayness and the others weren't. I find it especially irksome that one company in particular issued a blanket refusal for me to quote from any of the *dozens* of songs in their catalog in which I was interested, while at the same time an executive with an affiliated record label was defending the right of one of their artists to record and release a controversial song that had drawn tremendous public outcry. This executive cited "freedom of expression" in defense of song lyrics that countless people found dangerous and offensive. But another branch of his media conglomerate was simultaneously restricting my own freedom of expression, denying me permission to quote their song lyrics. This was hypocrisy at its most blatant.

As a result of this experience, I cut back significantly on the quoting of lyrics so that my usage of them would fall within the realm of fair use, which permits brief quotations in the context of critical reviews or educa-

16

tional analysis, such as those found in this book. If any of my readers, however, don't feel that my text provides enough direct lyrical evidence to support my views and hypotheses, I recommend that they obtain a copy of the recordings in question and decide for themselves. I've done what I can.

I want to express my great appreciation to the two music publishers whom I contacted who didn't hesitate to grant me permission to quote lyrics. Rondor Music International, publishers of the Joan Armatrading song "Rosie" and of the Dire Straits songs "Les Boys" and "Money for Nothing," gave me permission to quote from those songs, as did Gelfand, Rennert & Feldman, administrators for Six Pictures Music, who granted permission for quoting from Randy Newman's "Half a Man." The copyright lines for these songs appear elsewhere in this book. I'm sure that there were at least a few other publishers who would have granted permission had I contacted them before receiving my dozens of rejections and thereupon embarked upon my fair use strategy. I'm tempted to specifically identify the companies that *denied* permission, but it probably wouldn't be wise to do so.

One other important note: in a society such as ours that is both homophobic and litigious in the extreme—the latter even more than the former, I'm convinced—a book such as this is virtually unpublishable without the statement that follows: *This book includes names and photographs of heterosexual, homosexual, and bisexual people. The inclusion of any person's name or photo in this book does not necessarily indicate that he or she is of any particular sexual orientation. By the same token, the mention of, reference to, or quotation from any song in this book is not to be construed as an implication that the songwriter(s), performer(s), or any other person(s) associated with that song is homosexual or bisexual.* Honest.

About the Organization of This Book

The detailed discussions of songs in this book are arranged alphabetically according to artist. When several songs by a particular artist are discussed, those songs are arranged chronologically. For each song, key information is provided: the songwriter(s), the year of initial release, the album on which it originally appeared, chart performance, and current availability. "Chart performance" refers to the peak position achieved by a single on *Billboard* magazine's "Hot 100" chart, unless otherwise noted. If a song failed to chart or wasn't released as a single, the peak position of the album on *Billboard*'s album chart is cited instead. "Availability" refers to the original album, unless otherwise noted. "CD" means that it's currently available on compact disc, "CS" on cassette, and "LP" on 12-inch long-playing record album. The current record label and base catalog number, deleting prefixes or suffixes that distinguish the various formats, are also listed. (The label and catalog number often differ from those of the original release. They're also subject to change at any time, but are accurate as of the publication date of this book.) Only domestic releases are considered, not imports. If a song isn't currently available as a domestic release, it's listed as out of print. Used record stores are your best bet for finding an out-of-print single or album—and usually at a surprisingly low price.

▪ A C K N O W L E D G M E N T S ▪

I have some debts to pay. For one thing, this book would have been impossible were it not for the Twin Cities' used record shops. I also thank Leyland Publications for their willingness to publish my work. Additional thanks to Quatrefoil Library and A Brother's Touch bookstore for simply existing; to the writers and publishers of the many reference works that provided invaluable sources of information, especially Joel Whitburn's remarkable books of *Billboard* chart data; to the various record-company personnel who supplied publicity photos; to Roadrunner Records for offering useful material; to Ray Kush for editing an early version of the manuscript and for making some recommendations; to my longtime friend and fellow rock-fanatic David Dennie, who provided helpful input and insight; to the Rev. Dr. Nadean Bishop and members of University Baptist Church in Minneapolis, who gave me very good advice and moral support; to my pal Bob Moen for letting me borrow records and for suggesting a new way of looking at "Chains of Love"; to John Mikenas for telling me about "Feed Jake"; and to Claude Peck and Winston Leyland for loaning hard-to-find albums. Finally, George Knudson—my partner, lover, and best friend all rolled into one—provided more patience and encouragement than I deserved. And not once did he express jealousy of my Macintosh. Thank you, George, for the love.

Songwriters:	Steven Tyler – Joe Perry – Desmond Child
Year of Release:	1987
Original Album:	*Permanent Vacation*
Chart Performance:	The single reached #14
Availability:	CD, CS (Geffen 24162)

Welcome to our nightmares, at least metaphorically speaking. Or somebody *else's* nightmares. Heavy metal music, even the relatively light brand of metal practiced by Aerosmith, draws much of its appeal from the fact that it provides teenagers, especially teenage males, with a wonderful device for infuriating their elders. Not only is it raucous, raunchy, and rebellious, but its lyrics often deal with subjects that most parents would just as soon not have blaring into their children's ears at jackhammer decibel levels. By those standards, "Dude (Looks Like a Lady)" indeed qualifies as the stuff of parental nightmares. But in that respect it's hardly any different from several thousand other osmium anthems. What sets "Dude" apart is its other frightful dream—namely, every heterosexual male's dread of going to a bar and picking up a fine-looking chick, only later to find out that she's actually a rooster. As the title warns, "Dude looks like a lady."

Except the warning is celebratory in tone. And why shouldn't it be? The whole point is to be outrageous, particularly with the purpose of offending adult sensibilities, because offending adults is what it's all about. Then again, if you're not a parent, or at least not a conservative clod devoid of a sense of humor, there's really not much here to take offense at. Despite the tired old terror of homosexual panic at the root of this record, Aerosmith carries it off with such good-natured aplomb that there's little for gay people to be offended at, either. Steve Tyler and company betray not an ounce of anger or hatred. Regarding the case of mistaken identity at the core of the song, their attitude seems to be, "Oh well, it's just one of those things. Better luck next time." Another positive aspect of "Dude (Looks Like a Lady)" is its basic listenability. In a genre of rock not known for its tunefulness, "Dude" can grow on you.

The video, played in heavy rotation on MTV, bears all of this out. Most of it consists of typical stage performance-style antics, with Aerosmith hamming up the heavy metal nightmare role. It's the bits of imagery that flash across the screen between performance shots that are most interesting. For the briefest moments, Tyler himself appears in full drag—and very good drag, I should add. You can barely tell that she's him. Other scenes show cross-dressing men and women, including a bearded bride arm-in-arm with a female groom. Tyler shrieks and hops about straddling his microphone stand, Joe Perry performs standard-fare guitar acrobatics, and knowing smiles abound among bandmates as tight-assed parents everywhere worry about what all of this might be doing to their adolescent sons' psycho-sexual development. It's the very essence of soft-core heavy metal, distilled to slightly over four minutes.

▪ PETER ALLEN ▪ "TWO BOYS" ▪

Songwriters:	Marvin Hamlisch – Carole Bayer Sager – Peter Allen
Year of Release:	1977
Original Album:	*I Could Have Been a Sailor*
Chart Performance:	Not released as a single, but the album reached #171
Availability:	CS (A&M 4739)

Peter Woolnaugh truly broke the bank for audacity. While in his late teens, already a veteran club singer and pianist in his native Australia, he left school and hooked up with another aspiring young man named Chris Bell. They changed their last names and toured the world as a cabaret act billed "Chris and Peter Allen." Judy Garland saw them perform, loved them, and signed them up as her opening act. Within a year Peter was engaged to Judy's daughter, Liza Minnelli. Three years later, in 1967, they married. Three more years later they separated. Reportedly on the very same day, Peter and Chris Allen also broke up, ending their partnership. Again after three years, the Allen-Minnelli divorce was finalized. By now it was 1973, and Peter Allen still hadn't hit his stride. That would begin a year later, when Olivia Newton-John turned one of his songs, "I Honestly Love You," into a huge international hit.

An aside: It was in the mid- or late seventies that I was visiting with my mother during a break from college. We sat watching television—the syndicated *Merv Griffin Show*, I think—and saw Peter Allen perform one of his best-known songs, "I Go to Rio." My mother was visibly distressed. "I don't like him," she said, if I recall correctly. He was dancing all over the stage, shaking his maracas, his big-puffed-sleeved silk shirt open to his waist. "He's so—so—*sissified*," she explained. I said nothing. I wasn't able to at that point in my life. (My mother would *never* say something like that to me now.)

Within a few years of that incident, Allen would release, back to back, a pair of records that boast two of my all-time favorite album titles: *I Could Have Been a Sailor* and *Bi-Coastal*. The title song of the latter manages quite nicely to delineate the narrator's fast-paced lifestyle and torn allegiance to both the East and West coasts in terms of his dual fascination with the boys of Broadway and the girls of Hollywood. Or is that the girls of

Broadway and the boys of Hollywood? I forget.

Far more worthy of our consideration, however, is the song "Two Boys" from *I Could Have Been a Sailor*. Despite a melody jarringly similar to Eric Carmen's earlier "All by Myself," it poignantly contrasts—you guessed it —two boys. Perhaps they are brothers, even twins (the first line indicates that they were born on the same day), or maybe they're not brothers at all but friends. Despite their superficial similarities, with them both being raised in that "good old-fashioned way," they do have significant differences. For one thing, one of them's a sports star, while the other has little or no interest in sports. Do you smell stereotypes in the air? Well, in view of the fact that this particular stereotype often turns out to be true, I suppose we can handle it. Besides, Allen (or whoever's responsible for the lyrics—most likely Carole Bayer Sager, with or without Allen's assistance) puts the kibosh on another stereotype, specifically discounting any hint of that old canard about dominating mothers. Good work, Carole and/or Peter.

The songwriters proceed to describe the developing differences in their protagonists' personalities, and then explain those differences as the boys become men. I'm not sure I like the implication that, because one "lets the girls go by," he therefore has reason to cry. But, then again, if he hasn't reconciled himself to his gayness, you can't deny the underlying truth of the inference. To be frank, a gay man who hasn't accepted the fact that he's gay is most likely *going* to cry—a lot. And I do like the double-edged assertion that the apparently heterosexual member of this duo will *never* cry. Presumably enjoying all the advantages of straight white maleness, he "never has a reason" to do so. Yet there's something sad, too, about someone who won't cry, someone who's missing a powerful emotional element in his life. I definitely think that's part of Allen's message here, especially since the final lines of the song stress the importance of emotional honesty:

> *And they never let their feelings show*
> *Afraid to let the other know*

And there's the great tragedy of this story: these two brothers or lifelong friends have a barrier of silence between them, a barrier that prevents them from sharing their true selves with each other. For the gay young man, the unspoken truth is obvious. He can't bring himself to tell his friend that he's gay. As for his friend, perhaps the very fact that he's emotionally constrained is his unshared burden.

Of course, there's another possibility. Maybe this other young man, the one who'll never cry, isn't as heterosexual as I've assumed all along. Yes, the song implies that he is, but it's sufficiently vague about it that he, too, could be gay. It may just be that, because of his particular circumstances, including his emotional makeup, he never feels the need to cry about it. Perhaps he's "out" to himself but not to his friend. So their mutual fear and the resulting silence ironically prevent them from sharing one of the most important things they have in common, their gayness. It's just a possibility, but even without it "Two Boys" remains a fine song.

Long before his death in June 1991 of AIDS-related illness, Peter Allen had proved himself a good songwriter, though he wasn't exactly my cup of soup as a performer. (I couldn't envision him as gangster Legs Diamond, and considering how badly that Broadway show flopped, hardly anybody else could, either.) But, as I said, he was an audacious one, and while audacity isn't exactly a rare commodity in show biz, Allen's style certainly was. I mean, *Bi-Coastal*. Really.

■ MARC ALMOND ■
■ "JACKY" AND "WHAT MAKES A MAN" ■

Songwriters:	Jacques Brel – Gerard Jouannest – Mort Shuman ("Jacky"); Charles Aznavour – Bradford Craig ("What Makes a Man")
Year of Release:	"Jacky" – 1991; "What Makes a Man" – 1993
Original Album:	"Jacky" – *Tenement Symphony*
	"What Makes a Man" – *12 Years of Tears*
Chart Performance:	Not released as singles, and albums didn't chart
Availability:	CD, CS (*Tenement Symphony* – Sire 26764; *12 Years of Tears* – Sire 45247)

Who is Marc Almond? He's an openly gay singer-songwriter and interpreter of other people's work. A writer for *The Advocate* once referred to him in print as a "shameless fag," meaning it, of course, as a compliment.

He's formerly one-half of the duo Soft Cell, best known for their hit single "Tainted Love." That song has, in fact, been Almond's chief exposure to the U.S. market, although he's had a number of solo hits in his native U.K.

He's pop music's *Campmeister Extraordinaire*. His take on the subject of masturbation, "Mother Fist and Her Five Daughters," has a tango beat. And regardless of what one might think of some of the other relatively tacky things he's done, anyone willing to christen one of his albums *Vermin in Ermine*, the cover of which displays him sitting atop a golden garbage can wearing a spangled jacket and matching devil horns, has my undying respect.

He's a kitsch-peddlar, he's good at it, and he knows it. It goes hand-in-hand with the camp. Almond takes as much delight in gussying up *faux* art and packaging it for a knowing audience as do the people who make those limited-edition gold-leaf-edged plates with unnaturally colored reproductions of scenes from *The Wizard of Oz*, Elvis Presley movies, or *Star Trek*

22

painted on them, ostensibly intended to function as investments but actually designed to cater to the bad taste of those who either don't know any better or do but don't give a damn. To be sure, Almond probably takes much *more* delight in it.

He's a torch singer at heart. Nearly everything he's done is a torch song. Even his speedy synth-pop dance tracks are little more than uptempo torch songs with lyrics as relentlessly gloomy as the slow ones. And as with all good torch singers, Almond's vocals tend toward the emotive, if not overly emotive.

I haven't quite made up my mind about him. He's at his best in those fast-paced dance-oriented numbers, when he seems to have fun without giving full vent to his inclinations for over-dramatization. His slower selections can also be quite enjoyable, as long as he chooses his material carefully. Often, however, he doesn't. I could cite various tracks to illustrate these points, but none do so better than a pair of French songs found on his conceptual live album *12 Years of Tears*. For instance, he turns Jacques Brel's ode to aspiration "Jacky" (which Almond previously recorded for his *Tenement Symphony* album) into a glitzy techno dance extravaganza, so uplifting in its sound that it's easy to forget the melancholy lyrics. This Marc Almond, who turns defeat into victory, is the one I most like listening to.

By contrast, there's Charles Aznavour's "What Makes a Man," a tiresome first-person narrative of what it means to be gay from the perspective of someone who doesn't sound any too happy about it. I don't suppose I'd be very comfortable, either, living with my mother deep into adulthood, scrubbing floors for her by day, working at night as a stripper in a "strange" bar, getting together afterwards with a gang of bitchy queens who spend their time exchanging tongue-in-cheek insults and gossiping viciously about absentees, but always going home "alone and friendless." As Almond sings histrionically to a piano accompaniment, his torchy ambitions given full rein, I wonder whether he realizes how dreadfully tedious this song is. Though he dedicates it to everyone who "dares to be different," I suspect he performs it either as an archival document of times thankfully past or as an attempt to achieve some sort of artsy ironic effect; that is to say, camp. Or maybe he's trying to become the male Edith Piaf.

But if camp is indeed what Almond's after, "What Makes a Man" doesn't so much miss the boat as sink it. Perhaps I'm narrow-minded, but I like humor in my camp, and that's something this track seems devoid of. Instead, it reeks of *pathos*. Too often, Almond's world appears desperate, dour, and depraved, inhabited by characters like the narrator of "What Makes a Man," who's nothing more than a grossly self-pitying if mildly defiant holdover from pre-Stonewall French cabaret. If you doubt this, listen to some of the other songs from *12 Years of Tears*: "Mr. Sad," "Waifs and Strays," "Tears Run Rings." A database of depression.

Yet everywhere you turn in the world of Marc Almond, there's an indomitable campiness that's often more memorable than the music itself. Take the cover of his *Enchanted* album, a Pierre et Gilles painted photograph that places him on the ocean floor (or is it an aquarium?) cheek-to-cheek with an anonymous female who, because of his gayness, serves as a mere figurine of pop sexuality. Or a bowtie, a tux, just a touch of makeup, and a thorny rose stem substituting for a baton on *Tenement Symphony*. Or stage costumes of leather, vinyl, and fake (I hope) leopard skin. Sometimes I think that if it weren't for the intellectual escape valve of camp, Almond would simply *pop*.

We don't have aphorisms like "There's no accounting for taste" (mine and anyone else's) and "One man's trash is another man's treasure" for nothing. It's just that trash and treasure are seldom so thoroughly intertwined as in Marc Almond. Again, I'm sure he knows it. Remember that *Vermin in Ermine* album cover?

▪ JON ANDERSSON ▪ "KEEP YOUR HANDS OFF" ▪

Songwriters:	Steven Blevins – Jeffrey Roy
Year of Release:	1987
Original Album:	*¡Verboten¡*
Chart Performance:	Not released as a single, and the album didn't chart
Availability:	CS, LP (Yea! 1287)

Not to be confused with Jon Anderson (the lead singer of Yes) and John Anderson (the country singer), Jon Andersson describes himself as a cabaret performer for whom "theatricality" is among the most important aspects of a song. Pretty much for this very reason, I'm not terribly fond of most of his album *¡Verboten¡*, in which he puts his dramatic voice to good use—leaving me cold in the process. Much of the music comes across as "supper-clubbish," theatrical-without-the-theatre. It would almost certainly sound better live than on record. It may well be just the kind of music that you would enjoy immensely, but to me it all seems so studied, so self-conscious, so much a *performance* that the performer himself gets in the way of enjoying the song itself. Kind of like Streisand at her worst. At her best (which, to be sure, is often) she's the greatest female vocalist—no, vocalist *period*—of her generation. At her worst, however, her technique overwhelms the song, so that I admire her larynx and attached muscles, but little else. Yet I'd love to watch even those performances *live*.

Several of the songs on Andersson's album are especially noteworthy, for good or for ill. For one thing, I detest the title tract for drawing implicit parallels among homosexuality, prostitution, and drug-dealing. Just because mainstream society often does so doesn't mean that gay people have to buy into that crap. On a perhaps more positive note, another selection, "Play with Me," provides wonderful insight into the Peter Pan syndrome that manifests itself in many gay men: "Here in my kingdom there's no one to tell us we can't, so won't you come play with me?"

One song in particular I find extremely interesting and enjoyable. In fact, I like it so much that I bought the album just for that one cut—something I rarely do. That song is "Keep Your Hands Off," which is unlike any "cabaret performance" I've ever heard. A delightfully light-hearted, New-Wavish, technopop workout on synthesizers and programmed percussion accompanies Andersson as he brashly warns everybody everywhere to leave his handsome, much-coveted boyfriend alone. As he puts it in the chorus:

> Get your hands off, he belongs to me
> He's mine and mine alone
> Get your hands off my property

What a catch this guy must be to inspire such possessiveness! Andersson's persona doesn't care a whit that his words may be politically and psychologically incorrect, not to mention personally unappealing. Correctness and appeal be damned; in the face of such all-consuming passion for another human being, all other considerations fall to the wayside. It's only incidental that both of the human beings involved in this particular primary relationship happen to be men.

To my ears, Andersson's intensely stylized vocals work better on "Keep Your Hands Off" than on all the rest of the album. Appropriate to the context of the song, he sounds a little crazy, fanatical, not quite "for real." But that's as it should be because it greatly enhances the song's humor. What a funny, marvelous thing it is to be so much in love. Of course, such obsessive devotion can also be unhealthy, even dangerous—and there's that edge of danger in Andersson's voice, too, almost as if he's the physical embodiment of tomorrow morning's headline, eager to go to press. Scary, funny, and touching, all at the same time—quite an achievement.

I'd be willing to bet that Jon Andersson's performances live are a sheer delight. Some of the same songs that I don't really care for on !Verboten¡ probably approach show-stopper status in Andersson's preferred cabaret setting. But until I get a chance to see him perform in person, I'll settle for "Keep Your Hands Off." And I'll be surprised if some mainstream performer (I have visions of Cyndi Lauper) doesn't eventually grab it and adapt it to his or her own use, perhaps in the process even turning it into a big hit.

Songwriter: Traditional blues; arranged by Alan Price
Year of Release: 1964
Original Album: *The Animals*
Chart Performance: The single was #1 in the U.S. for three weeks
Availability: Original album out of print; available on *Best of the Animals*, CD, CS, LP (ABKCO 4324)

This classic blues number about being trapped in a lifestyle of prostitution was traditionally sung from a female viewpoint. As the Animals perform it, it doesn't necessarily have to do with homosexuality, but male prostitution does provide the simplest, least contrived explanation of the young narrator's plight.

> *There is a house in New Orleans*
> *They call the Rising Sun*
> *And it's been the ruin of many a poor boy*
> *And, God, I know I'm one*

A later verse makes the situation still clearer, as the narrator warns mothers everywhere to tell their children not to repeat his mistakes, which have led to a "life in sin and misery." If you doubt the sexual nature of this warning, just listen to Dolly Parton's 1981 rendition or any other version in which the female persona is retained. No one can dispute that it's about prostitution—whether male or female.

When Dave Marsh writes about this record in *The Heart of Rock & Soul: The 1001 Greatest Singles Ever Made*, he says that the Animals' lead singer Eric Burdon "was far too macho . . . to sing the song from a female perspective, as it had always been sung. So he turned the lyric around, portraying the prostitute as a male and, thus, himself as a catamite." Catamite? I thought that term went out with "uranian" and "invert." And I thought *my* writing style was rococo. Then again, Marsh elsewhere describes Frankie Goes to Hollywood inappropriately as "a pack of androgynes." Two of the group's members were in fact gay, but they were hardly of the androgynous variety. Dave, you're probably Earth's single most brilliant rock critic (well, OK, along with Greil Marcus), but when it comes to the gay stuff, it sounds as though your thesaurus is running on autopilot.

▪ JOAN ARMATRADING ▪ "ROSIE" ▪

Songwriter:	Joan Armatrading
Year of Release:	1979
Original Album:	*How Cruel*
Chart Performance:	Not released as a single, but the album reached #136
Availability:	Original album out of print; available on *Track Record*, CD, CS (A&M 3319)

For those of you unfamiliar with Joan Armatrading, shame on you. Hailing from St. Kitts in the West Indies, she has an extremely eclectic approach to music, blending reggae, folk, rock, soul, and even occasional touches of blues and country-western to produce a unique sound—or, perhaps more accurately, body of sounds. When Tracy Chapman made it big a few years back, a lot of people compared her to Joan Armatrading. True, they're both black women who play acoustic guitar, and their voices are quite similar, but such a comparison still seems superficial to me. For one thing, relative newcomer Chapman benefits more from being categorized with veteran Armatrading than *vice versa*.

It's been suggested by some critics that several Armatrading songs carry covertly gay overtones, such as the vibrant "Join the Boys" ("Are you in, are you out?") from her eponymous 1976 LP. But when it comes to "Rosie" from the 1979 EP *How Cruel*, ain't nothin' covert about it:

> *Lipstick and rouge on his face*
> *He has his hair piled high*
> *Has a red umbrella*
> *And carries his head in the sky*

A reggae-ish number about a gay transvestite, "Rosie" features Armatrading assuming the role of the title character's friend, mildly admonishing him in the chorus for his coy ways:

> *And I said, "Aw, Rosie, don't you do that to the boys*
> *Don't you come on so willin'*
> *Don't you come on so strong*
> *It can be so chillin' when you act so willin'*
> *And your warmth sets like the sun"*

In other words, Rosie's a queenly prick-tease.

It's a fascinating portrait, if a nebulously unattractive one. The narrator disapproves of Rosie's behavior, though she seems to have a touch of grudging admiration for it as well. Rosie's a proud one, choosy and disdainful despite his coming from a very poor family ("His sister asks for dimes on the street"). He strikes me as a bitchy antihero, the kind of person you can't help but appreciate if you have the slightest feeling for human dignity in the face of overwhelming adversity. In short, there's a grandeur in his irresponsibility as he tries to "take things too far" (as Armatrading puts it), pushing the boundaries of what is commonly thought of as acceptable behavior. Kind of like the drag queens who stood up for themselves at Stonewall.

Meanwhile, more than a decade after "Rosie," Joan Armatrading presses on, regularly pleasing the critics and just as regularly being ignored by the record-buyers of America. Thank goodness she's developed a faithful cult audience that keeps her in business. A large portion of those faithful consists of lesbians who like her quasi-feminist style—and her highly distinctive, very enjoyable music.

▪ AUDIO TWO ▪ "WHATCHA LOOKIN' AT?" ▪

Songwriters:	Milk Dee – Gizmo
Year of Release:	1990
Original Album:	*I Don't Care—The Album*
Chart Performance:	Not released as a single, and the album didn't chart
Availability:	CD, CS, LP (First Priority 91358)

Many of the people who do rap music seem to have difficulty coping with the reality of gay people existing in the same universe with them. While rock music in general is infected with heterosexism, I find it especially disheartening that members of an oppressed minority feel the need to shore up their own status by oppressing other minorities. And, not so incidentally, it works both ways. African-Americans have to work out their homophobia, and white gays have to work out their racism.

In the meantime, people should be on guard against hatemongering like that expressed in the rap group Audio Two's reprehensible "Whatcha Lookin' At?": "gay mothers get punched in the face." The Robinson brothers, Milk Dee and Gizmo, succinctly let it be known that they "hate faggots," whom they regard as infesting Greenwich Village "like meat on some maggots." Never mind the careless, nonsensical inverted imagery of meat living on maggots. I mean, why let *logic* get in the way of such a perfect rhyme? It's not easy to find another word that rhymes with "faggots." Take my advice, guys, it's much simpler to rhyme "queers": beers, ears, gears, jeers, rears, tears—and fears.

■ JOAN BAEZ ■
■ "THE ALTER BOY AND THE THIEF" ■

Songwriter:	Joan Baez
Year of Release:	1977
Original Album:	*Blowin' Away*
Chart Performance:	Not released as a single, but the album reached #54
Availability:	CD (Epic 34697)

No, that's not a typographical error, at least not on my part or on the part of the publisher of this book. The name of the song is "The Alter Boy and the Thief." That's how it's printed several times on Joan Baez's *Blowin' Away* album, including the lyric sheet. *Not* "Altar Boy." So I guess my question is this: Were Ms. Baez and everyone else connected with the printing of this album's paper components extremely careless about their spelling, or is this seemingly incorrect spelling of "altar" intentional? Is there a subtle pun at work here? Let's see—

In a 1979 interview in *Christopher Street*, Baez (whose bisexuality is well documented) said that "The Alter Boy and the Thief" was inspired by a visit to a gay bar in Santa Monica called the Pink Elephant. There she spied a "marvelous, very tall, appealing-looking, muscular woman, a magnificent disco dancer," who, as it turned out, was male. The song that grew out of this experience has a lovely if somewhat fragmentary melody coupled with highly evocative lyrics about seeking out "the safety of shadows and numbers" where "nothing encumbers the buying and selling of casual looks."

Baez transports us to an almost dreamlike world, but one that many of us would find familiar—a gay bar. She says she has gone there, as have the others, "to find some relief." She briefly describes other habitués of this bar, including "the seven-foot black with the emerald ring" and "a trucker with kids and a wife." Another she imagines (though it probably doesn't take too much imagination) grew up in a disapproving household, "hardly your daddy's little man." With a delightful economy of language Baez manages to convey some sense of the great diversity of the gay world. But as the song progresses, she focuses her attention on one couple dancing together, describing the timeless quality that she observes in the romantic image they present, referring to them as "the alter boy and the thief."

For the time being I want to spell *altar boy* "correctly." An "altar boy" is, of course, a church acolyte—a symbol of innocence. A thief is, well, a thief—a symbol of anything but innocence. I don't for a minute think that Baez is suggesting that these two fellows dancing together are literally an altar boy and a thief. How would she know their backgrounds and avocations, observing a pair of dancing strangers from across a smoky, dimly lit room? They must look, however, like total opposites. One, the "altar

29

boy," is young, almost virginal in appearance. The "thief" is older, more experienced. They must seem to have come from different worlds. And yet they've found unity, peace, and love in this gay bar, if only for a short while. It's truly one of the most beautiful images to be found in the entire corpus of gay-related pop music. It's an extraordinarily beautiful image for pop music, period.

Now, back to the matter of the apparently misspelled "alter boy." It may simply be just that: a mistake, a misspelled word that Baez herself and no editor caught. On the other hand, perhaps the seeming error was intentional. Maybe Baez is punning on the words "alter" and "altar." Could it be that her altar boy figure is also an alter boy in that he has been altered somehow? After all, one of the characters she described earlier in the song —the one who was "hardly daddy's little man"—had plucked his eyebrows and presumably done other things to change his appearance. He had quit his job and changed his name. And she says, he's "nearly beyond belief." Maybe her "altar boy" has been similarly changed and is therefore also an "alter boy." Perhaps he's even meant to be taken for the same young man whom she described before.

So that's what I get from the spelling of "Alter Boy." Or at least that's what I would have gotten if it weren't for the fact that in a reprinting of the lyrics in the 1979 Robbins Music Corporation anthology *And Then I Wrote . . .* , the spelling is rendered "The Altar Boy and the Thief," which strongly indicates that the original spelling was a mistake after all. Sigh. So much for hot-shot lyrical analysis.

▪ BEATLES ▪
▪ "YOU'VE GOT TO HIDE YOUR LOVE AWAY" ▪

Songwriters:	John Lennon – Paul McCartney (primarily Lennon)
Year of Release:	1965
Original Album:	*Help!*
Chart Performance:	Not released as a single, but the album reached #1
Availability:	CD, CS, LP (Capitol 46439)

John Lennon reportedly wrote this song shortly after a visit with the Beatles' manager, Brian Epstein, who was gay. It has been suggested (by gay singer-songwriter Tom Robinson, among others) that Lennon derived the title and at least some of the sentiment that underlies the song from his awareness of the internal torment Epstein felt because of his homosexuality. Indeed, aside from a few heterosexual reference points (the pronoun "she"), the lyrics strongly lend themselves to such an interpretation.

However, in his 1984 biography of Lennon, Ray Coleman notes that the

"Head Beatle" could be horribly nasty to Epstein, often baiting and insulting him on account of his being both gay and Jewish. For instance, when Epstein asked Lennon's advice in 1964 as to a possible title for his autobiography, Lennon cruelly suggested *Queer Jew*. When the book came out it was called *A Cellarful of Noise*, but Lennon referred to it as *A Cellarful of Boys*. For a possible incidence of this sort of bigotry emerging in the Beatles' music itself, read on—

▪ BEATLES ▪ "BABY, YOU'RE A RICH MAN" ▪

Songwriters:	John Lennon – Paul McCartney (primarily Lennon)
Year of Release:	1967
Original Album:	*Magical Mystery Tour*
Chart Performance:	The single reached #34
Availability:	CD, CS, LP (Capitol 48062)

Everyone seems to agree that "Baby, You're a Rich Man" is about Brian Epstein. According to widespread rumor and even at least one source in a position to know, something very interesting occurs during the fadeout of this song. As the Beatles continue to chant, "Baby, you're a rich man, too," with the volume ever decreasing, it *sounds* at one point as though they vary the words to "Baby, you're a *rich fag Jew*." If this is actually the case (and not just a misinterpretation caused by distortion and/or the power of suggestion), then it's quite simply an ugly, ungrateful slur against Epstein —the man who did more than anyone else aside from themselves and their producer, George Martin, to make them the worldwide phenomenon that they were.

As the editors of *The Book of Rock Lists* have put it, Epstein "was certainly Jewish, definitely wealthy, and probably gay." They're being a bit demure there. Brian Epstein was as surely homosexual as he was rich and Jewish, although whether the word "gay" can be accurately applied to an apparently self-hating victim of pre-Stonewall society seems debatable. Epstein died of a drug overdose—generally acknowledged as accidental but believed by some to have been intentional—less than four months after the Beatles recorded "Baby, You're a Rich Man" and less than eight weeks after it was released.

Songwriters:	John Lennon – Paul McCartney (primarily McCartney)
Year of Release:	1968
Original Album:	*The Beatles* (commonly known as *The White Album*)
Chart Performance:	Not released as a single, but the album reached #1
Availability:	CD, CS, LP (Capitol 46443)

I include this song with some hesitation because any possibility that it has something to do with gay people may have been entirely accidental. On the surface, it appears to be a simple song about the fairly ordinary court-ship of a male-female couple, Desmond and Molly. But something interest-ing happens in the last verse, which is sung twice. The first time it's sung, our protagonists fulfill "traditional" gender expectations, with Desmond working in the "market place" and Molly staying at home and doing "her pretty face." But the second time McCartney sings this verse, there's a switch, with Molly working and Desmond staying home and doing "his pretty face." In the last line of the stanza, he's even referred to as a "she."

What's going on here? In his book *The Beatles, Lennon and Me*, Pete Shotton, a longtime friend of John Lennon's, described the recording session for "Ob-La-Di, Ob-La-Da." He writes that, after having cut a seemingly flawless version of the song, McCartney started laughing and declared they'd have to record the song all over again. When the others pro-tested, claiming the performance was perfect, McCartney disagreed, not-ing that he had accidentally sung, "Desmond stays at home and does his pretty face," when he should have sung "Molly." A quick playback con-firmed it. But then McCartney changed his mind about re-recording. "Oh, it sounds great anyway," he said. "Everyone will wonder whether Des-mond's a bisexual or a transvestite." At least that's how Pete Shotton tells the tale.

Indeed, McCartney was right, and I have firsthand proof. Back when I was in high school (around 1970, give or take a year), one of my teachers, a big-time rock music fan, told me that he thought "Ob-La-Di, Ob-La-Da" was about a homosexual couple. He attributed this to the fact that the Beatles were cool, daring, advanced, and "with it," and that they wanted to slip a little something into the song to titillate their fans.

I suppose you can look at this whole business three ways. One, that despite McCartney's retained blooper, "Ob-La-Di, Ob-La-Da" remains an innocuous (some would say revolting) piece of fluff about the courtship of a heterosexual couple named Desmond and Molly, and that's that. Two, that because McCartney consciously decided to retain the mistake and was fully aware of how it might be interpreted, he effectively rewrote the song on the spot and it therefore became a song in which one or both of its characters are gay, bisexual, transvestite, or whatever. And three, that maybe—just maybe—McCartney's "flub" was intentional and calculated, and that he very much *wanted* to produce a potentially controversial or at least perplexing song about sexually ambiguous characters. If this is true, then his recording studio "mistake" might have been his way of "sneaking it in" and seeing how his fellow Beatles would react.

This is all speculative, of course. It does seem strange, however, that McCartney's vocal "slip-up" involves the switching of more than just one word, as one might expect from a mere error. *Several* words are flipped about, including some—but notably not all—of the pronouns. As a result, the roles of Desmond and Molly are totally reversed, and Desmond himself becomes a drag queen. And one other thing—what do you make of that odd, pixie-demonic laughter that punctuates the song at times, particularly at the end?

For those of you who are familiar with the intentional fallacy (namely, the concept that what an artist "intends" in his or her work is utterly irrelevant because his or her subconscious mind may be at work and, besides, any artwork is a collaboration between the artist and the audience, in which the audience contributes as much to the total aesthetic experience as the artist), this discussion is moot, anyway. In short, what McCartney or the Beatles did or didn't intend "Ob-La-Di, Ob-La-Da" to be doesn't count for squat. What matters is what it means to us, the listeners. But just speaking for myself, mind you, it seems more than a little queer.

▪ BEATLES ▪ "GET BACK" ▪

Songwriters:	John Lennon – Paul McCartney (primarily McCartney)
Year of Release:	1969
Original Album:	*Let It Be*
Chart Performance:	The single reached #1 and stayed there for five weeks
Availability:	CD, CS, LP (Capitol 46447)

Are you intrigued as much as I am by the second verse of this McCartney classic—the one about "Sweet Loretta Martin" who "thought she was a woman, but she was another man"? Frankly, I'm not sure *what* to make of it. Is Loretta Martin, who is "sweet," after all, supposed to be a gay man? A lesbian? A transvestite? A transsexual? Is this just abject nonsense masquerading as profundity? Or is it merely a bad joke? And does anyone besides myself care?

■ BLACKBERRI & FRIENDS ■
■ "IT'S OKAY" and "PLEASE HELP ME TO FORGET" ■

Songwriter:	Blackberri (both songs)
Year of Release:	1981
Original Album:	*Finally*
Chart Performance:	Not released as singles, and the album didn't chart
Availability:	Out of print (Bea B. Queen 1001)

It's tempting but simplistic to describe Blackberri as a "gay Richie Havens." More accurately, he's a gay African-American folksinger who doesn't hesitate to incorporate elements of other musical idioms, ranging from blues to country-western to jazz, into his stylistic vocabulary. True, the Richie Havens influence comes through, but it doesn't dominate. Both a semi-legend and welcome fixture in the Bay-area music scene for nearly two decades, Blackberri offers pro-gay messages in a way that delights as it educates—musically as well as politically. Wasn't it Aristotle who said that delighting and educating were the hallmarks of great art? Well, even if this isn't great art, it *is* good music.

The LP *Finally* by Blackberri & Friends is a genuine classic in the field of "gay music." It has such quality, depth, and richness—both musical and lyrical—that I hesitate to focus on any particular songs. But that's my chosen format, so hey, here goes. My personal faves are the album opener, "It's Okay," and the song that closes the first side (with the advent of compact discs, how much longer is *that* terminology—"first side"—going to make sense to most people?), "Please Help Me to Forget." These two songs alone demonstrate Blackberri's versatility as a performer.

In "It's Okay," Blackberri describes the pain of losing an intimate boyhood friend, a "childhood lover," because of social pressure. With his rough, bluesy voice backed by a small acoustic ensemble of bongos, assorted percussion, and his own guitar, he paints an ideal (perhaps idealized) portrait of their innocent passion as they walked "hand in hand," deeply in love:

> But people didn't understand
> Their ridicule destroyed our plan

In spite of Blackberri's intense desire to continue their friendship, his friend couldn't bear the active disapproval of others, and broke it off, avoiding all contact with his former lover. It's a terribly sad story.

Except that Blackberri turns it into a triumph, reflected in the upbeat, lightly skipping tempo of the music. Looking back on this experience with the wisdom of years, he understands exactly what happened and why. And though he still feels some sadness about it, he also feels confidence and joy about himself. He, for one, knows who he is: "Can't you see? It's good for me. . . . And it feels so grand." Gay people can be victors in the war that

34

homophobic society wages against them. Knowledge, especially of oneself, is power.

By contrast, "Please Help Me to Forget" reveals a far more comic side of Blackberri. Or at least I hope it does, because it's funny whether he intends it to be or not. Lyrically, "Please Help Me to Forget" is just what the title implies—a song in which the narrator strives to get over the pain of an old relationship via a new one. But it's the music that really defines this piece: early-sixties Nashville, thick with nasal twang and pedal-steel guitar. Since it comes across like a black Porter Wagoner doing a gay "Help Me, Rhonda," it can only be a parody, and a very good, very campy one at that.

Actually, I think the only real lapse in taste on *Finally* is the track "Eat the Rich," which gives vent to some nasty socialistic sentiments. Sorry, but it's no more moral to dehumanize the rich than it is to dehumanize the poor. (Don't think I'm just saying that because I'm rich, because I'm *not*—rich, that is.) And in light of recent substantiated reports that during the communist revolution in China some zealous freedom-fighters really *did* make meals of their better-to-do neighbors, I can't bring myself to appreciate the humor of the song's puns and overall conceit. But that's an ahistorical quibble. The tremendous merits of the album greatly outweigh its minor flaws. I greatly appreciate Blackberri, his music-making friends, and *Finally*. As the record's own liner notes suggest, they all provide excellent examples of "Gay pride in action"—action that you can sing along with as you drum on your tabletop to your heart's content.

P.S.—As far as I can tell, *Finally* is no longer available, though I do hope I'm wrong about that. The letters I sent to the last known business address of Blackberri's record label and distributor returned unopened. If you want to hear it, you may have to do as I did and borrow it from a friend. So let's hear it for very old and deep record collections. May they never *totally* be replaced by CDs, if only for the sake of album cover art.

David Bowie, ca. 1972, during his Ziggy Stardust period. (Photo: Courtesy Rykodisc.)

▪ DAVID BOWIE ▪ "QUEEN BITCH" ▪

Songwriter:	David Bowie
Year of Release:	1971
Original Album:	*Hunky Dory*
Chart Performance:	Not released as a single, but the album reached #93
Availability:	CD, CS, LP (Rykodisc 10133)

The details, influence, and ch-ch-ch-changes of David Bowie's career are well enough documented that I hardly need to expound on them here. Suffice it to say that Bowie practically invented glam or glitter rock, whichever you want to call it, and became the first major rock star not only to *say* that he was gay or bisexual but also to employ an exaggeratedly gay and/or bisexual image as a drawing card. To be sure, Bowie wasn't the first rock star to capitalize on androgyny: Little Richard, the early Beatles with their revolutionary "long hair," Mick Jagger, and a host of "teen idols" all had their androgynous angles. As other pop-culture analysts have noted—perhaps simplistically but probably accurately—the androgyny of some male rock stars has always served a dual function: for adolescent males it represents a form of rebellion, while for adolescent females (at least those who are heterosexual) it offers a transitional, "safe" outlet for budding sexual desire.

David Bowie fit into this pattern, but with a vengeance. During the years in which he established his reputation, 1970 to 1974, Bowie played it Queer with a capital Q, creating a recording and stage persona that was so outrageous, so bizarre, that it was as if he knew that people wouldn't be able to help themselves but notice him, follow him, hang on his every move, the way that people are impelled to look at circus freak shows or automobile accidents.

One track from Bowie's 1971 album *Hunky Dory* (the cover of which features him doing his best Greta Garbo impersonation) exemplifies the early Bowie-as-Queer persona. Singing over a fast, hard-rocking beat, the narrator of "Queen Bitch" tells us about the scene he's witnessing from the window of his cheap hotel room, including the "cruisers below." As we quickly learn, the narrator is lonely and jealous because his boyfriend (who's "tryin' hard to pull sister Flo") is down in the street, hoping to pick up someone for sex.

Of course, being way up on the eleventh floor, he can't see any details, so he lets his imagination run wild. His dark, envious fantasy focuses on one particular character whom he knows all too well:

> She's so swishy in her satin and tat
> In her frockcoat and bipperty bopperty hat
> Oh God, I could do better than that

What a marvelously ambiguous line! Does Bowie's lonesome narrator mean that even he could find a better trick than that swishy creature, or does he mean that even he could do better drag? Either way, the irony is devastating.

Our antihero proceeds to dish out the lowdown on the subject of his loathing, the Queen Bitch of the title, who's "known in the darkest clubs." The narrator then returns to his fantasy, imagining how this rival is seducing his boyfriend. When he says, "It could have been me," he's probably visualizing himself in place of the Queen Bitch, seducing his lover. But in his miserable, desperate state of mind he might be imagining himself in place of his boyfriend, being seduced by the Queen Bitch. It hardly matters since, in either case, he's totally consumed by sorrow and self-pity. His loneliness turns to anger and he decides to call it quits with his boyfriend. Still, despite this moment of pride and/or spite, he lets us know that he has his regrets about how things have turned out between them. And then it's back to the chorus, with the "bipperty bopperty hat" and "God, I could do better than that."

On its own, "Queen Bitch" is a remarkable track, a testament to the demons lurking in the human psyche. It makes you wonder the extent to which the Queen Bitch him/herself may be a fabrication of a morbid mind, a symbolic scapegoat "Everyqueen" onto which the narrator can project his envy and rage. It even makes you wonder whether the narrator himself may be the true Queen Bitch of the title—the queen of bitchiness, bitching about his own miserable lot in life.

Taking all of that into consideration, Bowie's work here is skillful, rich, and complex in a disturbing sort of way—but it's that disturbing quality that, well, disturbs me, especially when viewed in a larger context. "Queen Bitch" is but one example of the way in which David Bowie, at least during the early 1970s, would brazenly and repeatedly exploit homosexuality. It was obvious that he was exploiting it for its shock value, for the attention it would bring him as something new, daring, and different, but that angle doesn't bother me in the least. What concerns me is the relentlessly gloomy, depraved vision of homosexuality that emerges from the Bowie corpus. There's nothing "gay" about it. It's all bitchiness, shock, pain, misery, loathing, and decadence. And "Queen Bitch" is far from the last time we'll see it.

Songwriter: David Bowie
Year of Release: 1972
Original Album: *Changesonebowie*
Chart Performance: The single didn't chart, but the album (released several years after the single itself) reached #10
Availability: CD, CS, LP (Rykodisc 20171, retitled *Changesbowie*)

Atop a raging current of strummed acoustic guitars and a throbbing bass, Bowie virtually squeals out the lyrics to this song in his queenliest voice. The words, heavily distorted by echo, mauled by Bowie's own bizarre inflections, and periodically punctuated by campy shrieks, are almost unintelligible. Thank heaven for published sheet music, allowing us to read what can't be gleaned from mere listening. That way, we get to learn about Joe, who's "awful strong," but you can "bet your life he's putting us on." About *what*, pray tell?

Bowie proves himself at his stereotypically bitchy best/worst here. That dishy remark about "Joe" might have been repeated in any given gay bar twenty years ago, around the time when this was recorded. As the song progresses, it becomes obvious that we're overhearing a spat between lovers, replete with brickbats and sarcastic hyperbole. And the chorus is perfectly clear:

John, I'm only dancing
She turns me on

The narrator's boyfriend is miffed because he's been dancing with someone else, identified only by the pronoun "she." This suggests that the other party is female, but given the traditional penchant of queens to switch pronouns, one can't be too certain of that. Whichever is the case, Bowie's persona assures his companion that he's just dancing with this other person and nothing more.

Long before the end of the song, electric guitars have joined in—wailing, slightly out of tune and key, Bowie's tried-and-true musical motif for queerdom. Early in his career, Bowie flaunted apparent homosexuality at every opportunity (and I know that "flaunted" is a loaded word, often used by heterosexists, but it's totally appropriate here), using gayness as an attention-getting gimmick. For instance, the original cover of his album *The Man Who Sold the World*, released during the same period, shows a very long-haired Bowie lounging on a sofa wearing what can only be described as a dress. This image apparently so alarmed U.S. record executives that, for the album's American release, they gave it not one but two new covers: the first with a strange Pop-Art-influenced comic book motif, and the second featuring a performance shot of Bowie, still looking androgynous enough to be titillating but not so much so as to alienate masses of potential consumers.

But all the while it seemed as though Bowie relished queerness *because* it was queer, *not* because it was natural. Those out-of-whack guitars paralleled his personae, which were also out-of-whack. In other words, it's hard to tell whether Bowie was pandering to his listeners' stereotypical concepts about gay people or whether he was actually performing a sort of media cross between a drag ball and a Queer Nation kiss-in. Was he exhibiting internalized homophobia, outlandish liberationism, or shrewd marketing? Probably a little of each. As we shall see, throughout his fascinating career—it's become a cliché to describe it as "chameleon-like"—Bowie has generally managed to have his gay cake and eat it, too.

▪ DAVID BOWIE ▪ "THE JEAN GENIE" ▪

Songwriter:	David Bowie
Year of Release:	1973
Original Album:	*Aladdin Sane*
Chart Performance:	The single reached #71
Availability:	CD, CS, LP (Rykodisc 10135)

It was around this period that Bowie in concert would often get down on his knees in front of his lead guitarist, Mick Ronson, and "fellate" his instrument. A consummate showman, he.

One of Bowie's best-known, most popular numbers, "The Jean Genie" was reportedly dually inspired by the author Jean Genet (that much is obvious from the title) and the legendary proto-punk rocker Iggy Pop, who was known for intentionally injuring himself with multiple cuts and bruises during his performances. I have no idea how one is supposed to interpret lyrics that include references to being "strung out on lasers" and eating razors, to keeping "all your dead hair for making up underwear," and to biting on neon and sleeping in a capsule. My best guess is that it means absolutely nothing at all and is simply meant to *sound* profoundly decadent. But only David Bowie knows for sure, and I don't think he's talking. However, I just *love* the chorus with its infectious clap-along beat and lines about how the screaming, bawling Jean Genie "lives on his back" and "loves chimney stacks." *Oh, don't ask.* I'm not altogether sure I could tell you, but the imagination reels at the prospect.

▪ DAVID BOWIE ▪ "CRACKED ACTOR" ▪

Songwriter:	David Bowie
Year of Release:	1973
Original Album:	*Aladdin Sane*
Chart Performance:	Not released as a single, but the album reached #17
Availability:	CD, CS, LP (Rykodisc 10135)

I'm sorry, but this is the sickest puppy of a bad litter. The song's narrator—the "cracked actor" of the title, which sums up Bowie's attitude toward him—is talking to a prostitute he's just picked up. And though the gender of that prostitute is never stated, it's almost certainly male. The narrator is middle-aged, a has-been in the film industry, but convinced of his own legendary status—essentially a male Norma Desmond. In the chorus, Bowie leaves no doubt as to what this actor wants from his hustler, including the demand that he "Suck, baby, suck, give me your head." I couldn't believe my ears the first time I heard *that* on my college radio station back in 1973.

There's more, but I'm sure you've caught the drift. Actually, I consider *Aladdin Sane* an excellent LP, one of Bowie's best. "Drive-in Saturday," "Panic in Detroit, and "The Jean Genie" are all great rock songs, and I personally find the enigmatic title cut of the album fascinating. But I can't help feeling that Bowie has anything but disdain for most of his characters, this aging gay actor in particular. Recorded during the very height of his orange-haired androgyne *qua* space-alien pose (queerness as a sci-fi conceit), "Cracked Actor" may just be the most unpleasant and exploitive of Bowie's attempts to cash in on the "bisexual chic" that he himself did so much to establish in rock music of the early seventies.

■ DAVID BOWIE ■
■ "SWEET THING" AND "REBEL REBEL" ■

Songwriter:	David Bowie (both songs)
Year of Release:	1974
Original Album:	*Diamond Dogs*
Chart Performance:	"Rebel Rebel" reached #64; "Sweet Thing" wasn't released as a single
Availability:	CD, CS, LP (Rykodisc 10137)

Here we have the perfect example of Bowie's gaydom-as-freakshow *schtick*. Our first clue resides in the cover of the *Diamond Dogs* album itself, with a now magenta-haired, earringed, braceleted, heavily made-up Bowie lounging naked on a wooden stage as a circus sideshow attraction, the lower half of his body metamorphosing centaur-like into that of a dog (a decidedly *male* dog, the prominent and offending organ being air-brushed out on early pressings), behind him a sign hawking "The Strangest Living Curiosities." I mean, I do see the humor in it; I suppose I even see the point Bowie was presumably making in relation to the album's general theme of the Great Decay to Come. But *really*. As Bowie himself cries in "Rebel Rebel," "You tacky thing!"

Diamond Dogs is set in a bleak, depraved futuristic landscape in which human beings exploit each other almost carnivorously. Three interconnected tracks—"Sweet Thing," "Candidate," and "Sweet Thing (Reprise)"—constitute a dark, brooding, creepy mini-epic about backrooms, cellars, consensual pain, and thoroughly impersonal sex. Amidst some of the most disturbing, discordant, *queerest*-sounding music ever recorded, we hear Bowie intone, "Hope, boys, it's a sweet thing," immediately adding that it's a "cheap thing," too. Bowie then volunteers insights into how "weird" a place the world is and offers sage advice about committing suicide by jumping into the river. No wonder this stuff depressed and scared the hell out of me when I was a young gay man, barely out of his teens, not yet "out" to himself. *Not* a positive image.

But Bowie wasn't interested in positive images. He was interested in a form of success (and, to his credit, a thoroughly original albeit warped pop-artistic vision) that virtually required shock and dismay. After the "Sweet Thing" trilogy has segued into "Rebel Rebel," Bowie's first lines of the new song constitute quintessential genderfuck, but with a mildly self-parodying edge, the pot calling the kettle fuchsia:

> *You've got your mother in a whirl*
> *She's not sure if you're a boy or a girl*

Ah, words guaranteed to resonate in the hearts of most teenagers, male and female, who live to send their parents in a tizzy.

Not me, of course. I was a good boy.

■ DAVID BOWIE ■ "BOYS KEEP SWINGING" ■

Songwriters:	David Bowie – Brian Eno
Year of Release:	1979
Original Album:	*Lodger*
Chart Performance:	The single failed to make the charts, but the album reached #20
Availability:	CD, CS, LP (Rykodisc 10146)

I could go on for a dozen pages or more about this one, but I'll constrain myself. David Bowie's "Boys Keep Swinging," while not at all ostensibly a gay song, boasts more layers than a wedding cake, and at least one of those layers is decidedly homoerotic.

Take the title itself. Given Bowie's history of ambisexual music, one might expect "swinging" here to refer to sexual swinging—either in a more "traditional" sense, meaning "freewheeling," as in "swinging singles," or in an overtly bisexual sense, as in swinging from one gender of partner to another. And it may indeed mean that. Or you might even think of swinging hips, as in a particularly "swishy" boy. But, when you examine the lyrics closely, you'll see that at least on an uppermost level, the swinging actually being evoked is the swinging of *fists*, as in boxing—as in "stay in there swinging"—so that the words "boys keep swinging" is in fact a highly metaphorical way of saying "boys keep trying" or "boys keep pressing on." This becomes quite apparent when you consider the recurring words "Boys keep swinging, boys always work it out." Boys—presumably as opposed to girls—always keep at it, whatever "it" may be.

Now, let's take the blatant sexism of such a supposition for what it is—blatant sexism, yes, but of an especially silly variety that begs to be interpreted satirically. What else sounds a wee bit satirical here? Basically the song turns out to be a litany of all the great things there are about being a boy—all of the fun you have, all of the challenges you face, all of the advantages you enjoy (over girls, of course). The words "When you're a boy" are repeated over and over again as Bowie proclaims how nifty it is that boys get to wear uniforms (!). And, if that weren't enough—

> *Other boys check you out*
> *You get a girl when you're a boy*

—the first line an obvious double-entendre emphasized by the fact that it's immediately followed by the self-consciously heterosexual assertion "You get a girl," as if the narrator were suddenly aware of the homoerotic implications of what he had just said and therefore immediately tries to "cover" for himself. It's a virtual definition of the closet.

Between the song's repetitive "When you're a boy" and its equally repetitive cry of "Boys!" sung by an all-male chorus of multi-tracked Bowie —which manages to sound both fey and brutal, almost like a mob of *femme* Nazis—the whole thing starts to take on a somewhat fascistic air, which may not be at all surprising in light of the overt sexism of the lyrics. In fact, the cold, dissonant, mechanistic, thudding, grating instrumental track of the song, typical of many Bowie–Eno collaborations, only serves to heighten the fascist mood. Taken altogether, it's a singularly unattractive piece of music about a singularly unattractive idea—that boys have it better than girls, perhaps even that boys are *better* than girls— which is made more bitterly ironic by the idealization of maleness, *boyness* if you will, implicit in many forms of homoeroticism.

I mean, what is Bowie *saying* here? Is he criticizing the idealization of masculinity or celebrating it? Is he attacking sexism or promoting it? Is he advocating dogged persistence or is he ridiculing it? Is he parodying fascism or evoking it? Is he campy or serious? Is he being heterosexual, homosexual, or bisexual? I just don't know where to stop.

And I haven't even mentioned the video yet! If you haven't seen it, you haven't seen Bowie at both his most dismaying and genderfucking brilliant. Though this song drones on and on about how great it is to be a boy, chanting "Boys!" over and over again, the focus of the video is on a trio of drag queens—all three of them Bowie himself—singing male background vocals together via the miracle of trick photography. Near the end of the video, each strolls out on stage (of a beauty pageant? a model's runway?), one by one, glaring directly at the viewer, only to pull off his wig and disdainfully smear his lipstick on the back of his hand—a variation on a common, even traditional gesture of drag queens at the end of their performances. The last of the three is the most disturbing of all, in which Bowie plays the drag not only with gender but with age, mimicking an elderly woman (possibly Bette Davis, one can't be sure) complete with wrinkles, walking slowly, delicately, painfully up to the camera until— after just the slightest of pauses, one final tease—the wig is again torn off and the lipstick is smeared. Despite the fact that we've seen it happen twice before, this third, almost violent destruction of the drag illusion is the most shocking of all.

Boys keep swinging indeed!

▪ DAVID BOWIE ▪ "MODERN LOVE" ▪

Songwriter:	David Bowie
Year of Release:	1983
Original Album:	*Let's Dance*
Chart Performance:	The single reached #14
Availability:	CD, CS, LP (EMI 46002)

The Gay Trivia Book cites David Bowie's "Modern Love" as a song with gay subject matter. This assertion appears to be based on the song's opening line, "I catch the paper boy." Speaking for myself, I don't really see much evidence there or anywhere else in the song. The chorus, which asserts how Bowie's persona is "never gonna fall for modern love," may provide additional clues. Since the thought of getting "to the church on time" (an apparent reference to *My Fair Lady*, of all things) seems to "terrify" the narrator, perhaps there's an implicit criticism of traditional heterosexual marriage.

I don't know. It all seems so tenuous to me, especially considering that it's coming from a one-time admitted bisexual who had long been married and who, in recent years on different occasions, has taken either to stating that his earlier flirtations with homosexuality were mere youthful experimentations, over and done with, or to denying that his gayness was ever anything more than an act. Besides, Bowie has quite a few other songs that are much "gayer" than this, regardless of whether they're mere act or experimentation. I would relegate "Modern Love" to the "maybe, maybe not" category and move on to more fruitful territory, if you'll pardon the expression.

▪ BOY GEORGE ▪ "NO CLAUSE 28" ▪

Songwriters:	George O'Dowd – Ian Maidman – Glen Nightingale – Richie Stevens – Fletcher
Year of Release:	1988
Original Album:	*The Martyr Mantras*
Chart Performance:	Both the single and the album failed to make the charts
Availability:	CD, CS (Virgin 91596)

When, in 1988, the Thatcher government of Great Britain backed discriminatory anti-gay legislation that came to be known by the shorthand designation "Clause 28," a firestorm of protest erupted in the British gay community—and in decent non-gay quarters, too. Perhaps the most famous protest came in the form of the technopop dance record "No Clause 28" (according to some accounts originally titled "Stop Clause 28") by none other than Boy George, late of Culture Club. (More about them later.) It was available in the U.S. only as an import until 1991, when a remixed version appeared on *The Martyr Mantras*, an LP that bespoke of the Boy's recent conversion to or at least fascination with Hare Krishna. Ah, life's strange journeys.

Aesthetically nondescript—the melody, what there is of one, is so trivial and repetitive that Boy George might just as well have been rapping—"No Clause 28" is chock-full of synthesized pops, squiggles, wheezes, and electronically distorted background vocals, employing advanced technology to make up in interesting sounds what it lacks in musical substance. Its importance, however, lies not in melodic terms but rather in political ones. As an in-your-face assault on bigotry as a policy of right-wing governmental social engineering, it's hard to beat.

Not content merely to parody anti-gay prejudices, George takes turns hurling accusations and tweaking the conservative noses of the Thatcherites:

> *You want to make us hated*
> *You want to make us slide*
> *No Clause 28*
> *Brother, you're much too late*

Too late to turn back the hands of time—that is, to push gay people back into their closets and throw away the key.

Rest assured, Boy George knows that there's a lot at stake. An undercurrent of fear gives urgency to his words as he warns about what Clause 28 and the reactionary notions that inspired it would mean for gay people. He boldly asserts, "You don't need this scare, don't need this fascist groove." The lyrics wind down with some fashionable jibes against pornography (an issue on which the extreme right and the extreme left too often find themselves snuggling uncomfortably) and Ms. Thatcher herself, finally resorting to repetition for no other reason than to stretch the track out to a length palatable to latter-day discos. But the point's made. "No Clause 28" very ably serves its purpose as well-intentioned, highly danceable propaganda.

46

▪ *BOY MEETS BOY* (THE ENTIRE CAST ALBUM) ▪

Songwriter:	Bill Solly
Year of Release:	1980
Original Album:	*Boy Meets Boy*
Chart Performance:	The album didn't chart
Availability:	Out of print (Private Editions FRC/PES-1)

Given the well-known fondness many if not most gay men have for the musical theater, it was only a matter of time before somebody would write a gay—*very* gay—musical comedy. And I don't mean *La Cage Aux Folles*. I mean *Boy Meets Boy*, first performed in 1979 (several years before *La Cage*) by Minneapolis' dearly departed Out & About Theatre company and released on record the following year. I cite here the entire album because it would be both foolish and unjust to single out any one or two songs as standouts (although, just between you and me, the marvelously silly "It's a Dolly" is one of my favorites).

With music and lyrics by Bill Solly, who also collaborated with Donald Ward on the book, *Boy Meets Boy* is a joyous, delightful show that harkens back to the pre-World War II days of musical comedy, when the Broadway stage was dominated by the Gershwins and by Rodgers and Hart. Its plot is no great shakes—basically, as the title suggests, it's a variation on the old boy-meets-girl, boy-loses-girl, boy-gets-girl formula, except, of course, the "girl" is *also* a boy in this particular mix. The love that dared not speak its name in the days of *Anything Goes* is now celebrating itself in song and dance with all the gusto of its earlier heterosexual parallels.

One of the things that I find especially wonderful about *Boy Meets Boy* is the fact that its gayness is no issue at all. Gayness simply *is*, and the musical assumes of its audience the same acceptance of and acquaintance with homosexuality that they afford to heterosexuality. To be sure, the overwhelming majority of the show's audience has always consisted of gay people, so this is no great stretch.

While a tad amateurish in some ways, *Boy Meets Boy* is nonetheless a terrific work, full of hummable melodies, witty lyrics, and even a winking innocence that more than makes up for any flaws. I remember attending a performance during its original Minneapolis production—back when I was in the early flush of my own coming out process—absolutely thrilled by what I was seeing and hearing on stage. It was, without question, one of the most positive evenings in the theater I have ever spent. For that, I'll always be grateful to Bill Solly and everyone else who had anything to do with creating *Boy Meets Boy*. It deserves perennial restaging across the country, anywhere where there are gay people—which, I don't have to tell you, is everywhere.

▪ BOYS TOWN GANG ▪ "CRUISIN' THE STREETS" ▪

Songwriter:	Bill Motley
Year of Release:	1981
Original Album:	*Cruisin' the Streets*
Chart Performance:	Not released as a single, and the album failed to chart
Availability:	Out of print (Moby Dick BTG-231)

Let's say, for a moment, that it's 1981. You're a gay man in the mood for a little new music, so you cruise on down to your local record shop. While perusing the bins you spy a brand new album by a group called the Boys Town Gang. The record jacket depicts a San Francisco street scene. Real macho types hanging around a pickup truck. There's a construction worker—or at least a guy dressed like a construction worker—leaning against a wall. Another guy wears a T-shirt, leather vest, and leather cap. A burly type has on a flannel shirt and jeans. Seven butch fellows in all. Might as well plunk down your cash.

Back at your humble abode, you give your new acquisition a spin on the old turntable. (Remember, this is before the CD revolution.) The record features just two extended cuts, one per side. Side One is a "suite" that blends the Ashford and Simpson classics "Remember Me" and "Ain't No Mountain High Enough." But it's Side Two that really makes you sit up and listen. Not because of the music. "Cruisin' the Streets" is basic, functional disco. No polyrhythms, studio wizardry, gaudy synthesizer flourishes, or grand orchestral passages. Just guitars, bass, keyboards, horns, and that thump-thump-thump-thump percussion.

But those lyrics! Sung by a woman, they sound like a female habitué of the gay bar scene offering sisterly advice to the gay men of the world:

Hey there all you hunky guys dancing to the beat
Listen good, I'll tell you about a new way to meet

This "new way," as it turns out, is simply the "cruisin' the streets" of the title. You don't know what's so "new" about that. But you're in no mood to argue. Besides, your female friend gets more explicit:

You might find a big ol' boy, nine inches or more
It's all true, I promise you, it might make you sore

My, my. She even catalogues some of the locales where you're liable to find such action: Folsom, Castro, Christopher Street, Fire Island.

Then things get *really* interesting. The vocals cease and the music is pared down to little more than that omnipresent thump-thump-thump-thump. You get to eavesdrop on the after-midnight street scene. A couple of the boys compare notes on a well-endowed fellow they've both been cruising. Another twosome check each other out, only to learn that they don't share each other's particular sexual interests. Two more guys start getting it on right there on the street as an enraptured woman watches. But this three-some is interrupted by a pair of verbally abusive cops who, as luck would have it, are themselves drawn into the lusty thick of things. Then the vocals kick in again, carrying you to the fade-out. You like it. You like it a lot.

• • • • •

It's now 1984. There's a new album by the Boys Town Gang, this one titled *A Cast of Thousands*. Naturally, you buy it, too. "A Good Man Is Hard to Find," as well as most of the rest of the album, is again sung by women—only this time, instead of sounding like sisterly advice, it bears the aura of pretend heterosexuality. Why the veneer of *women* singing about how hard it is to find a good man? As if they couldn't find enough good male singers. Besides, the music this time is duller than the butter knives in a reform-school cafeteria.

You take it back to the store. Fortunately, you know the clerk; you tricked with him once in a former life. "This album is embarrassing," you complain. "Any chance of a refund, or at least of exchanging it for something else?"

"Sweetcakes," he says with an exasperated smile, "you buys your record and you takes your chances. This is *not* a charitable institution!"

So you take it back home. Who knows? Maybe it'll grow on you. Maybe it'll become a collector's item. And maybe flying monkeys will come to your next birthday party.

▪ BILLY BRAGG ▪ "SEXUALITY" ▪

Songwriters:	Billy Bragg – Johnny Marr
Year of Release:	1991
Original Album:	*Don't Try This at Home*
Chart Performance:	Both the single and the album failed to reach the charts
Availability:	CD, CS, LP (Elektra 61121)

What's a superb piece of guitar-driven power-pop—it's as though New Wave never got old—with some chest-thumpingly heterosexual opening lines ("I've had relations with girls of many nations") sung by a guy with a thick cockney accent doing in a book like this? Well, quicker than you can say "politically correct," Billy Bragg informs us,

And just because you're gay
I won't turn you away

immediately adding that he has no doubt we can find "common ground."

That's in the first verse of "Sexuality," a bouncy, ringing celebration of healthy, open-minded, live-and-let-live attitudes about the human body and human relationships. Bragg, a left-wing British semi-folkie who's not afraid to rock out every now and then, provides an extra-special treat in the chorus: "Sexuality—your laws do not apply to me," followed by a demand for equality. And in a later stanza, Bragg assures us that "safe sex doesn't mean no sex," that all you need is "imagination" to keep your love-life alive. Highly recommended.

Also worth noting: "Trust," from the same album, in which Bragg adopts the role of either a woman or a gay man concerned about AIDS. "He's already been inside me." When was the last time you heard an avowedly straight man sing anything like *that*?

▪ BRONSKI BEAT ▪ "SMALLTOWN BOY" ▪

Songwriters:	Jimmy Somerville – Larry Steinbachek – Steve Bronski
Year of Release:	1984
Original Album:	*The Age of Consent*
Chart Performance:	The single reached #48
Availability:	CD, CS, LP (MCA 5538)

During its brief but notable existence, Bronski Beat was an openly gay British technopop trio whose music distinguished itself with throbbing post-disco rhythms, heavy use of synthesizers, and the thin but piercing falsetto lead vocals of Jimmy Somerville. Although several of their songs were played extensively in dance clubs—especially the gay dance clubs—"Smalltown Boy" became their only single to make it onto the U.S. charts, and even then it failed to crack the Top Forty. No doubt its subject matter clashed with its potential for greater success.

"Smalltown Boy" is, in essence, a socially conscious domestic drama set to a dance beat. The lyrics (written by Somerville) concern a young man who leaves home because of his sexual orientation. It isn't entirely clear whether he is leaving willingly or has been thrown out, though the fact that he stands alone on a platform at the train station strongly suggests the latter. "Mother will never understand," sings Somerville, "For the love that you need will never be found at home."

Our unnamed hero has long led a somewhat tortured life, tormented physically, verbally, and emotionally by his "peers." But he has nonetheless managed to maintain his dignity, refusing to let his abusers see him cry. The repeated, haunting, "run away, run away, run away" background vocal only adds to the song's overall air of uptempo melancholy.

The video for "Smalltown Boy" features Somerville himself in the role

50

Bronski Beat, ca. 1984: Jimmy Somerville (top center), Steve Bronski, and Larry Stein-
bachek. (Photo: Courtesy MCA Records.)

of the central character and makes it more apparent that his leaving home isn't entirely voluntary. We see him not altogether successful in concealing his desire for his male schoolmates as he watches them swimming and diving. We also see how at some point he's been attacked and beaten for being gay, and then brought home by the police. For most of the video, he is indeed "sad and lonely," as the lyrics say, but a happy ending is provided. On the train he's greeted by the smiling, friendly faces of a pair of young men like himself, and they begin to laugh and talk together as the train makes its way to the big city where, presumably, a happier life awaits them.

This ending is, in fact, at the very root of "gayness" as opposed to mere homosexuality. The hero of "Smalltown Boy" is a victim, but he's not *just* a victim. He always holds on to his dignity ("you'd never cry to them") and, though he "runs away," the video makes it clear that he is running away to a better, more fulfilling life with a new "gay family" to take the place of the old, unsupportive one. The "Smalltown Boy" transcends his victim status to become a victor.

▪ BRONSKI BEAT ▪ "WHY?" ▪

Songwriters:	Jimmy Somerville – Larry Steinbachek – Steve Bronski
Year of Release:	1984
Original Album:	*The Age of Consent*
Chart Performance:	The single didn't make it onto the charts, but the album reached #36
Availability:	CD, CS, LP (MCA 5538)

"Why?" received some airplay on some of the more adventurous U.S. radio stations and, as noted previously, was also widely played in gay dance clubs. It's basically a protest song, its central "why?" being as much an accusation as a question. Lead singer and lyricist Jimmy Somerville addresses a gay-basher, noting the contempt in his eyes: "Blood on your fist—can you tell me why?" Of course, society has given the gay-basher all the reasons he needs for hatred and violence, citing gay sexuality as an "illness" and a "sin."

The narrator then turns to his lover and affirms their relationship, despite society's disapproval—"You and me together, fighting for our love"—but there remains an intense feeling of injustice and resentment. "Can you tell me why?" That is, why should they or anybody else have to fight for their love? Why should it be that way?

"Why?" stands as a powerful indictment of society, an attempt to heighten the awareness of complacent listeners, and an affirming statement of defiance. Even now, a decade after its release, it remains one of the boldest "gay" songs ever to be recorded and released on a major record label (MCA Records). No wonder it wasn't a hit.

Incidentally, the entire album from which "Smalltown Boy" and "Why?" came, *The Age of Consent*, consists of one gay-affirming song after another, although some more obviously so than others. Especially noteworthy are "Screaming," "Heatwave," and "Need a Man Blues." The one *faux pas* is "I Feel Love/Johnny Remember Me"; more about that in a moment. Even the album's back cover and inner sleeve, with their prominent pink triangles, are statements of gay pride. It's a pity that Jimmy Somerville left Bronski Beat after this first album and Bronski Beat itself all but faded away after a second album with a different lead singer and lyricist. Somerville went on to further success, first as the vocalist for another group, the Communards, and then as a solo performer. Still, Bronski Beat deserves a highly honored place in that small—but potentially much larger—pantheon of openly gay recording artists.

- ■ BRONSKI BEAT ■
- ■ "I FEEL LOVE / JOHNNY REMEMBER ME" ■

Songwriters:	Donna Summer – Giorgio Moroder – Pete Bellotte ("I Feel Love"); Geoffrey Goddard ("Johnny Remember Me")
Year of Release:	1984
Original Album:	*The Age of Consent*
Chart Performance:	The single failed to make the charts, but (as I noted before) the album reached #36
Availability:	CD, CS, LP (MCA 5538)

Now that I've sung the praises of Bronski Beat, I couldn't let them off the hook without putting in my two cents' worth about the final track on *The Age of Consent*. Jimmy Somerville's penchant for revamping disco oldies has served him well in his career, but this early example was, shall we say, inauspicious. I'll never fathom why he and his cohorts picked "I Feel Love." They couldn't possibly have hoped to improve upon or even do justice to the original. Donna Summer's 1977 hit was a shockingly innovative track; in retrospect one can hardly overstate its subsequent influence. With its unexpected blending of the sensuous (Summer's voice and overtly sexual lyrics) with the coldly robotic (the mechanistic, totally synthesized instrumental track—which took on a bizarre sexuality of its own), it all but defined the technopop of the decade to follow.

To sum it up, the Bronski Beat rendition pales miserably by comparison. Tacking on "Johnny Remember Me," a much older tune given an explicitly gay twist, didn't help matters in the least. And to top it all off was one of the cheesiest videos ever, the cheap tackiness of which is indicative either of camp miscalculation or a lack of support and enthusiasm from the record label. It even features as guest vocalist ex-Soft Cell mainman Marc Almond, the cultic prince of sleezoid pop decadence. For most of the video he and Somerville do nothing but gently sway in one place, lip-synching badly. If this was the direction in which Bronski Beat was headed, no wonder Somerville jumped ship.

Yes, gay is definitely good, but some gay things leave a bit to be desired.

▪ GARTH BROOKS ▪ "WE SHALL BE FREE" ▪

Songwriters:	Stephanie Davis – Garth Brooks
Year of Release:	1992
Original Album:	*The Chase*
Chart Performance:	The single failed to make the pop charts, though it reached #12 country, and the album spent seven weeks at #1 pop
Availability:	CD, CS (Liberty 98743)

Who would've guessed that Garth Brooks would emerge as *the* musical phenomenon of the early 1990s, his albums outselling Michael Jackson, Prince, Madonna, and anyone else you can name. Widely interpreted as white baby-boomers' somewhat unpredictable reaction to the ascendancy of rap, heavy metal, and nondescript dance music on the mainstream pop charts, Brooks is an unlikely superstar—a balding, slightly chubby country singer with a good but unexceptional voice, his chief talents lying in his abilities to write or select first-rate material and to put on a damn good stage show. (Come to think of it, note the many similarities to Elton John.) Speaking of first-rate material, we have "We Shall Be Free" as a case in point.

Though by no means the first country hit to refer, however obliquely, to homosexuality (there are more to come later in this book), it *is* the first to be unabashedly supportive of full-fledged freedom and equality for gay people. No, it doesn't come right out and put it like that. Rather, it simply states, in the midst of its catalog of all the things that must be done in this world to ensure freedom for everyone, that "when we're free to love anyone we choose . . . we shall be free." To be sure, this sentiment refers to *any* type of love that others may disapprove of and wish to prohibit, such as interracial love, but it indisputably includes gay love as well. Just to erase any doubts, Brooks repeatedly confirmed this fact in interviews conducted shortly after the song's release as a single.

That's enough for me. When the Brooks phenomenon first hit, I viewed it quite cynically, seeing it as just another short-term mass infatuation, another trendy flash in the pop-culture pan. It may yet prove to be just that. But in light of "We Shall Be Free" and other high-quality music to his credit, I sure hope not. Garth, with folks like you helping out, maybe we all really *shall* be free someday.

▪ JOHN BUCCHINO ▪ "IF I'D BEEN WITH HIM" AND "UNTIL THE BALANCE TIPS" ▪

Songwriter:	John Bucchino
Year of Release:	1991
Original Album:	*Solitude Lessons*
Chart Performance:	Not released as singles, and the album didn't chart
Availability:	CS (Dinosaur 302)

As if you needed any further evidence, John Bucchino's album *Solitude Lessons* provides proof positive that it takes a lot more than first-rate talent to get a big-time recording contract. While by no means absolutely essential, heterosexuality—or at least a reasonable facsimile thereof—certainly helps. Or, perhaps more accurately, open gayness certainly doesn't help.

Solitude Lessons features a slew of marvelous songs with fine lyrics and highly inventive melodies, superbly performed within the budgetary and technological confines of home recording on a four-track system. The resulting sound is, not surprisingly, somewhat muddy (more noticeable than ever in this CD/digital age), but that turns out to be only a minor distraction. The music all but transcends such limitations. In *Solitude Lessons*, Bucchino has composed a virtual song-cycle about the end of a love affair and its aftermath. Though only a couple of songs are "overtly" gay— that is, taken out of context, they would be recognized as such by your average heterosexual listener—the entire album holds together as an important statement of gay sensibilities in the face of a personal romantic crisis. Oh, I know, it's probably grotesque of me to generalize in this way: "Just what *are* these 'gay sensibilities'?" you ask. So sue me.

As for those aforementioned "overt" songs, first we have "If I'd Been with Him," a wistful piece that expresses how you can torment yourself by thinking of ways in which you could make an ex-lover's life a little better, offering solace and advice, if only the two of you were still together. Its unusual, innovative melody takes some getting used to, but in this case familiarity breeds admiration. In his liner notes, Bucchino specifically cites

Stephen Sondheim and Joni Mitchell as "artists who follow their muses through some pretty dense underbrush," and, indeed, "If I'd Been with Him" betrays their musical influences. Another superb song on the album, "Love Quiz," is particularly Mitchell-esque.

Other great songs include "If I Ever Say I'm Over You" and "Love Will Find a Way," both introspective and beautiful. But the real standout—the one that in a fairer world surely would have been a hit single—is the final song on the album, the infectious, vaguely Latin "Until the Balance Tips." With its socially conscious lyrics that touch upon AIDS, the end of the Cold War, and environmental issues, it deviates from the thematic consistency of the other songs. That is, unless you consider its outward-looking as an ultimate triumph over the almost self-absorbed viewpoint of the previous songs. Maybe the best way to get over a breakup is to consider the larger problems of the world and what you can do to help. Paralleling this outward lyrical movement is the arrangement: not only does the music fairly lift you up out of your seat, but "Until the Balance Tips" is also the only song on the album that features musicians other than Bucchino himself. It's almost as if he were saying, "OK, so much for my little troubles. Now it's time to let myself out and to let the rest of the world in!" And then there's its tremendous optimism:

> The pain we pull through, the good we can do
> Is a prayer on our lips—until the balance tips

Bucchino seems confident that the balance *is* going to tip and that things are going to get better. And, cynic though I am, I think I'm almost persuaded.

John Bucchino is a supremely gifted songwriter, singer, and musician who deserves a major recording contract (assuming he wants one). I would love to hear his work well produced in a state-of-the-art recording studio. As good as it is, without such amenities, I can only imagine how much better it would be *with* them.

▪ MICHAEL CALLEN ▪ "HOW TO HAVE SEX" ▪

Songwriter:	Michael Callen
Year of Release:	1988
Original Album:	*Purple Heart*
Chart Performance:	Not released as a single, and the album didn't chart
Availability:	CD, CS (Significant Other 881)

A phenomenon that I find endlessly fascinating, one that demonstrates about as well as anything else the sheer resilience of human beings in the face of horrible adversity, is the way in which people can wrench humor out of the most tragic of circumstances. For instance, a Jewish friend of mine once told me a Holocaust joke. Sorry, I won't repeat it here, but it was one of those admittedly hilarious things that make you terribly ashamed of yourself for laughing at it. After getting over my uncomfortable laughter, I expressed my shock and dismay. "How can you, of all people," I asked (for I knew that he had lost relatives in the Nazi concentration camps), "tell such a joke?"

Placing his hand on my forearm, he replied, "Honey"—he's gay as well as Jewish—"sometimes the only way to keep from crying about it is to laugh about it."

That, I believe, is precisely what's going on in Michael Callen's excellent song "How to Have Sex." Callen, a very openly gay singer who has lived with AIDS for many years, apparently decided to have a little fun with the confusion, fear, and frustration surrounding the tragic consequences of the disease, both in his own life and in the gay community in general. In the process, he pulled off an amazing feat: he created a shining, cathartic tune that manages to make light of a terrible situation, yet without diminishing its seriousness in the least.

In a nutshell, the lyrics of "How to Have Sex" deal with the inner turmoil an unattached gay man can experience looking for gratification in an age in which lovemaking can be deadly. He spies a hot man in a bar who finds him equally attractive. But whereas in earlier days this would have been all that was needed to ensure a night of wild abandon, now his would-be partner isn't taking any chances, saying that he doesn't even kiss anymore. Rather, "I keep it in my pants."

Faced by this unfortunate turn of events, our lonesome narrator confides that he's "goin' crazy" being unable to do all the naughty things he'd like to do. And, like his erstwhile trick, he waxes nostalgic—

> *Can't it be like the fantasy?*
> *Can't it be like it used to be?*

—which leads to Callen's rhetorical refrain, featuring an unexpected rhyme worthy of Cole Porter:

How to have sex in an epidemic
Without getting caught up in polemic

Adding to the mood of humorous frustration is Callen's vocal performance. By turns he muses, growls, booms, sounds quizzical, becomes hesitant, and periodically soars into his absolutely killer falsetto, a wonderful example of really *acting* with one's singing voice. And then there's the music itself, a fabulous pastiche of styles: jerky, new-wavish, synth-pop with hints of disco and fifties doo-wop. Or is it early-sixties girl-group? It's hard to be sure exactly what Callen had in mind. Nor does it really matter. It all *fits*.

Later in the song, after a brief consideration of masturbation, porn, and the p.c. implications of said diversions, Callen returns to his nostalgic thoughts of the seventies, when the prevailing philosophy was "so many men, so little time." But then he suddenly switches back to reality, offering safe-sex advice in the process and urging his listeners always to use condoms so that "it's OK to get laid." Still, despite this optimistic turn, the troubling reality of AIDS and our society's reaction to it remains just under the surface. "How to Have Sex" soon dissolves into a reiterating, staccato sequence of synthesized beeps and burps, with Callen's multi-tracked falsetto voice mimicking assorted slogans of the day ("Safe sex is good sex," "Just say no," and the like) before grinding to a halt. It's a fantastic piece of work that is amusingly serious and seriously amusing.

Though I consider "How to Have Sex" to be the far-and-away standout on Callen's *Purple Heart* album, most of it is quite worthwhile. Personally, I could have done without his odd remake of "Where the Boys Are," which opens the album and sounds as if it were recorded in a stainless steel shower stall, but hey, you can't have everything. Meanwhile, for the further adventures of Michael Callen, check out the Flirtations. *I* certainly do, once we get around to the F's.

▪ VIC CAMPBELL ▪ "STALLIONS" ▪

Songwriter:	Vic Campbell
Year of Release:	1983
Original Album:	*West Fourteenth*
Chart Performance:	Not released as a single, and the album didn't chart
Availability:	CS (George Colin Stewart Productions 2)

Vic Campbell is a singer-songwriter-pianist little known outside Minneapolis, where he lives, but that's not as it should be. His music, though blatantly influenced by Billy Joel and Elton John—whom I happen to regard as pretty good musical role models—is generally so enjoyable that I think it's a crying shame that, at least as far as his work as a performer goes, he now seems to be in semi-retirement. But back in the early 1980s he recorded *West Fourteenth* (a reference to the street on which he lived at the time), a marvelous collection of songs, several of which are piano instrumentals. Although it's something of a "homemade" recording and has had only limited distribution, it nonetheless has the kind of quality that one would expect from music with far more economic clout to back it up.

My favorite *West Fourteenth* selection (and also the one most obviously "gay") is "Stallions," a rollicking waltz featuring just Campbell's piano and his multi-tracked vocals. If, like me, you're not terribly fond of horses, have no fear. Campbell's stallions are young men, and his song is a driving, joyous celebration of them and the environment in which so many can be found: gay bars. In essence, Campbell reminds us that, just about wherever you go, you can find a bar with the appropriate clientele: "No matter what city, the boys are so pretty." He doesn't go quite so far as the Beach Boys did in "California Girls," when they elaborated in turn on the special virtues of females in each U.S. region, but he does express a sense of almost religious awe at the plenitude of this particular aspect of creation. You can go to a "disco cathedral" in search of love (or whatever), where the services are anything but solemn. Campbell, in fact, assumes the role of evangelist, urging his listeners

> So return, tonight, to your favorite spot
> Down the street, tonight, give it just one more shot

You'd think the local taverns were giving him kickbacks.

Campbell hasn't been pursuing his musical career very aggressively in recent years, though he still performs sporadically in and around the Twin Cities. In fact, I've seen several of his live performances, and he's just as good in person as on tape, if not better. If you're reading this, Vic, tell you what—consider this a little push. Give it just one more shot. Or two.

Songwriter:	Shel Silverstein
Year of Release:	1969
Original Album:	*Johnny Cash at San Quentin*
Chart Performance:	The single reached #2
Availability:	CD, CS (Columbia 33639, the *San Quentin* album now combined with *Johnny Cash at Folsom Prison*)

Although I doubt whether Shel Silverstein (the songwriter) or Johnny Cash would see it this way, the central, essential ingredient of this song is the typical heterosexual male's immense fear of being thought homosexual. This fear, and the pervasive hatred of gay people that causes it, results in the paranoid-macho violence so ably depicted in the lyrics—as well as in the headlines of your daily newspaper. The irony of this song having been recorded live before a highly appreciative audience of convicts at San Quentin should be lost on no one.

Songwriters:	Tommy Chong – Richard "Cheech" Marin – Gay DeLorme
Year of Release:	1974
Original Album:	*Cheech and Chong's Wedding Album*
Chart Performance:	The single reached #9
Availability:	CD, CS (Warner Brothers 3253)

A parody not of gay people but rather of the exploitive gender-bending pretensions of Alice Cooper, David Bowie, and their early-seventies ilk, who were hot properties when this track became a surprise hit. Side-splitting in 1974 and still amusing today, "Earache My Eye" also satirized heavy metal while it was yet in its infancy, long before Rob Reiner and friends dreamed up Spinal Tap.

It's indicative of Cheech and Chong's astute awareness of how pop culture works that they not only linked the more macabre aspects of glam rock with metal but also allowed their opus to serve as the soundtrack to a furious father's screaming at his teenage son to turn down that god-awful music. This, after all, is what it's all about. If it involves a guy named Alice, so be it. If it calls for a very hairy man to wear a pink tutu, a Mickey Mouse hat, and "high-heel sneakers" (as Cheech Marin did when performing the song live) as he sings about looking "like a queen," so much the better. If it takes loud, repetitive, monotonous, cacophonous power chords, right on. The goal is to upset your elders, and anything that contributes to that end isn't merely applauded but embraced. So long as it's just an *act*, of course.

Frankly, I'm surprised a lot of "straight" teenagers don't pretend to "go gay" just to drive their parents up the proverbial wall. Perhaps that's going too far even for rebels without a cause. Instead they settle for decibels without a pause and let their rock heroes do the screwing around with superficial gender expectations for them. Cheech and Chong obviously knew this long before the rest of us did, or at least before we were able to articulate it nearly as well.

▪ COMMUNARDS ▪ "NEVER CAN SAY GOODBYE" ▪

Songwriter:	Clifton Davis
Year of Release:	1987
Original Album:	*Red*
Chart Performance:	The single reached #51
Availability:	CD, CS, LP (MCA 42106)

After he left Bronski Beat, Jimmy Somerville hooked up with keyboardist Richard Coles to form the Communards. They put out two albums before going their separate ways, the second of which, *Red*, contains the most aesthetically successful of Somerville's disco remakes.

Before the Communards got a hold of it, "Never Can Say Goodbye" was basically an ordinary love song with an extraordinary history. Granted, it had an inventive melody and very pleasant lyrics, but it was hardly unique in those respects. Nothing very special set it apart—aside from the fact that it had already been a Top Forty hit three times over: by both the Jackson Five and Isaac Hayes in 1971 and by Gloria Gaynor in 1975. However, using Gaynor's rousing disco version as a model, the Communards transformed it into something very special indeed. They did this not so much with Somerville's instantly recognizable falsetto (admittedly an acquired taste) but rather by refusing to change a single word from Gaynor's version—that single word being "boy," as in "I never can say goodbye, boy." Virtually every other male performer seeking mainstream success, gay ones included, would have sung, "I never can say goodbye, *girl*," *à la* the Jackson Five and Isaac Hayes renditions. But not Jimmy. This boy's gay pride ain't for sale. And while the Communards' version certainly didn't burn up the charts, it did receive some airplay on mainstream Top Forty radio stations. If I hadn't heard it on my own car radio I wouldn't have believed it.

And it made me feel very, very good to hear it, too.

Not surprisingly, the *Red* album contains a number of other valuable songs from a gay vantage point. Especially noteworthy are the touching AIDS protest song "Victims" and the enigmatically titled "TMT♥TBMG" (what hath Prince wrought, or does it matter much 2 U?), which, as it turns out, stands for "There's More to Love Than Boy Meets Girl." I should say.

■ JOSIE COTTON ■
■ "JOHNNY, ARE YOU QUEER?" ■

Songwriters:	Bobby Paine – Larson Paine
Year of Release:	1981
Original Album:	*Convertible Music*
Chart Performance:	The single didn't make the U.S. charts, but the album reached #147
Availability:	Out of print (Elektra 60140)

In this fast and furious New Wave rock song—reportedly offered to the Go-Go's but rejected—the narrator asks her boyfriend why "when the lights are low, you never hold me close." She then tells him that she thinks she knows:

> *I saw you today, boy*
> *Walkin' with them gay boys*

So she asks him if he's queer. What could be simpler?

Surprisingly, the use of "queer" by a presumably heterosexual female singer doesn't seem offensive, largely because the song is so tongue-in-cheek. The confused, spoiled-girl ache that Ms. Cotton sometimes allows to creep into her voice tips us off. That, plus the fact that the picture sleeve of the twelve-inch single is a parody of those old romance comics, with the heroine in tears as she notices that her boyfriend is exchanging longing glances with another boy they've just passed. There's even a hysterical caption: "Josie feared the shocking truth . . . but she *had* to know!"

Though Cotton repeatedly uses the word "queer," she never appears to do so with spite or contempt. It merely seems to be just another word on a par with "gay." (This was, of course, years before "queer" became fashionable in gay circles.) Also, the song wouldn't be nearly so funny had she said, "Johnny, are you gay?" And humor, often of a satirical nature, was an important but often overlooked component of New Wave rock music of the late seventies and early eighties.

We might even sympathize with our heroine's plight because she seems genuine and honest in wanting to come to terms with the possibility that her boyfriend may be gay. As the music starts to fade out, Cotton speaks rather than sings, in a conversational tone, "Johnny—are you—you know—" and suddenly, as she starts to say "queer" one last time, her voice soars siren-like into a shout. Superb.

Before I heard this, I wouldn't have thought that any song that used the word "queer" so liberally could be simultaneously so heartwarming and amusing. Besides, it's got a great beat and it's fun to dance to.

▪ WAYNE COUNTY AND THE BACK STREET BOYS ▪
▪ "FLIP YOUR WIG" ▪

Songwriter:	Wayne County
Year of Release:	1976
Original Album:	*New York New Wave – Max's Kansas City*
Chart Performance:	Not released as a single, and the album didn't make the charts
Availability:	Out of print (CBS 82670)

In the mid- and late-1970s, Max's Kansas City in Lower Manhattan was one of the chief venues of the burgeoning punk/New Wave scene. New acts like the Ramones, the New York Dolls, Blondie, Talking Heads, Television, Suicide, and Pere Ubu, as well as more established performers like Lou Reed and Iggy Pop, made it a favored spot among kids who liked their music fast, lean, and alienated. Another frequent performer at Max's Kansas City was the Georgia-born Wayne County—who, by later becoming Jayne County, would earn the epithet "rock and roll's most famous transsexual."

In the course of his/her career, Wayne/Jayne fronted several bands, including Queen Elizabeth, the Back Street Boys, and the Electric Chairs. Amidst these changing lineups and banners, County developed a head-turning stage image that included a platinum wig, fishnet stockings, sheer dresses, and makeup for days. One publicity photo from the mid-seventies shows him (and he still was a he at the time) not only dressed in this manner but also bearing a remarkable facial resemblance to Boy George, who wouldn't make his grand entrance in pop music for several years yet. But for all of the supposed "femininity" of his wardrobe, County's music was as loud and hard as anything else the frequenters of Max's Kansas City wanted to hear. Further, County sang with a subtle but persistent lisp, doing for that stereotypically "gay" speech impediment what the Who's Roger Daltry had done for the stutter a decade before in the song "My Generation"—that is, turn it into a symbol of defiance and nonconformity, an almost revolutionary expression of pride in one's inability or unwillingness to meet "establishment" expectations. Articulate inarticulateness, if you will.

Several recordings by Wayne County and the Back Street Boys appear on a 1976 compilation album titled *New York New Wave – Max's Kansas City*, along with tracks by Pere Ubu, The Fast, Suicide, and others. Among the County songs are the scandalously titled "Cream in My Jeans" (more than 50% of the lyrics of which consist of repeating "You make me cream in my jeans") and the more clearly gay-specific "Flip Your Wig." In the latter song, County addresses a young man (we know he's male because he's referred to as a "boy" in the lyrics) who surprises him with the brazenness of his manner of dress. County says that he looks "like last year's Christmas tree" and mildly scolds, "You've really flipped your wig, babe. . . . You must be wearing everything but a lampshade."

Although nowhere is it forthrightly stated that he's talking about drag, the "shock" County feigns, the elaborateness of his descriptions, and the repeated references to the flipping of wigs leaves no question of what's going on. In fact, I seriously doubt whether County himself is supposed to be the narrator here. Rather, I suspect that he's the person being addressed, what with his own penchant for drag, and that his narrative persona is mouthing the words of friends and acquaintances who are dismayed by his behavior. As such, this song is anything but an expression of disapproval for public drag, despite the reprimands found in the lyrics. On the contrary, it's a parody of such disapproving attitudes. Think about it: what a sight it must have been to see this guy up on stage, dressed in full drag, berating some unseen person for dressing outrageously! It must have been a hoot—a fully intentional hoot.

Strangely, "Flip Your Wig" eventually degenerates into an assertion of the craziness that supposedly underlies life in New York City. County starts rapping about how he's going to kill all of the city's pigeons, stuff them into CARE packages, and ship them to India to feed the starving people there who refuse to eat their sacred cows. Then maniacal laughter. A regrettable end to an otherwise fascinating song. Mind you, "Flip Your Wig" is by no means a great song. Actually, I'd have to say it's a pretty bad song. But it makes for a nifty selection from the historical soundtrack of drag-rock theatre.

▪ CULTURE CLUB ▪ "MISS ME BLIND" ▪

Songwriters:	George O'Dowd – Jon Moss – Roy Hay – Mikey Craig
Year of Release:	1983
Original Album:	*Colour by Numbers*
Chart Performance:	The single reached #5
Availability:	CD, CS (Virgin 91391)

For about a year and a half, from early 1983 to mid-1984, Culture Club was just about the most successful pop group in the world. Their first six singles to hit the U.S. charts all made the Top Ten, including a Number One, "Karma Chameleon." And the principal factor behind their success lay in one person: George O'Dowd, better known as Boy George. Boy George not only had one of the finest voices of the early eighties; he also boasted one of the most singularly original and outrageous images in the history of rock music.

To say that androgyny was core to the image of the Boy is only part of it. David Bowie and a score of imitators used androgyny, as do many heavy metal acts to this day. But these other brands of androgyny have always been aggressive, have always brandished an intense, overt sexuality. Not so with Boy George. His was an all-but-sexless androgyny—safe, endearing, almost comfortable. (Bowie in his heyday was *never* safe, endearing, and almost comfortable.) With his heavy makeup, plucked eyebrows, dreadlocks, childish pouts on album covers but bright smiles nearly everywhere else, and costumes that chaotically blended not only the masculine with the feminine but also the European with the Asian and African, he was an embodiment of the multiculturalism that the name of his group implied. In short, Boy George made stark contradictions seem pleasantly compatible. And he was totally new.

In European interviews, Boy George was generally quite forthright in discussing his homosexuality. He reportedly acknowledged, for instance, that the group's drummer, Jon Moss, was for a time his lover. In the United States, however, he had to be far more coy about it, tending to avoid questions of his sexual orientation or, when pressed, giving conflicting answers. Sometimes he suggested he was bisexual. Sometimes he indicated he was asexual. (That was a change of pace in rock!) Sometimes he said that it was irrelevant since he didn't have time for sex anyway. But it was nevertheless widely assumed that he was primarily if not totally gay. After all, while accepting Culture Club's award for Best New Artist of 1983 on the nationally televised Grammy Awards show, he boldly thanked America for knowing "a good drag queen when you see one."

The music of Culture Club itself rarely offered any substantive insight into the matter, with most references to the specific genders of the characters in their songs scrupulously avoided. For instance, although it has been asserted that their first hit, "Do You Really Want to Hurt Me?" was based on the broken love relationship of Boy George with his former roommate, there's nothing in the song to suggest a male-male context *per se*. "Miss Me Blind," however, is a notable exception to the rule:

> *Bet you got a good gun*
> *Bet you know how to have some fun in bed*

The person to whom Boy George (or his persona, which would actually be a persona of a persona since the character of Boy George is itself a persona of George O'Dowd) sings is clearly male (the phallic imagery of the "gun" is unmistakable, especially considering the juxtaposition with the bed in the next line), as is the narrator himself ("I'm better than the rest of the men"). No doubt about it: "Miss Me Blind" is one man's assertion that his erstwhile male lover will miss him when he's gone. And it was all but saturating the airwaves in early 1984.

As I said, Boy George was totally new. But nothing can be totally new for long. After a little over a year at the top, the Boy suffered badly from overexposure, what with a flood of videos, scores of magazine articles, and visits to the Joan Rivers talk show. A strongly adverse reaction set in, especially when the Boy began to adopt an even more "girlish" image, as seen on the cover of Culture Club's third album, *Waking Up with the House on Fire*. Magazines with his picture on the cover were being defaced on the newsstand. He became more outspoken, too, both in interviews and in song. A single—the forthrightly sociopolitical "The War Song"—that loudly proclaimed "People are stupid" couldn't have helped matters much, either. I assume that most record-buyers consider themselves people, and most people don't appreciate being called stupid, especially to their face. "The War Song" was political, but hardly politic.

The hits began to dry up, the group broke up after Boy George failed in his attempt at changing his image (from cuddly sexless gender-bender to quasi-masculine punk butchette), and George O'Dowd fell victim to a very well publicized drug addiction. (As gay music historian Boze Hadleigh has suggested, the tremendous extent to which it was publicized exemplified as well as exacerbated the increasingly negative feelings much of the public had about him.) Boy George has since apparently recovered from the drugs, but his career has yet to rebound in kind. He keeps trying, however, now as a solo act. He's had some success so far in Britain, even scoring a #1 hit there. His new music, however, appears to be pretty much shut out in the States, though he scored mildly with the title song from the notorious film *The Crying Game*. (To be sure, George was a natural for *that* one.) Meanwhile, he has adopted an even more outspokenly positive gay stance, as evidenced in "No Clause 28," discussed earlier. The coyness seems to be a thing of the past. And, until recently, I would have said the same thing of his career. But I'm not so sure about that anymore. I suspect we've yet to hear more from the Boy.

▪ CULTURE CLUB ▪ "KARMA CHAMELEON" ▪

Songwriters:	George O'Dowd – Jon Moss – Roy Hay – Mikey Craig – Phil Pickett
Year of Release:	1983
Original Album:	*Colour by Numbers*
Chart Performance:	The single hit #1 and stayed there for three weeks
Availability:	CD, CS (Virgin 91391)

"Karma Chameleon" may not be a "gay" song—its somewhat opaque lyrics seem universalized, perhaps largely because of that very opacity—but it does boast one of Boy George's most profound lyrical statements: "I'm a man who doesn't know how to sell a contradiction."

If, as Jean Cocteau via Philip Core asserts, camp is "the lie that tells the truth," then these must be the campiest lines ever to reach #1. (The only real competition is when Frankie Valli sang, "Walk like a man, talk like a man" in his piercing falsetto.) The lie, obviously, comes from the fact that the Boy's career was *built* on selling contradictions. The truth, far less obviously, is that the contradictions he sold were false social constructs, existing not so much in himself as in the minds of his audience. What, pray tell, was inherently contradictory about Boy George? His only contradictions lay in the realm of shallow, ephemeral sociosexual expectations. In his best moments he himself came across as one of the most honest creations of pop culture. And as for that business about being without convictions—where does the playfulness end and the irony begin?

Songwriter:	Richard O'Brien
Year of Release:	1975
Original Album:	*The Rocky Horror Show* (Original Cast Album)
Chart Performance:	Not released as a single, and the album failed to reach the pop charts (although the later, very similar *Rocky Horror Picture Show* movie soundtrack album, in which Curry also performed, hit #49)
Availability:	CD, CS, LP (Rhino 70090)

Do you know the "Insider/Outsider Rule"? It's a guideline for people who want to be sensitive and politically correct in their references to other people, minority groups in particular. The rule has two major tenets:

1. People who do not belong to a certain group should refer to people who do belong to that group by the term that they (the "insiders") have themselves chosen as the term that "outsiders" should use when referring to them.
2. There are terms that "insiders" may appropriately use when referring to themselves and each other (primarily for the purpose of disarming the harmful power of those words) that, when used by "outsiders," are insulting and should therefore be avoided by the outsiders.

Let me give you an example. Most gay men would almost certainly agree that "gay men" is a good term for non-gay people to use when referring to them. This is the term that the "insiders" have chosen for themselves. On the other hand, gay men can refer to themselves and each other as "faggots," "fags," "fairies," "queens," "queers," and assorted other epithets, but "outsiders" should not. It's all very simple, really.

Now, the reason I bring this up is that I find the Insider/Outsider Rule helpful in figuring out what to think of something like *The Rocky Horror Show*—or, in its more familiar filmed incarnation, *The Rocky Horror Picture Show*. You know the story: the depraved alien transvestite mad scientist, Dr. Frank-n-Furter, played as a heavily mascaraed, rouged, and lipsticked (or is that "lipstuck"?) queen by Tim Curry, creates a gorgeous, muscular hunk of a monster (the Rocky of the title) in gold lamé briefs. Widely regarded as an all-out assault on conventional sexual mores (as well as on good taste in general), the movie became the center of a macabre audience-participation pop-cult of near-religious magnitude, complete with liturgy (shouting out lines from the script as the actors recite them) and ritual (shooting squirt-guns during the rainstorm scene, tossing pieces of toast at the screen when one of the characters calls for a toast, and so on).

The musical centerpiece of the show—the closest thing it had to a "hit" aside from the infamous "Time Warp"—is a tune called "Sweet Transvestite," sung by Curry in all of Frank-n-Furter's stereotypically gender-twisting splendor. In addition to the song's refrain, "I'm just a sweet transvestite from transsexual Transylvania," we're treated to assorted references to the mad scientist's sexual inclinations, such as when he admits a fondness for old Steve Reeves movies. In an especially telling line, Frank confesses that his motives for creating such a hunky monster aren't entirely academic: "He's good for relieving my tension." Ultimately, in true Frankensteinian fashion, both creature and creator must be destroyed in order to save the world from their evil. Not to give it away to any of you who may never have seen the show, but they're both zapped to death by a laser gun, with Frank-n-Furter apparently deriving some sort of aesthetic-sexual pleasure from the experience.

Which brings us to the question: from a "gay" point of view, what are we to make of this?

Well, I can only give *my* point of view, which is somewhat bifurcated. And that's where the Insider/Outsider Rule comes in. If the people who masterminded this affair—writer of the book, music, and lyrics Richard O'Brien, as well as Tim Curry, who originated the role of Frank—were gay, I'd be inclined to cheer it all on as a marvelously funny, campy trampling of traditional gender expectations.

But I don't know whether O'Brien and Curry are gay. And I'm going to do what is perhaps a risky thing: I'm going to assume they're not.

In which case *The Rocky Horror Show*, specifically Dr. Frank-n-Furter himself, takes on more insidious overtones. Without a doubt, he's one of the most malicious, over-the-board portrayals of an alleged homosexual ever to appear on the screen—and in light of the competition, that's quite a feat. Forget the screaming queen aspect of his character. Far more significantly, he's every homophobe's dream/nightmare-come-to-life of what gay people are "really" like: decadent, corrupting, murderous, unquestionably wicked, albeit in a humorous sort of way, but a threat nonetheless to decency, moral values, and civilization itself. His well-deserved death is not only inevitable—it's pleasurable. In short, it's nauseating.

To be sure, I know of many gay people who would disagree with me in that assessment. To take one especially notable example, the late Vito Russo, in his classic analysis of the depiction of gay men and lesbians in the movies, *The Celluloid Closet*, described *The Rocky Horror Picture Show* as "a truly subversive and anarchistic film on the subjects of sexuality, movies, sex roles and the homosexual as monster." He hailed the film version of the musical "as both a catalog and spoof of old monster movies and science fiction films" in which "its most expert satire is of the age-old fear with which straight society encounters deviant sexuality." With his usual brilliant insight, Russo further observes that "Tim Curry's performance . . . is the essence of what every parent in America fears will happen if our sexual standards are relaxed. It becomes the living horror of making deviant sexuality visible and tangible[.]" Only in a creepy old house inhabited by "lesbians, transvestites, acid freaks and goons who sing rock and roll" does the seduction of "innocent youth" by allegedly alien, perverse values seem to make any sense at all to mainstream America. But Russo prefers to view the movie as a spoof of mainstream attitudes *about* "deviant sexuality" rather than as a satire of those forms of sexuality themselves.

Me, I'm not so sure. Maybe Russo knew something I don't. (Well, I don't doubt that.) Maybe *The Rocky Horror Show* manages to skin its queer cat in more ways than one, poking fun simultaneously at *both* "conventional" and "unconventional" sexuality. But I just can't help but think about all of those young people for whom Dr. Frank-n-Furter may be the most memorable homosexual character they've ever seen on film, and for whom "Sweet Transvestite" may be the only song they've ever heard in which the narrator is so obviously "gay." And when I think about that, I don't like it.

- **DEPECHE MODE** -
- **"BOYS SAY GO!"** AND **"WHAT'S YOUR NAME?"** -

Songwriter: Vince Clarke (both songs)
Year of Release: 1981
Original Album: *Speak & Spell*
Chart Performance: Neither song was released as a single, but the album reached #192
Availability: CD, CS (Sire 3642)

"Depeche mode" means "fast fashion" in French. And Depeche Mode the British band means lots of synthesizers, percussion, and those robotic-style vocals so trendy in the early eighties. Or at least that's what it meant when synthesizer hot-shot Vince Clarke was leading the show. He left after a couple of albums, later forming Yaz with Alison Moyet and still later Erasure with openly gay vocalist Andy Bell. Meanwhile, Depeche Mode carried on—and achieved far greater popular success—without him. But *Speak & Spell*, their debut album from 1981, features not only Clarke but also a pair of delightfully gay bits of technopop.

The first of these, "Boys Say Go!" starts off with the title exclamation shouted four times, followed by the male narrator's invitation to an unnamed young man to take him "for a ride." Then, after saying that he wants to get to know him better, he sings:

> *Boys meet boys, get together!*
> *Boys meet boys, it's forever!*
> *Don't say no, boys say go!*

As the song continues, the background cry "Boys!" periodically punctuates the proceedings, and the fade-out urges listeners onward: "Go—Go—Go—Go—Go—Go." It's really quite remarkable, especially coming from an avowed heterosexual like Clarke.

The second song of note is "What's Your Name?" which offers a chorus of "Hey, you're such a pretty boy" repeated several times. Campy background vocals embellish the affair with such things as "Hey, hey, what's your name?" and "P–R–E–double–T–Y." The singer also echoes the earlier song, asserting, "All the boys, we've got to get together." I mean, who can resist?

Well, lots of heterosexual record-buyers could. It wasn't until Depeche Mode toned down the gay-sounding stuff that they started to take off commercially. Ah, but it was nice while it lasted.

■ DEPECHE MODE ■ "PEOPLE ARE PEOPLE" ■

Songwriter:	Martin L. Gore
Year of Release:	1984
Original Album:	*People Are People*
Chart Performance:	The single reached #13
Availability:	CD, CS (Sire 25124)

A good friend of mine insists that this classic of percussion-heavy electronic pop belongs here. He concedes that the lyrics are not gay-specific, though the line "Different people have different needs" does leave open the possible inclusion of gay people in the mind of the songwriter, Depeche Mode member Martin Gore.

Essentially, the song is a plea for mutual respect and tolerance among human beings, daring those who would despise the narrator to tell him the reasons for their feelings, thus opening a line of communication and perhaps ending the cycle of hate. There's even a clear reference to violent hate crime, for which gay-bashing certainly qualifies. So I understand my friend's argument that I should include "People Are People" in this book. What's more, he distinctly remembers hearing this song sung-chanted at gay pride rallies during the mid-1980s. Personally, I recall no such thing, and I've attended my share of gay pride rallies. Maybe it was an East Coast thing; I live in the Midwest.

▪ DIONNE AND FRIENDS ▪
▪ "THAT'S WHAT FRIENDS ARE FOR" ▪

Songwriters:	Burt Bacharach – Carole Bayer Sager
Year of Release:	1985
Original Album:	*Friends*
Chart Performance:	The single reached #1 and stayed there for four weeks
Availability:	CD, CS (Arista 8398)

Not a gay song, but gay-sensitive, plus absolute proof that in the right hands a piece of fluff can be turned into something truly important. A neglected Bacharach-Sager tune, "That's What Friends Are For" had previously been performed by Rod Stewart for the soundtrack of the movie *Night Shift* and then promptly forgotten.

Well, obviously *almost* forgotten but not quite, for it was transformed by Dionne Warwick, Stevie Wonder, Elton John, and Gladys Knight into a profession of steadfast friendship in the face of adversity, the specific adversity in this case being AIDS. It slowly climbed the charts to become the most popular song in the country, not to mention one of the two or three biggest hits of 1986. A charitable enterprise, it raised a passel of money for AIDS research and assistance for people with HIV.

As for the performance itself, Dionne (who deserves blessings for her leadership of the project) was her usual stately, elegant self; Stevie's vocal was good, but it was his harmonica that served as the delightful fulcrum upon which the whole track pivoted; Elton was white, avowedly bi, and an essential spark in making the song work as well as it did, both musically and commercially; and the matchless Gladys could strip wallpaper with her voice alone. I wanted to hear much more of her—the way she stretches a simple word like "for" out to six perfectly natural-sounding syllables is incredible.

By the time the single finished its run on the charts, it had raised public awareness of AIDS to new heights without being the least bit negative or sensationalistic. Kudos to everyone involved in making "That's What Friends Are For" a great, grand testament of love.

▪ DIRE STRAITS ▪ "LES BOYS" ▪

Songwriter:	Mark Knopfler
Year of Release:	1980
Original Album:	*Making Movies*
Chart Performance:	Not released as a single, but the album reached #19
Availability:	CD, CS (Warner Brothers 3480)

Gay music journalist Adam Block has characterized this song as a "smug affront," and I'm inclined to agree. In "Les Boys," Mark Knopfler has composed one of his most trivial tunes using melodic phraseology borrowed from European cabaret tradition, resulting in the weakest cut on an otherwise terrific album. The rinky-tink arrangement indicates an at least partly comic intention, confirmed by the intentional (I assume) mispronunciation of the French article *les* throughout. (For the record, the *s* should be silent when the next word starts with a consonant.) And Knopfler's usually stellar guitar work sounds lackluster at best.

What's more, the way that Knopfler seems to appropriate—maybe even satirize—Tom Robinson's "Glad to Be Gay" refrain of a few years earlier borders on the downright nasty:

> *Les boys do cabaret*
> *Les boys are glad to be gay*
> *They're not afraid now*
> *Disco bar in Germany*
> *Les boys are glad to be upon parade now*

Knopfler takes no pains to conceal his sense of superiority as he ridicules certain trappings of one small segment of the gay male community. Unfortunately, the fact that some of these trappings do indeed merit ridicule (such as Nazi regalia) lends some credence to his stance.

> *Les boys got leather straps*
> *Les boys got SS caps*
> *But they got no gun now*
> *Get dressed up, get a little risque*
> *Get to do a little S&M these days*
> *It's all in fun now*

The implication is that, back in Nazi Germany, gay men were engaged in real-life oppression and torture. Again, the fact that *some* members of the SS were undoubtedly gay (and that large numbers of the SA were as well before the SS exterminated them) makes Knopfler's intimations not altogether incorrect. Of course, he seems to ignore the fact that homosexuals were among the Nazis' victims, and that while some Nazis were themselves homosexuals, the number of queer Nazis was certainly far less than the number of gay people the Nazis murdered in cold blood.

But back to "Les Boys." Knopfler's lyrics become a little less precise in the middle part of the song. He mentions closeted businessmen driving Mercedes Benz who meet with "les boys." And he refers somewhat unclearly to changes in attitudes on the part of the people who run a local disco, to the jokes of deejays and the embarrassing photographs of tourists. Where Knopfler had previously only had snide, caustically ironic things to say about these gay young men, a slight note of pity—very slight—seems to creep in. Of course, pity is hardly the most positive of emotions.

The final verse strikes me as ambiguous, but it definitely verges on the sympathetic. In terms of simple, elegant pop lyricism, it's also the most effective portion of the song:

> *Late at night when they've gone away*
> *Les boys dream of Jean Genet*
> *High-heel shoes and a black beret*
> *And the posters on the wall that say*
> *Les boys do cabaret*
> *Les boys are glad to be gay*

Overall, I get mixed signals from "Les Boys." Mark Knopfler makes some astute and legitimate points about the hypocrisy of gay men getting done up in Nazi drag. And the general harshness of his tone definitely appears to soften toward the end of the song. But still I get the distinct sense that Knopfler has no great fondness for gay people. At its worst, "Les Boys" is just plain self-righteous and demeaning.

▪ DIRE STRAITS ▪ "MONEY FOR NOTHING" ▪

Songwriters:	Mark Knopfler – Sting
Year of Release:	1985
Original Album:	*Brothers in Arms*
Chart Performance:	The single was #1 for three weeks
Availability:	CD, CS (Warner Brothers 25264)

This song, ostensibly a hapless Average Joe's view of the world of rock stardom, is notorious for a verse that many radio stations refused to broadcast, preferring instead to play an edited version in which it was deleted:

> *The little faggot with the earring and the mink coat*
> *Yeah, buddy, that's his own hair*
> *That little faggot's got his own jet airplane*
> *That little faggot is a millionaire*

Singer and principal author Mark Knopfler has maintained that these are merely the nasty opinions of his ignorant blue-collar persona in the song, which is not at all like himself. In a vacuum, I could buy that. The song undoubtedly has a fundamentally ironic intention (reinforced by the popular video), what with rock stars singing about how easy and lucrative it is to be a rock star. But coming from the writer of "Les Boys," which similarly has very little good to say about gay people, you have to wonder. In the meantime, however you look at it, "Money for Nothing" holds the dubious distinction of being the only #1 song so far that uses the word "faggot" not once but three times. Maybe these Straits are a little *too* dire.

■ DISPOSABLE HEROES OF HIPHOPRISY ■
■ "THE LANGUAGE OF VIOLENCE" ■

Songwriters: Michael Franti – Mark Pistel
Year of Release: 1992
Original Album: *Hypocrisy Is the Greatest Luxury*
Chart Performance: Neither the single nor the album reached the pop charts
Availability: CD, CS (4th and Broadway 162-444043)

I'd been waiting a long time for this one: a medicinal dose of anti-gay-bashing rap. Verbose lyricist Michael Franti's grim tale initially focuses on a fifteen-year-old kid—gay, though he's never had sex with anyone—who's been cornered by a violent teenage gang. They hurl all the standard insults at him: sissy, queer, faggot. But mere words and threats aren't enough. They begin to beat him mercilessly, a beating that ends in his death. It's not a pretty picture, but then there's nothing pretty about gay-bashing.

The story doesn't end there, however. Attention shifts to a member of the attacking mob, apparently the oldest of the bunch, who's captured and tried as an adult. Convicted, he's sent to prison, where he's subjected to the same taunts that he and his cohorts had used against their victim: sissy, queer, faggot. In a horrible turn of poetic justice, he's ultimately gang-raped in the prison shower.

As the mad pun in their name suggests ("hip hop" + "hypocrisy"), the biracial duo who call themselves the Disposable Heroes of Hiphoprisy preach relentlessly against the evils of hypocrisy in its various manifestations in virtually every track of their debut album. Homophobia is but one of their many targets. Despite the record's regrettably poor sales, we need more of this sort of thing. *Support socially responsible rap!* With all the anti-gay prejudice and other forms of bigotry polluting rap music, popular music in general, and the world at large, I don't understand why the Disposable Heroes consider themselves "disposable." If you ask me, they're damn near indispensable.

▪ DIVINE ▪ "JUNGLE JEZEBEL" ▪

Songwriter:	Bobby Orlando
Year of Release:	1983
Original Album:	*Jungle Jezebel*
Chart Performance:	Neither the single nor the album made the pop charts
Availability:	Original album out of print; available on *The Best of Divine*, CD, CS, LP (O Records 16)

   The brilliance of the late, lamented Divine lay in the fact that a 300-plus-pound transvestite could parody stereotypical femininity and gender roles, as all drag queens do, while simultaneously parodying drag itself. He didn't ask his audience to suspend its disbelief so much as its inability to have a good time without doing so. It was more than bad drag; it was *preposterous* drag, which is why it worked. Of course, he also had the good fortune to hook up with director John Waters and share in his singularly warped vision of the universe. Divine couldn't really act—aside from the acting it took to turn bad drag into highly functional drag—but lack of acting skill isn't necessarily a liability in a John Waters film. Likewise, he couldn't sing, but that's not necessarily a liability in the world of pop music, where any producer with a modicum of studio savvy can transform the weakest voice into an acceptable accompaniment to the instrumental track.

   In the case of Divine's best-known disco hit, "Jungle Jezebel," he worked with prolific songwriter-producer Bobby Orlando. Surely nobody bought "Jungle Jezebel" for its dubious musical value, but rather for its status as an artifact of camp. The title itself is camp shorthand for Divine's success at making us "accept" him as everything he clearly was not—with "accept" in quotes because we really *didn't* accept him as a Jungle Jezebel, but we accepted the fact that we weren't really *meant* to and therefore became full participants in the joke. What this ultimately signifies is an amazing talent at turning shit into a successful consumer commodity. Divine did it in *Pink Flamingos*—in more ways than one—so why not on the dance floor?

The inimitable Divine (1945–1988) in concert, ca. 1983. (Photo: Walter McBride. Retna Ltd.)

• DONOVAN • "TO TRY FOR THE SUN" •

Songwriter:	Donovan Leitch
Year of Release:	1965
Original Album:	*Fairy Tale*
Chart Performance:	The single didn't chart, but the album reached #85
Availability:	Out of print (Pye 18128)

Most people remember Donovan as the quintessential singing flower child—all frizzed hair and love beads, flowing caftans and cross-legged meditations, a purveyor of gentle, happy, and sometimes vaguely druggy singles like "Sunshine Superman," "Mellow Yellow," "Jennifer Juniper," and "Hurdy Gurdy Man," songs that could only have emerged from the sixties. What most people don't remember is that before he became hippie-dom incarnate, Donovan was something of the Scottish Dylan, a prole-tarian folkie right down to the denim jacket, badly played harmonica, and ubiquitous acoustic guitar. "To Try for the Sun" is from that earlier, more derivative phase of Donovan's career.

Accompanied only by that guitar and harmonica, Donovan sets the per-fect pseudo-folk, Dylanesque backdrop in this appealing if musically unex-ceptional little song. But the story he tells is hardly typical for "folk music." Oh, the highly mannered, self-consciously poetic language is there, all right, as are the idealized depictions of the down and out—stock material for this genre of pop music. But I don't recall the Kingston Trio singing anything about sleeping with a "gypsy boy," as Donovan does in this song.

Now I must digress at this point. As reported by Fred Bronson in his richly informative *Billboard Book of Number One Hits*, Donovan dropped out of school at the age of fifteen and set out traveling around Britain and the European continent. He was accompanied on these journeys by another youngster curiously called "Gypsy Dave." They earned money along the way by playing music—Donovan on the guitar and Gypsy Dave on kazoo. Almost without question, Gypsy Dave is the inspiration for the beloved gypsy boy of these lyrics.

Back to the song. The chorus defiantly asserts the goodness of the rela-tionship between these two young men: "Who's going . . . to say it was no good what we done?" The narrator maintains that his love for this gypsy boy is part and parcel with his determination "to try for the sun"—to move forward, to push the boundaries, to aim for the highest goals he possibly can. And it's no mere physical attraction. Though they seem to be impoverished outcasts (because of their relationship?), they enrich and support each other with a deep, self-sacrificing love, sharing their meager possessions as well as their love.

They're very young—the narrator says that their ages added together total less than thirty (Donovan was in fact still in his teens when he wrote this song)—but, through their experiences together, they've become wise beyond their years. Such, presumably, is what living a gay life as a teenager meant back in the mid-1960s. Indeed, many gay teenagers today, in the 1990s, are still forced to grow up all too quickly when they're rejected by their families.

In the final verse of the song (aside from a restatement of the first), Donovan gets a little too undergraduately "poetic" for my taste, but he nevertheless manages an effective metaphor about singing to "the flowers so very few people really know." The gypsy boy (and perhaps the narrator as well, if Donovan is speaking here in a voice distinct from that of the narrative persona in the rest of the song) can be thought of as among these "flowers"—beautiful, delicate, precious, yet largely unknown things, despite the fact that they can be found all around. Donovan may be saying that gay people in general, as well as other traditional social outcasts, are such "flowers." And he prays for some justice, even a little help from above, on behalf of these misunderstood, unappreciated flowers. While I'm not sure whether many gay people today would cotton to the idea of being thought of as flowers (please, no pansy jokes!), I'm sure most of them would have appreciated a friend like Donovan when they, too, were teenagers.

▪ DORIAN ▪ "MEN'S ROOM" ▪

Songwriters:	K.D. Passante – D. Chromfeld
Year of Release:	1977
Original Album:	*Dorian*
Chart Performance:	Not released as a single, and the album didn't chart
Availability:	Out of print (Amerama 1001)

As we probe into the darkest, most hidden cavities of gay music history, we come across a brief six-song LP less than twenty minutes in length. Its front cover depicts a mutton-chopped young man dressed in a white tuxedo and top hat. Even his skin is painted white, the only dashes of color provided by his dark hair and a trickle of red streaming from the right corner of his mouth. (Vampire imagery? A wound?) At any rate, this must be the Dorian of the album's title—also the K.D. Passante of the songwriting credits, we suspect. We turn our attention to the back cover, which includes a smaller picture of Dorian, this time clutching a microphone in mid-song. The lyrics are there, too. As we read them we observe that we can easily read gayness into most of them. The most unquestionably gay song, however, appears to be the first one, titled "Men's Room." Fetching, very fetching.

So we put the record on our trusty old turntable and have a listen. Basic guitar rock, nothing out of the ordinary. The music, and for that matter Dorian's voice as well, could have been produced by any of a thousand or so garage bands across the country. The words tell of meeting someone "in the men's room" and the activities that ensue, which sound as though they involve oral sex followed by murder. Oddly tossing in quotations from the Rosary, Dorian pleads repeatedly for us to meet him in the men's room. But with all this talk of post-fellation death, we're not inclined to do so.

Meanwhile, as the record continues to play in its own forgettable way, we examine the album cover more closely. Beneath Dorian's photo on the back is a tiny quote: "I have no one to thank for this album but myself." Yes, we've heard this kind of thing before, direct from the egocentric, masturbatory self-aggrandizement school of modern thought, whose adherents are wont to spend their time reveling in the astounding wonderfulness of themselves. But before moving on to far better music, we post a reminder that when we have no one to thank but ourselves, we have no one else to blame, either. Which isn't such a bad idea, except it usually doesn't work out that way. More often than not, we're only too willing to take the credit, but none too eager to accept the responsibility.

▪ EMERSON, LAKE AND PALMER ▪
▪ "JEREMY BENDER" ▪

Songwriters:	Keith Emerson – Greg Lake
Year of Release:	1971
Original Album:	*Tarkus*
Chart Performance:	Not released as a single, but the album reached #9
Availability:	CD, CS (Atlantic 19121)

If the gatefold cartoon graphics on Emerson, Lake and Palmer's second album, *Tarkus*, can be taken at face value, the side-long title suite is a vaguely anti-war allegory about a half-tank, half-armadillo creature, born from an egg in a volcano, who confronts a succession of equally fearsome conglomerate beings and destroys them all, only to meet ultimate defeat when it gets poked in the eye (its sole weak spot) by the barbed tail of a manticore (one-third each of human, lion, and scorpion), which sends it lumbering off to the sea, presumably to die.

If all that sounds ridiculously pretentious and muddled, I assure you, it is.

The first song on the second side of the album suffers from much the same problem, though on a smaller scale. Less than two minutes in length,

"Jeremy Bender" is little more than a throwaway. To a comical, some-what Copland-ish melody played by Keith Emerson on a rinky-tink piano, Greg Lake sings the confused and confusing tale of one Jeremy Bender, "a man of leisure" who "decided to become a nun." Later Jeremy and another person of uncertain gender are described as asking "one another if the other's a queen." And later still we find our hero "Diggin' the sister—she was a mister."

But why go on? The alleged "story" never goes anywhere. It's just an excuse for the nebulous expression of sniggering, superior attitudes about ambisexuality. Without a doubt, gender anarchy is the order of the day (Jeremy Bender = gender-bender, plus "bent" is common British slang for "queer"), but this gender-play isn't of the sort that gay people sometimes do as a form of social satire. Rather, it's hateful and exploitative. It's not the gender-benders who are making fun of "straight" society, but rather it's the "straights" who are making fun of the gender-benders. There's even the faint sound of laughter in the background throughout the track, as if a coterie of Emerson, Lake and Palmer's select friends and acquaintances were present at the recording session, being tremendously entertained by this presumably naughty, naughty song about those silly, silly bent people.

I really shouldn't have expected any better. Emerson, Lake and Palmer always was the most vacuous of the "progressive rock" bands of the seventies.

▪ ERASURE ▪ "HIDEAWAY" ▪

Songwriters:	Vince Clarke – Andy Bell
Year of Release:	1987
Original Album:	*The Circus*
Chart Performance:	Not released as a single, but the album reached #190
Availability:	CD, CS (Sire 25554)

Erasure is a British technopop duo composed of ex-Depeche Mode, ex-Yaz synthesist Vince Clarke and openly gay lyricist-vocalist Andy Bell—whose voice bears an eerie resemblance to that of Clarke's earlier Yaz partner, Alison Moyet. Their song "Hideaway" charts much the same territory as Bronski Beat's "Smalltown Boy" from a few years before, telling the tale of a youngster rejected by his family because of his gayness—an occurrence that is, unfortunately, all to predictable both in the real world and on the melodramatic stage of pop music.

The music starts out slow and builds in speed and intensity. As it does so, it tells how our hero must leave home and head out on his own. Along

Erasure, 1989: (l-r) Andy Bell and Vince Clark. (Photo: David Scheinmann. Courtesy Sire-Reprise Records.)

the way, it lends support where his family would not, affirming him as well as any real-life gay teenagers who might be listening. "Don't be afraid," sings Bell, "you don't have to hide away." But this is no pie-in-the-sky slice of idealism. Young gay people face a world not only of possibilities but also of challenges and dangers for which they need to be strong: "There's a new world—you can make it on your own." While, as far as I'm concerned, "Hideaway" is hardly a first-rate piece of music, I nevertheless wish I had songs like it when I was growing up.

▪ ERASURE ▪ "GIMME GIMME GIMME (A MAN AFTER MIDNIGHT)" ▪

Songwriters:	Benny Andersson – Björn Ulvaeus
Year of Release:	1987
Original Album:	*The Two Ring Circus* (CD and cassette versions only)
Chart Performance:	The single didn't make the charts, but the album reached #186
Availability:	CD, CS (Sire 25667)

I remember thinking back in 1979 when Abba released "Gimme Gimme Gimme (A Man After Midnight)" what a wonderful tune it would be for some gay artist to record. "But no," I told myself, "it'll never be." Shows how much I knew. Erasure took it and made it their own. And our own. The Erasure version is perhaps not as frothily delicious as Abba's original musical milkshake, but it's no less amusingly lascivious. If only horniness were always this much fun.

▪ ERASURE ▪ "CHAINS OF LOVE" ▪

Songwriters: Vince Clarke – Andy Bell
Year of Release: 1988
Original Album: *The Innocents*
Chart Performance: The single reached #12
Availability: CD, CS (Sire 25730)

Confronted with the almost insurmountable challenge of saying exactly what he wants on pop radio, Andy Bell opens this remarkable record with a slow, solemn confession of his dilemma: "How can I explain when there are few words I can choose?" Then, backed by Vince Clarke's bank of synthesizers, he launches into a percolating, irresistibly danceable piece of social commentary. Although deep thought isn't commonly linked to dancing, at least of the rock-related variety, Bell asks us to think back to another era: "Do you remember . . . when people on the street were walking hand-in-hand-in-hand?" He then adds the bittersweet insight, "Days would last forever."

That was then. Now days grow short. This is language you might expect from a middle-aged or elderly person. But Bell is a young man. Why should days no longer seem to last forever? Why has time grown so precious?

AIDS. And with it have come changes in the social climate: more struggle, more fear, greater challenges. As Bell goes on to suggest, the old days—the warmer, more carefree, yet still caring days before AIDS—now seem like a children's fable. But faced with this loss, we can do more than simply whine nostalgically about the past. We can affirm ourselves and each other, lending each other our love and support. The chorus says it all:

> *Come to me, cover me, hold me*
> *Together we'll break these chains of love*
> *Don't give up, don't give up*
> *Together with me and my baby break the chains of love*

It took me a while to understand the metaphor here. The first few times I heard this song, I thought "chains of love" referred to the way in which love, under some unfortunate circumstances, can entrap and entwine people, binding them in unhealthy relationships. But that's not what's going on here at all. "Chains of love" is, in fact, a strangely appropriate metaphor for AIDS and the fears it has inspired. Think about it. Most commonly spread through an act of love, AIDS has therefore caused a restricting, a chaining of love. People aren't as free to share their love (OK, OK, in this case a euphemism for sex) as they once were. Furthermore, AIDS has also revealed a dismaying lack of love in some quarters—not that it ever surprised us—as too many people have responded to the epidemic with fear, reproach, and bigotry. Fortunately, by contrast, almost paradoxically, it has also resulted in greater loving and caring among gay people and their non-gay friends than ever before. These, too, are chains of love.

I have no idea if this is really what Bell and Clarke intended when they wrote "Chains of Love." It hardly matters. All I know is that when Bell urges us again and again, gliding in and out of his falsetto, singing that unforgettable chorus so forcefully, so soulfully—"Don't give up, don't give up"—I feel stronger. I feel more hopeful. Yes, *together* we can do it.

And, in a small way, you know what's the best part of all? That Andy Bell, with so few words to choose, succeeded in getting his message across on pop radio, even producing a significant hit in the process. True, most listeners and record-buyers probably haven't heard in it what I and many others have heard. But at least they danced. And it's important to keep dancing.

■ ROBERTA FLACK ■
■ "BALLAD OF THE SAD YOUNG MEN" ■

Songwriters: Frances Landesman – Thomas J. Wolf, Jr.
Year of Release: 1969
Original Album: *First Take*
Chart Performance: Not released as a single, but the album was #1
                      for five weeks
Availability: CD, CS (Atlantic 8230)

Originally composed for an obscure 1959 musical, *The Nervous Set*—all about Greenwich Village beatniks and other artistic types—this relic of pre-Stonewall sensibilities would at one time have been considered liberal, open-minded, and supportive. You see, it expresses deep, deep pity for those poor, poor—you know—*artistic* types. But nowadays it seems quaint, depressing, and more than a little offensive. Essentially, "Ballad of the Sad Young Men" is the musical equivalent of *The Boys in the Band*, with all of the loathsome pathos but none of the almost-redeeming humor of Mart Crowley's equally antiquated play.

The song's arrangement is typical early Flack. Think of "The First Time Ever I Saw Your Face" (from the same album), with its nightclub-style ballad-jazzoid piano, upright bass, barely audible drums, and slow, stately tempo—you pretty much have it. When you get right down to it, "Ballad of the Sad Young Men" is the perfect vehicle for this sort of treatment, which probably explains why Flack chose it. Nearly every stanza (and there are quite a few of them in this seven-minute-plus song) begins with the words "All the sad young men," used over and over again, repeated *ad nauseum* from one verse to the next. And, as anyone can see, these sad young men are so sad because they're so lonely, and they're so lonely because they're gay.

In some ways the lyrics are as closeted as the sad young men, who are never specifically identified as homosexuals. For the most part you have to read between the lines, noting the references to drinking, bars, and, most stereotypically, recurring suggestions that the one thing that weighs most heavily on these sad young men's minds is the inevitability of aging. For instance, we're told that one major source of their misery is the fact that they're "running from the truth" of growing old. It's that malevolent "Nobody loves you when you're old and gay" cliché, employed here not only to explain in part why these young men are sad, but also as a tip-off to the root cause of their sadness. After all, "normal" men aren't supposed to dwell on aging in this way, are they? (But if that's the case, then what accounts for all those "Hair Club for Men" commercials on late-night TV?)

The song goes on to hint at another source of their sadness: the fleeting nature of love in the gay world. Another stereotype, this time the pervasive loneliness of gay people and the transience of their sexual relationships. These have always been modern society's "big guns," so to speak, in its continuing battle against homosexuality—the claim that gay people are invariably both miserable and immoral.

This all begins to get quite tedious, but then the most interesting stanza of the song comes when a lone female character is introduced to the narrative. She's a "tired little girl" who tries her best "to be gay for a sad young man." What else can this be but the pathetic image of a woman trying to "change" a gay man, or at least trying to meet his needs in order to gain or retain his love? To help out those listeners who still haven't figured out why all these young men are so sad, the lyricist drops a code word, "gay," for the benefit of those in the know. (Remember, this song was written in the 1950s, when you still could have counted on most people not instantly associating "gay" with homosexuality.) This young woman is doomed to failure because her sad young man can only find satisfaction in another gay (read *homosexual*) man, not in a gay (read *gleeful*) woman. It's a devastating pun, the sole truly imaginative thing in the song. If it didn't appear in such a dreary context, it would even be amusing.

The final stanzas are the worst of all, not only because of their moronically transparent moon images (oh, moon—sad, sad, sad—lonely, lonely, lonely) but also because of their implications for what it means to be gay, when you "play at making love." In short, even gay love-making is fake. Gay people are incapable of true love. The lyrical and psychosexual clichés simply pile atop one another. It's as reprehensible as it is depressing.

For all of the obvious pity expended on the young men of its title, "Ballad of the Sad Young Men" is ultimately a sermonette against the lifestyle that it professes to describe. It practically screams out, "You wouldn't want to be like *that*, would you?" Granted, such sermonizing is better coupled

86

with pleas for pity than with pleas for imprisonment or execution. For 1959, or even the 1969 of Flack's version, I suppose "Ballad of the Sad Young Men" could have been worse. But it's dreadful for anything thereafter, especially for the way in which it reinforces vicious stereotypes. Like the similarly flawed *The Boys in the Band*, "Ballad of the Sad Young Men" belongs in a museum somewhere as a reminder of how bad things have been in the past. And in a particularly dusty corner of the museum at that.

Would you believe that Johnny Mathis also recorded a version of this thing 'way back when, and that Rickie Lee Jones even revived it for her 1991 *Pop Pop* album?—an act of musical necrophilia if there ever was one. I would've given them both more credit than that. But at least Mathis can claim the ignorance of the period in which the record was made. I don't know what Jones' excuse is.

▪ ROBERTA FLACK ▪ "MAKING LOVE" ▪

Songwriters:	Carole Bayer Sager – Burt Bacharach – Bruce Roberts
Year of Release:	1982
Original Album:	*I'm the One*
Chart Performance:	The single reached #13
Availability:	CS (Atlantic 19354)

"Making Love" is the pretty but antiseptic title song from the almost-as-pretty, almost-as-antiseptic movie about a young husband who leaves his young wife after discovering his own homosexuality. Both the film and the single were mild successes. In order to ensure maximum mileage for the record (and perhaps even to help lure unsuspecting movie patrons), such words as "gay" and "homosexual" are nowhere to be found in the lyrics. Instead, the language is so universalized that only those who already know about the film's subject matter truly understand what the song's copious references to love and confusion allude to.

The recurring line "There's more to love than making love" essentially means that you don't have to continue having sex with someone (such as your gay ex-husband) to continue loving him—a fact that was at the very heart of the movie. And, after a while, the pain of learning that the one you love sexually is unable to return that sexual love goes away. "Some things never change. Some things sometimes do." How's that for stating the obvious?

At any rate, Roberta Flack delivers a warm, aching reading of the quiet, contemplative lyrics on this, her only solo Top Forty single of the 1980s. I do assume that she knew what the movie would be about when she recorded "Making Love" (which, considering the general nature of the lyrics, would by no means have been essential), in which case I give her credit. Actually, I appreciate the fact that everyone involved in the making of the film and single took such pains to make them as inoffensive as possible so that they might reach a wider audience and engender the greatest support. As they say, you catch more flies with honey than with vinegar. And a spoonful of sugar makes the medicine go down.

▪ FLIRTATIONS ▪
▪ "TO KNOW HIM IS TO LOVE HIM" ▪

Songwriter:	Phil Spector
Year of Release:	1990
Original Album:	*The Flirtations*
Chart Performance:	Not released as a single, and the album didn't chart
Availability:	CD, CS (Significant Other 902)

I suppose that when openly gay performers take an old pop/rock chestnut like this (a 1958 #1 hit for Phil Spector's original group, the Teddy Bears) and neglect to change the pronouns as a heterosexual performer of the opposite sex would almost certainly do (the Teddy Bears had a female lead vocalist), it's only poetic justice—revenge, if you will, for all those years of absolutely no music for gay teenagers, or at least for gay teenagers to be gay to. (My favorite example of this, since not a single song in the entire Beach Boys *oeuvre* can even remotely be considered "gay," is the remake of "Surfer Girl" by the openly lesbian artist Phranc.) Besides, the sentimentality that underlies songs like "To Know Him Is to Love Him" is equally viable for gay and non-gay people alike. And, with regard to this song in particular, I would further argue that it takes gay ears, or at least ears well informed by gay sensibilities, to glean fully the inherent humor in those parallel "know-know-knows" and "love-love-loves."

To make a long story short, "To Know Him Is to Love Him" was just *waiting* for openly gay voices.

In this case, the openly gay voices belong to the Flirtations, a five-man *a cappella* group. They're every bit as good as a certain other, far more famous *a cappella* group whom a great many people believe also to be gay despite their lack of openness on the subject (though the occasional lyric provides hints, and one of the original members reportedly died of complications from AIDS), which, of course, accounts at least in part for the disparity between the levels of commercial success for the two groups. The Flirtations, by contrast, *flaunt* their gayness—and I mean that in a wholly

The Flirtations, 1992: (l-r) Jon Arterton, Cliff Townsend, Aurelio Font, Michael Callen, and Jimmy Rutland. (Photo: Gene Bagnato. Courtesy Fleming Tamulevich & Associates.)

positive sense. In fact, they're a tremendous joy to see and to hear.

Although it may be unfair of me to single out any single Flirtation, I should note that, at the time of this recording, one of them was Michael Callen (who later, unfortunately, had to retire from the group because of his own AIDS-related illness). Callen possesses perhaps the most astounding, songbird-like falsetto in the business today. I love ya', Jimmy Somerville, but you can't touch this. And while Frankie Valli in his heyday definitely *could* touch it—hell, *surpass* it—it's been a long, long time since Dawn went away. At any rate, Michael and his pals put their respective vocal skills to superb use in "To Know Him Is to Love Him."

What makes this track so special—aside from the general excellence of the vocal performance—is its multiple strands of campiness. Within the basic framework of a sweetly harmonized love song barely over three minutes in length, the Flirtations toss in assorted pseudo-operatic flourishes, fifties-style doo-wops, a spoken recitative lifted directly from "Ain't No Mountain High Enough" as interpreted by Diana Ross, occasional images of ordinary domestic bliss ("I'll make lunch for him") not at all part of Spector's original (except in the way that they similarly pursue the mundane implications of sublime emotions), and enough breathiness to fill half the balloons at a gay pride parade. Essentially, they take this song where no cliché has gone before, into a musical borderland where it's neither a fishy parody nor a foul lounge piece. It manages to be both beautiful and comical at the same time, and if you can listen to it without smiling, then I certainly don't ever want to run into you in a dark alley.

"This," I want to shout, "is why we're called *gay!*"

Lest I mislead you, I should add that "To Know Him Is to Love Him" is only one of sixteen wonderful reasons to rush out and buy *The Flirtations*, though you'll probably have to go to your local gay bookstore to do it. I especially like "Breaths," "Shooting Star," "Something Inside So Strong," and the group's signature tune, "The Flirt Song." If you like terrific vocal harmonies—spiced with warm humor and just a touch of naughtiness—then you're doing yourself a great disservice until you get this album. Meanwhile, I can't resist indulging in that grand Spectorian cliché one more time: when it comes to the Flirtations, to know, know, know them is to love, love, love them.

Songwriter:	Bill Folk
Year of Release:	1991
Original Album:	*Lookin' for Mr. Right*
Chart Performance:	Not released as a single, and the album didn't chart
Availability:	CD, CS (Bright Moon 91732)

In order to do Bill Folk's music justice, I have to split myself temporarily into two different observers: the Nice Gay Boy and the Nasty, Cynical, Jaded Record Reviewer.

• • • • •

The Nice Gay Boy

"Lookin' for Mr. Right"—not just the title track, but the whole album —is a warm, whimsical, wonderful celebration of gayness. Bill Folk's gentle, sincere style makes you feel good all over, even when he sings the occasional sad song. He keenly observes modern gay urban life and comments on it in a witty, loving manner. The music moves from one style to another, from folk to pop to soft rock, but always retains a heartfelt, personal style.

Mr. Folk looks and sounds like a very nice man, someone who would make a marvelous friend, and that friendliness—as well as a tremendously gay-positive attitude—comes across clearly on every number. In short, *Lookin' for Mr. Right* is a very, very nice record. It makes you feel really, really good to be gay.

• • • • •

The Nasty, Cynical, Jaded Record Reviewer

"Lookin' for Mr. Right"—not just the title track, but the whole album— is a major disappointment. No matter how hard he tries with his gentle, sincere style, Bill Folk can't make up for the fact that his singing voice can graciously be described as mediocre. Meanwhile, his lyrics are unrelentingly sappy, stilted, and/or clichéd. And though they're hardly unique in that respect—at least 95% of all pop music lyrics of the past forty years are equally awful or worse—at least a good or even merely interesting singer can transform bad lyrics into a satisfying experience. Not here. The music moves from one style to another, from folk to pop to soft rock, mangling each in the process. The melodies are repetitive, both within individual songs and from one song to another, and the instrumentation, aside from some good keyboard and acoustic guitar (the latter courtesy of Folk himself), is amateurish. I have trouble believing that anybody aside from the people who worked on this record could find repeated listenings anything but intolerable. But, then again, I'm a nasty, cynical, jaded record reviewer. Don't you just *hate* me?

Mr. Folk looks and sounds like a very nice man, someone who would make a marvelous friend, and that friendliness comes across clearly on every number. But it takes more than friendliness to make a good record. Even a good *gay* record. In short, a tremendously gay-positive attitude (and, heaven knows, that's important) and an overriding sense of niceness are just about the only things to recommend *Lookin' for Mr. Right*. But you certainly don't need music like this to make you feel good to be gay. If you do, I feel very, very sorry for you.

● ● ● ● ●

Which of these two observers should you take to heart? If supporting earnest, openly gay performers is important to you—as perhaps it should be—then by all means do as I did and buy Bill Folk's album. If you're a Nice Gay Boy, you may enjoy it more than any Nasty, Cynical, Jaded Record Reviewer would.

▪ TED FOX ▪ "TELL ME WHY" AND "WHEN WE WERE FRIENDS" ▪

Songwriter:	Ted Fox (both songs)
Year of Release:	1992
Original Album:	*One of Us*
Chart Performance:	Not released as singles, and the album didn't chart
Availability:	CS (Heymanee – no number)

Not to be callous about it, but now to some "gay music" of superior quality. "Tell Me Why" and "When We Were Friends" are the opening tracks on *One of Us* by Ted Fox, a folkish singer-guitarist based in New Mexico. Fox writes songs from an unflinchingly gay viewpoint, and he has a strong yet intimate voice that all but demands you to share in his equally intimate acoustic music.

"Tell Me Why" is a near-anthemic, activist-oriented call for gay people everywhere to stand up for themselves and each other. Fox's relentless optimism is tempered by a sense of realism that only serves to strengthen his positive outlook:

> *I realize we have an uphill fight*
> *But tell me why we should sit back and wait*
> *Or pretend we're straight when we feel this great*

The mood is infectious, a driving musical force for change.

"When We Were Friends" is just as optimistic, though in an angrier, more personal context: being rejected by a heterosexual friend who has just learned that you're gay. (I know how *that* feels.) Although Fox says that he wishes "things could be like they were back when we were friends," he won't plead or apologize. Rather than surrender "to a brain-dead schmuck" like his former friend, he tells him to "get the hell away" because he "ain't got time for bigotry." Fox leaves open the possibility that the friendship might be renewed at a later date, but only after his erstwhile buddy has "gotten some therapy."

While we're on the subject of therapy, let me say that that's pretty much what *One of Us* is all about. It's a marvelously therapeutic album that doesn't sacrifice musical quality for the sake of its many empowering, affirming messages. Other standout numbers include a "pride song" titled "Sink or Swim," the lovely keyboard instrumental "Song for the Quilt," and the title track, which is yet another pride song. Though occasionally heavy-handed in its pervasive air of activism, Ted Fox's *One of Us* remains totally enjoyable to listen to. Sort of like hearing a sermon by a *really good* preacher. A really good *gay* preacher.

▪ FRANKIE GOES TO HOLLYWOOD ▪ "RELAX" ▪

Songwriters:	Peter Gill – Holly Johnson – Mark O'Toole
Year of Release:	1984
Original Album:	*Welcome to the Pleasuredome*
Chart Performance:	The single originally failed to chart, but it reached #10 upon re-release a few months later
Availability:	CD, CS, LP (Island 422-824052)

In his wonderfully informative albeit somewhat controversial book about the "hidden gays" in the music industry, *The Vinyl Closet* (the fun of trying to guess the names of his anonymous interviewees alone is worth the price), Boze Hadleigh notes that "Relax" has been called "the first love song ever addressed to an anus." I wish I knew who said that.

So you take a five-man group with a very odd name, two of whose members (lead singer Holly Johnson and background vocalist-dancer Paul Rutherford) are openly gay, and let them record a song with such lyrics as "Relax, don't do it when you wanna come." If that's not enough to send the Jesse Helmses of this world into paroxysms of righteous rage, add a line about "shooting it off." Then serve it up with an initial video (banned from the BBC and mainstream American television, which is always good for business) that depicts scenes from something that resembles a cross between a circus, a Roman orgy, and an upscale S&M bar, including a visual euphemism for so-called "water sports." And what have you got? One of the most astounding hits of the 1980s, that's what.

"Relax" was anything but subtle, with a hammering bass line that mechanistically drove home the fact that it was all about SEX, and without too great a leap of the imagination, about male-male sex to boot. Near the end of the song you can hear Johnson's almost-buried-beneath-the-mix cries of "I'm comin', I'm comin'." There's even the sound of rushing water, directly related to the bar scenes of the original video. American viewers rarely got to see this, however. Instead they were treated to a lip-synching stage-performance video in which Johnson spends much of his time shining a large flashlight (metaphor, anyone?) on his bandmates and members of the audience, most of which consists of young girls intent upon leaping to the stage to plant kisses on members of the group. The craven dishonesty and hypocrisy of the record industry can be disgusting at times.

"Frankiemania" was an intense but short-lived phenomenon in Great Britain that never took off in the United States. After "Relax" came a second hit, the latter-day Cold War protest song "Two Tribes." The inner sleeves of the two-record *Welcome to the Pleasuredome* album hawked such merchandise as "Frankie Say" T-shirts and "Jean Genet boxer shorts" so crassly that it's hard to say for sure whether it was cynical get-rich-quick capitalism gone rampant or a clever parody of that very impulse. Unfortunately, despite a cut titled "Krisco Kisses," the LP was largely ignoble aside from the hits themselves. After a second album bombed miserably, Frankie fell apart. But you had to hand it to them. In their fifteen minutes of glory, they were wild, if calculatedly wild, and they managed to produce a riveting, pulsating classic of gay rock that still sounds as exciting today as when it first appeared.

▪ LEWIS FUREY ▪
▪ "HUSTLER'S TANGO" AND "LAST NIGHT" ▪

Songwriter: Lewis Furey (both songs)
Year of Release: 1975
Original Album: *Lewis Furey*
Chart Performance: Neither song was released as a single, and the
                       album failed to chart
Availability: Out of print (A&M 4522)

Lewis Furey, a British singer and keyboardist who released a couple of albums on A&M Records in the mid-seventies, was a highly original talent. The reason that you probably haven't heard of him is that his career never really took off. But his debut album is interesting from a "gay" viewpoint. The personae he adopts on various songs seem by turns to be heterosexual, homosexual, and bisexual. On the surface, the opening number, "Hustler's Tango," seems the "gayest" of the lot. Yes, it's a tango, with a stuttering arrangement that adds a comic tone to the proceedings. Furey assumes the role of a male prostitute negotiating with a prospective client: "You say you want to rape me, baby . . . you know you've got to pay." To remove any doubt as to the gender of the person to whom he's speaking, he addresses him as "my brother, my lover." The client, however, seems apprehensive, so the narrator tries to assure him. "Don't feel guilty . . . c'mon decide."

The last lines of "Hustler's Tango" provide a weird twist:

Hey, baby, do you want me?
Faustus, can you hear me?

In other words, Furey has recast the Faust story—the man who sells his soul to the Devil—with Satan in the role of a male prostitute. Very clever. Also very insidious; I'll leave it to you to contemplate the propriety of employing a "gay" image to describe seductive evil.

The song "Last Night" doesn't carry such metaphysical weight. Rather, it appears to be the tale of a miserable man who's in the habit of "picking up boys, faking a love"—a self-described "mean old churl" who considers himself "unnatural." But suddenly he finds himself literally singing with joy.

I met a lady last night
Made me feel so loving and so gay

So whereas the narrator could never find love in his stream of pick-up boys, he does find it in a woman who, ironically, makes him feel "gay."

I don't think I need to go into this any further, do you?

Lewis Furey made some enjoyable music, and he wasn't afraid to evoke gayness in his lyrics. I just don't care for the *ways* in which he evokes gayness, using it as an allegorical device for portraying the Devil or offering it as a negative contrast to positive heterosexual love.

▪ GENESIS ▪ "THE BATTLE OF EPPING FOREST" ▪

Songwriters:	Genesis (Peter Gabriel – Tony Banks – Mike Rutherford – Phil Collins – Steve Hackett)
Year of Release:	1973
Original Album:	*Selling England by the Pound*
Chart Performance:	Not released as a single, but the album reached #70
Availability:	CD, CS (Atlantic 19277)

Long before Peter Gabriel and Phil Collins had solo careers, they were two-fifths of Genesis, perhaps the most intelligent and melodic of the British progressive-art-rock bands of the seventies. In this selection from their excellent *Selling England by the Pound* album, they describe a teenage gang fight in their typically baroque style of the period. One of the characters in this mini-epic is obviously meant to be taken as gay, betrayed by the fact that Gabriel affects a haughty but slightly lisping voice as he sings the lines,

> *And Harold Demure, from Art Literature*
> *Nips up the nearest tree*

Facile gay stereotype #1: Gayness equals effeminacy equals cowardice. True, Harold partly redeems himself later in the song as he "fires acorns from out of his sling." But he's still not exactly a paragon and, besides, Gabriel compounds his sin by adding a falsetto sweep, verging on girlish giggliness, the second time around.

Oh, well—perhaps the enlightened social awareness demonstrated by Gabriel and his chums in recent years now extends to gay people, too. I suppose we all did things back in the seventies that we regret now.

▪ GENESIS ▪ "JESUS HE KNOWS ME" ▪

Songwriters:	Tony Banks – Phil Collins – Mike Rutherford
Year of Release:	1991
Original Album:	*We Can't Dance*
Chart Performance:	The single reached #23
Availability:	CD, CS (Atlantic 82344)

Eighteen years later, in this scathing satire of televangelism, the faithful core of Genesis offers up a straw-man T.V. preacher who extols "family values" by day but surreptitiously engages in extramarital affairs by night. And just to underscore his hypocrisy, they have him fooling around with men as well as with women. In essence, Phil Collins and company make a statement implicitly supportive of gay people while using a villainous closet bisexual as the brunt of their joke. In this way they manage to please everyone and offend no one—except, of course, televangelists and their fundamentalist flocks. And perhaps some bisexuals, though I suppose most of them won't mind small sacrifices like this in the ongoing war against anti-gay bigotry, which certainly has an impact on them, too.

▪ BOBBIE GENTRY ▪ "ODE TO BILLIE JOE" ▪

Songwriter:	Bobbie Gentry
Year of Release:	1967
Original Album:	*Ode to Billie Joe*
Chart Performance:	The single was #1 for four weeks
Availability:	Original album out of print; available on *Bobbie Gentry's Greatest Hits*, CD, CS (Curb 77387)

During the late summer of 1967, it seemed that more than half the country was totally preoccupied with either the Beatles' *Sgt. Pepper's Lonely Hearts Club Band* or Bobbie Gentry's "Ode to Billie Joe." The latter was a genuine mystery set to music. Just what did the song's narrator and Billie Joe McAllister throw off the Tallahatchee Bridge? And why did Billie Joe commit suicide by jumping off that same bridge shortly afterwards? There were all sorts of speculations, but Bobbie Gentry kept quiet about it. She wisely let her mesmerizing composition, with its oddly detached vocal, haunting melody, and folksy acoustic guitar backed by mournful, swooping strings, do all of the talking for her. Some mysteries are far more eloquent left unsolved.

Unfortunately, Gentry's recording career floundered—she was never able to come up with anything else with even a fraction of the appeal of "Ode to Billie Joe"—and she surrendered to the temptation to allow her masterpiece to become the basis for a 1976 movie. The producers of the film just couldn't resist spilling *all* the beans, including ones that probably never existed before screenwriters got a hold of the story. According to *Ode to Billie Joe* the movie, the object that got tossed off the Tallahatchee Bridge was a rag doll long cherished by the female protagonist as a sort of "security blanket," its disposal unsubtly symbolizing her loss of innocence. And, wouldn't you know it, Billie Joe McAllister (portrayed by Robby Benson) jumps off the bridge because he found out he was queer, or at least bisexual enough to be distraught about it. As the heroine later says accusingly to the man with whom Billie Joe had "done it," he killed himself because he had "been with a man—a sin against God and nature."

Now this is what I have to say about that. While gay teen suicide is a horrible reality that should be honestly dealt with in the media, the film *Ode to Billie Joe* doesn't so much "deal" with it as exploit it. Despite its presumed sensationalism and shock value, teenage homosexuality serves as the movie's clichéd, predictable excuse for the theretofore mysterious death of a fictional character. The movie makes no attempt to criticize the terrible social attitudes that have driven gay and lesbian youngsters to kill themselves before, during, and after the 1950s, when the *Billie Joe* story was set. Instead, homosexuality is this awful, sinful thing that, in the context of the film, becomes a perfectly rational explanation if not justification for suicide.

Getting back to the song, it's hard for me to believe that homosexuality played any role whatsoever in the original concept. I seriously doubt whether Bobbie Gentry had any one explanation in mind for Billie Joe's suicide. As she herself has said, it wasn't very important: "Anyone who hears the song can think anything they want . . . but the real 'message' of the song, if there must be a message, revolves around the nonchalant way the family talks about the suicide. They sit there eating their peas and apple pie and talking, without even realizing that Billie Joe's girlfriend is sitting at the table, *a member of the family*" (as quoted by Fred Bronson in *The Billboard Book of Number One Hits*). Thus, from Gentry's own words, we can see that Billie Joe's suicide is a Hitchcockian "MacGuffin" —a mere plot device that motivates the actions of fictional characters, those actions themselves being the real focus of the story. I find it interesting that Gentry's description of her song involves people sitting around a dinner table, thoughtlessly saying things that are painful for one of their family members to hear—a parallel to the way in which non-gay people so often say hurtful, homophobic things in the presence of their closeted (and sometimes even uncloseted) gay and lesbian friends and family members.

So here's to "Ode to Billie Joe"—a classic song, a regrettable movie, and in both cases an eloquent testimonial to the callousness of humanity.

■ STEVE GOODMAN ■
■ "MEN WHO LOVE WOMEN WHO LOVE MEN" ■

Songwriter:	Steve Goodman
Year of Release:	1979
Original Album:	*High and Outside*
Chart Performance:	Both the single and the album failed to make the charts
Availability:	Out of print (Asylum 174)

Here's a rousing, toe-tapping, hand-clapping, quasi-gospel number for you, based on "When the Saints Go Marching In," complete with horn section. The late singer-songwriter Steve Goodman, best known for his classic train song "The City of New Orleans," always had a streak of unpredictable whimsy about him, and it certainly shines in "Men Who Love Women Who Love Men." You can hear him smiling as he sings it.

Basically, "Men Who Love Women Who Love Men" is an equal-opportunity celebration of human sexual behavior. Goodman looks up and down "42nd Street" and sees "every kind of man and woman" there, which leads him to his chorus, where he refers not only to heterosexuals and lesbians but also to

> *Men who love men because they can't pretend they are*
> *Men who love women who love men*

As the song continues, Goodman flippantly but nonjudgmentally describes all manner of sexual beings, ranging from prostitutes to voyeurs to exhibitionists, always returning to his straight-lesbian-gay refrain.

The underlying irony of the "When the Saints Go Marching In" music is never far from the surface. On the one hand, it serves as a delightful contrast with the catalog of sexual "malefactors" in the lyrics, the implication of course being that "Men Who Love Women Who Love Men" is a sort of inverted "When the Sinners Go Marching In"—or "Out," as the case may be. At the same time, Goodman is so joyful in his mood that you get the sense that he regards these folks as true saints in their own way: saints of sexuality, so to speak, affirming sexual pleasure-seeking.

At any rate, "Men Who Love Women Who Love Men" may be somewhat on the frivolous side, but a little frivolity never hurt anybody. Besides, didn't some wise person once observe that, when you actually think about it, sex really is pretty ridiculous?

Yes, it is. Wonderfully so.

■ STEVEN GROSSMAN ■ "CARAVAN TONIGHT" ■

Songwriter:	Steven Grossman
Year of Release:	1974
Original Album:	*Caravan Tonight*
Chart Performance:	Not released as a single, and the album didn't chart
Availability:	Out of print (Mercury 1-702)

Don't make the mistake I used to and confuse this guy with Steve Goodman or with jazz saxophonist Steve Grossman. Steven Grossman is an openly gay singer-songwriter who recorded the groundbreaking but largely forgotten album *Caravan Tonight* in the early seventies. What made it so revolutionary wasn't just the upfront gayness of the lyrics, but also the fact that it was released by a major record label, Mercury. While major record labels had already shown some willingness to release songs by gay (or gay-pretend) artists working in the genre of glitter rock, Grossman was no Bowie clone. His music bore a far stronger resemblance to that of James Taylor or Cat Stevens. And if anything was hotter in the early seventies than glitter, it was sensitive singer-songwriters.

Nearly every song on *Caravan Tonight* is unambiguously gay. "Out," for instance, finds Grossman telling each member of his (or his narrator's) family, one by one, about his gayness, employing the clever lyrical device of never saying "gay" until the very last word of the song—though he comes close a couple of times to using the words "fag" and "queer," only to leave them out and allow the unspoken, implied rhymes with the previous lines' "brag" and "fear" as clues for filling in the blanks. Another track, "Dry Dock Dreaming," utilizes shifting rhythms and styles to parallel a stream-of-consciousness description of the narrator's sexual adventures and/or fantasies "at the docks by the cold Hudson River."

But the song that stands out most in my mind is the one that gives the album its title. "Caravan Tonight" is a lovely song with highly evocative lyrics. Its appealing arrangement—acoustic guitar supported by piano, light percussion, and strings—heightens the almost magical aura as Grossman sings metaphorically of a crisis point in a youthful gay relationship: "Austin, you got that gypsy in your eye." The narrator, so deeply in love, imagines a caravan outside their window that will soon draw Austin away. There's sadness in his voice, but understanding as well, for he knows that any attempts to restrain his lover will only serve to drive them farther apart. So he decides to let Austin go—doing so with the hope that, by granting him freedom, he will strengthen their love.

> And if the freedom your heart embraces
> Is nothing but a vision in the sand
> Oh, I'll be your oasis . . . I'll be your promised land

"Caravan Tonight" is filled with marvelous rhymes and images like this, carried along by a gorgeous melody. Absolutely stunning.

Find this record if you can. Search local libraries. Haunt used record stores. Find a friend who has it. (Is it unethical to suggest taping an out-of-print record?) Hell, write to Mercury Records and *beg* them to re-release it on CD. Unless you're so jaded that you refuse to reduce yourself to listening to a "sensitive singer-songwriter," you simply *must* hear "Caravan Tonight," if only once. It should be a required part of your personal gay education.

▪ GUNS N' ROSES ▪ "ONE IN A MILLION" ▪

Songwriters:	Guns N' Roses
Year of Release:	1988
Original Album:	*G N' R Lies*
Chart Performance:	Not released as a single, but the album reached #2
Availability:	CD, CS (Geffen 24198)

A notoriously racist, xenophobic, and homophobic song in which the narrator warns "niggers" to stay out of his way and then rails at immigrants and "faggots" who "come to our country and . . . spread some fuckin' disease." More than anything else (except perhaps guitarist Slash's repeated use of obscenities on live network television during the 1991 American Music Awards), "One in a Million" established Guns N' Roses' reputation as one of the supreme malignancies of rock. (I'm not going to discuss some of the hideously misogynistic songs they've recorded.) At least they had the decency to give the album an honest title.

I've read that lead singer and chief lyricist Axl Rose has gotten some therapy and has now become a more compassionate person, as exemplified by his participation in the big Freddie Mercury tribute–AIDS fundraising concert, in which he sang "Bohemian Rhapsody" with Elton John. Let's hope his new appreciation for gay people extends beyond his fellow rock stars.

▪ LARRY HAVLUCK ▪ "PIANO ROLLS" ▪

Songwriter:	Larry Bob Havluck
Year of Release:	1992
Original Album:	*Half-Life*
Chart Performance:	Not released as a single, and the album didn't chart
Availability:	CS (Larry Bob Havluck – no number)

In the world of gay men's music, they don't get much "folkier" than Larry Havluck. You can sometimes see him performing on the sidewalks of downtown Minneapolis, his base of operations, with his guitar case open to catch any spare change or paper currency passers-by may toss his way. He also performs with some regularity in various coffeehouses and gay bars around town. When he records, Havluck does so in a decidedly low-budget environment, often accompanied only by his acoustic guitar, though he's sometimes supplemented by harmonica, kazoo, keyboards, violin, or other instruments, but rarely more than one or two others at a time. He also composes his own songs, ranging from intense pieces that tug at your heart-strings to tongue-in-cheek celebrations of the ironies and absurdities of life. Perhaps Havluck's best-known number is "Must've Been Drunk," which Romanovsky & Phillips have turned into a nationwide favorite among gay audiences. Too bad more royalties aren't forthcoming from that sort of thing.

As is the case with most "folk-oriented" music, Havluck's performances generally come across much better live than on recordings. But there's still plenty to enjoy on *Half-Life* (the title of which I suspect is a self-deprecating play on his surname). Consider, for instance, the jaunty, highly melodic opening cut, "Separate Beds," the slightly lewd "Fireman Song," and the delightfully strange "Bearnaise (On the Bare Knees of Bernice)," which, if there's no such thing as "camp folk," goes a long way toward inventing the genre.

I want to make special mention, however, of the final track, "Piano Rolls." It's a beautiful, touching song that laments the AIDS-related death of an unnamed fellow musician—a self-hating pianist friend and erstwhile sex partner. Though Havluck chastises the spirit of the dead man for his refusal to truly love another person (because he felt no love for himself), he grieves nonetheless. And, in a chillingly honest statement, he confesses, "I'm full of wonders that I am still alive." In this way, "Piano Rolls" moves beyond a simple song of grief, into a therapeutic attempt to cope with survival. As the song fades, a haunting piano takes up a counter-melody. It sounds distant, like a memory, or perhaps like a refrain from the realm of the dead. Very moving.

A few poor selections mar *Half-Life* somewhat—particularly several Jeffrey Dahmer references of questionable taste and "Die, Yuppie Scum," a parody of "The Ballad of the Green Berets" that cruelly stereotypes those who thrive in the capitalistic system without deigning to toss money into street musicians' guitar cases—but, otherwise, it would make a fine addition to your music collection, especially if you're fonder of somewhat "folky" music than I. And the next time you see a sidewalk musician performing for the harried pedestrians of urban America, just remember: he or she may be gay. He may even be Larry Havluck.

▪ JIMI HENDRIX EXPERIENCE ▪ "PURPLE HAZE" ▪

Songwriter:	Jimi Hendrix
Year of Release:	1967
Original Album:	*Are You Experienced?*
Chart Performance:	The single reached #65
Availability:	CD, CS, LP (Reprise 6261)

Get ready for a good laugh. I've heard on good authority that some people believe that when Hendrix sings his famous line, "'Scuse me while I kiss the sky," he's actually singing, "'Scuse me while I kiss *this guy*." Patently ludicrous—all you need is one good ear to know the difference.

Now that you've had your laugh, I must add that on at least one live version of "Purple Haze" recorded in 1969 (found on the four-CD boxed set *Stages*), Hendrix does indeed unmistakably sing, "'Scuse me while I kiss *that guy*" with a slight chuckle in his voice. Was this perhaps a playful nod to the rumor about the original version? Or was it (and other live performances in which he may have sung the same thing) the source of the rumor to begin with? We'll probably never know exactly what the voraciously heterosexual Hendrix had in mind when he did this.

▪ JANIS IAN ▪ "QUEEN MERKA AND ME" ▪

Songwriter:	Janis Ian
Year of Release:	1968
Original Album:	*. . . For All the Seasons of Your Mind*
Chart Performance:	Not released as a single, but the album reached #179
Availability:	Out of print (Verve 3024)

A friend of mine in college, aware of Janis Ian's relatively open bisexuality, used to have fun parodying the opening lines of her big hit "At Seventeen," singing, "I learned the truth at seventeen that love was meant for closet queens." True, it was sophomoric. But, then again, we were sophomores at the time, so I suppose we were par for the course.

From the start of her recording career at the age of fifteen, Janis Ian had shown a willingness to tackle subjects that put her older, more reticent peers to shame. Her first hit, "Society's Child" from 1967, dealt with interracial romance (which explains why it wasn't played on the radio in my native Virginia and I never heard it until nearly a decade later). After such a remarkable debut, it was surprising that she didn't have another hit single until 1975, when "At Seventeen" all but redefined the "sensitive singer-songwriter," transcending that genre's typical self-pitying confessionals with a brutal, anti-romantic remembrance that dwells on the pain of being an "ugly girl." It can still hurt to hear it.

Between these two commercial highwater marks, Ian produced some intriguing if less marketable music. One example is "Queen Merka and Me," a delightful Donovan-ish song with a driving, soaring, yet paradoxically delicate melody. The lyrics are told from the perspective of a girl intent on observing the late-night goings-on of the big city. Most of the people she talks about might be considered among society's outcasts, a favored Ian topic. One verse in particular describes a fascinating scene in which a "childless wife-beater . . . walks with his boyfriend, . . . saying, 'I love you, babe.'" Nearby, as Ian describes it, there's a fountain that reverberates in sympathy with this pair, saying, "Your love is not wrong." She then adds, "Nobody sees but Queen Merka and me." Here and now, after 11 p.m. (as Ian informs us) in the midst of the anonymous city, a male couple can find a moment of peace and even acceptance.

In 1993 Ian released the album *Breaking Silence*, which made news not only because it was her first record in more than a decade, but also because it contained more upfront references to her lesbianism than ever before. The album coincided with an interview in *The Advocate* in which she identified herself as gay rather than bisexual. In that interview, Ian cited "Queen Merka and Me" as evidence of her long-standing interest in recording gay-related material. (Another is the lesbian love song "Maria" from her *Miracle Row* album.) I just wish I could figure out who Queen Merka is. The elaborate, sometimes self-consciously poetic lyrics are vague on that point. But that doesn't prevent it from being a wonderful song. Too bad hardly anyone's heard it.

▪ JOE JACKSON ▪ "FIT" ▪

Songwriter:	Joe Jackson
Year of Release:	1980
Original Album:	*Beat Crazy*
Chart Performance:	Not released as a single, but the album reached #41
Availability:	CD, CS (A&M 3241)

The melody of the final song on the album *Beat Crazy* by Joe Jackson is nothing to skip classes for. That's unusual for the generally highly melodic Jackson. But what "Fit" lacks in tunefulness it makes up for with a powerful and poignant lyric.

Jackson's no fool. He knows his listeners well. The rock music audience is as permeated by cruelty and prejudice as most other audiences—perhaps even more than many—so he bids them right off the bat not to laugh. He's going to be discussing things that are more often the subjects of jokes than songs. But it's no joke this time. He wants to talk about people who are "born as boys—and fighting to be girls." But they face opposition from others, both straight and gay, who label them "drag queens" and blame them for not conforming to assorted expectations. "You can't be one of us. . . . You don't fit."

Whether Jackson's talking about transvestites, transsexuals, or both, it hardly matters. I find it particularly insightful—not to mention pointedly correct—that he accuses both heterosexuals and homosexuals of creating a world in which these people don't "fit." Yes, the gay community does (or, more accurately, gay communities do) exhibit homophobia absorbed from the culture at large and often directs it toward those among them who are a little *too* gay.

Jackson goes on to note others who don't easily "fit" in society, such as persons of mixed racial ancestry. In the final stanza, however, he brings his message close to home, if in a somewhat contrived manner. He suggests that perhaps, "in some other lifetime, you won't fit." And then you'll know the pain of nonconformity and ostracism. Because, after all, "if you don't fit, you're fit for nothing."

Of course, I don't think for one minute that Joe Jackson truly believes that people who don't fit in aren't fit for anything. Nor do I think he really believes that the lives of "social outcasts" are necessarily incomplete. Those assertions are simply part of his indictment of the world we live in. In a better world—one that we can presumably still create (otherwise why would he bother writing and singing a song like this?)—everyone will "fit." He reminds us in the meantime that, but for the grace of God (or, as you may prefer to view it, *because* of the grace of God), we ourselves might be the ones who don't fit in. That's something most gay people have some experience with anyway.

▪ JOE JACKSON ▪ "REAL MEN" ▪

Songwriter:	Joe Jackson
Year of Release:	1982
Original Album:	*Night and Day*
Chart Performance:	Not released as a single, but the album reached #4
Availability:	CD, CS (A&M 3334)

With "Real Men" Joe Jackson created one of the most remarkable pop music compositions of the early 1980s. The song starts off by telling us to think back on years past, to a time in our lives when the whole world seemed divided into "just us and them." And who makes up these opposing camps? Not only "girls that wore pink and boys that wore blue"— referring, of course, to our culture's virtually automatic typecasting of people into gender roles, dividing and distinguishing us even from infancy —but also different groups of boys, including those who grew up to become, as Jackson says, "better men than me and you." Already we can tell that this is no ordinary pop song. Jackson proceeds to ask a series of questions that delve into what it means to be a man. These are questions that wrestle with definitions, stereotypes, and expectations. At the heart of "Real Men" is a painfully honest, searching examination of what it means to be a "real man" in today's world.

The second verse provides the primary impetus behind the song's appearance here. He points out a group of "nice boys" dancing together in pairs. Their blow-waved looks, as he describes them, are stereotypically gay, but he assures us they're all "straight as a line." By contrast, "all the gays are macho," right down to the shine of their leather. But if those words are interesting, what follows shortly thereafter is simply astounding coming from a mainstream pop musician: "Don't call me a faggot, not unless you are a friend." These words can be interpreted any number of ways. They might be read as a possible acknowledgment of gayness on the part of Jackson himself—or of his lyrical persona, assuming there is one other than himself. Then again, Jackson may not at all be saying that he's gay. "Real Men" is full of heterosexual references and, after all, heterosexual as well as homosexual friends can get away with jokingly calling each other "faggot" (though there's an underlying element of homophobia at work when they do so). In either case such name-calling would be quite another matter coming from an enemy or stranger.

And what should we make of the subsequent reference to how "you can wear the uniform," but only if you meet certain requirements of physical strength and stature? This could be an echo of the message of Jackson's earlier song "Fit," in which he accused gay as well as straight people of harmful attitudes and behavior toward those who don't meet various standards. Here Jackson may be saying that only those gay men who are tall

106

enough, strong enough, and handsome enough can wear the metaphorical uniform of macho status, thus qualifying as "real men."

Jackson briefly suggests that he might "play along" with the uniformed, handsome, strong pose that he assigns to the listener. Perhaps he's saying that he'd accept the masculine conceit on the part of a gay man—as long as he's tall and handsome and strong. In other words, this macho stuff is all a game anyway, and *especially* so for gay men. There might also be a hint (strengthened by the reference to a uniform) of the role-playing that often accompanies some "hypermasculine" segments of the gay community—S&M, B&D, and so on.

By the time "Real Men" concludes, Jackson has given vent to the fear and insecurity that many if not most men feel in the modern western world, especially regarding competition with women in the work place and other aspects of daily life. Jackson also thoroughly condemns the violent, aggressive aspects of traditional masculinity as it is all too often reflected in the world. He directly links it to war, militarism, and various forms of bigotry, including racism and sexism. Which brings him back to his refrain: "Now and then we wonder who the real men are."

It's really one of the high points of Jackson's career thus far—a career that, in my opinion, has had several very noteworthy high points. In fact, Joe Jackson is, along with Elvis Costello, one of the most significant, enduring artists to have emerged from the New Wave scene of the late seventies, having long ago moved far beyond the "New Wave" tag into producing a large, impressively diverse body of work. As for "Real Men," there's so much more going on in this song than just the "gay angle." Like a great deal of what Jackson has produced, it's much richer than can easily be absorbed even after repeated listenings.

▪ JAMES GANG ▪ "CLOSET QUEEN" ▪

Songwriters:	Jim Fox – Dale Peters – Joe Walsh
Year of Release:	1970
Original Album:	*The James Gang Rides Again*
Chart Performance:	Not released as a single, but the album reached #20
Availability:	CD, CS (MCA 31145)

I almost feel dirty writing about this one, it's so nasty. Overtop a crunching proto-heavy-metal guitar riff, Joe Walsh sings the role of a young man who, having just "come of age," goes knocking on a certain person's "back door." This "back door" reference carries long-standing connotations of furtiveness and social stigma, as in requiring servants, delivery boys, and non-white people to "go around back." It's also a euphemism, lifted from old blues songs, for anal sex, though here that meaning probably only serves to create an obscure pun. At any rate, whom does our protagonist meet at the back door?

> *The closet queen, the bus-stop fiend*
> *She wants to shake my hand*

Oh, ick, letting a closet queen *touch* him! But if the narrator considers this creature who cruises bus-stops (presumably in search of "prey") such a fiend, then why did he go knocking on his back door?—unless this tale is told retrospectively, with him realizing only later this other character's true nature. It's all so terribly muddled.

After a few more snide remarks about this object of the narrator's derision, the track goes instrumental, interpolating that haunting chestnut "Cast Your Fate to the Wind." Then back for a final verse of vitriol, during which our protagonist concedes that he'll soon be back "for the punch line of the joke," whatever that means. As far as I'm concerned, he needn't bother. This is a grim piece of work that says a lot more about the pseudo-sophisticated but ultimately ignorant people who produced it than the closet queens they thought they were talking about.

▪ JEFFERSON AIRPLANE ▪ "TRIAD" ▪

Songwriter:	David Crosby
Year of Release:	1968
Original Album:	*Crown of Creation*
Chart Performance:	Not released as a single, but the album reached #6
Availability:	CD, CS (RCA 4058)

David Crosby wrote "Triad" for the Byrds and recorded it with them during the sessions for *The Notorious Byrd Brothers*, but the rest of the group ultimately rejected it for inclusion on the album. This was reportedly one of the proverbial last straws, inspiring Crosby to leave the group. He turned the song over to the Jefferson Airplane, who apparently had far fewer qualms about releasing controversial material. Meanwhile, the Byrds' version remained unheard for many years, finally appearing on a post-mortem (the band's mortem, not Crosby's) compilation of previously unreleased tracks.

"Triad" is perhaps the supreme example in song of a notion that was commonly though not uniquely held by the hippies, that in sexual experimentation lay the path to utopia. This was a product of a pampered generation that arrogantly thought it had discovered free love. Grace Slick sings oh, so somberly, about how the person to whom she's speaking wants to know "how it will be: me and him or you and me." The enclosed lyric sheet, however, reads: "Me and him *and* you and me" (my emphasis). An intriguing difference, don't you think? As if to underscore the sense of sub-cultural specialness that the narrator feels within her circle, not to mention her generation (long hair as revolutionary statement), Slick comments, "You both stand there, your long hair flowin'." How very sixties-con-textual. We're offered no clues as to whether her lovers are a man and a woman or two men. (The "me and him" reference rules out two women.) In either case it suggests bisexuality.

The title of the song is "Triad," not "Triangle." This is no mere domes-tic dispute over who gets whom and who's left in the cold. At the very core of the song is the narrator's repeated wish that the three could go on to-gether in their intertwined relationship, just as they are. She's posing much more than a challenge to the parties directly involved; she's hurling the gauntlet down before society. She mocks the hesitancy of her two lovers, summoning the ghosts of their mothers, who feebly warn them about breaking the rules they "learned in school."

Youth Rule #1: If you want to get people to do something, tell them that their parents and/or schools *don't* want them to do it.

What makes "Triad" particularly interesting isn't that the narrator wants to revel openly in the enjoyment of two lovers, nor even the implicit bisex-uality of the situation. Rather, it's the oddly visionary turn that the song takes, hoping that "in time—maybe others" would be willing to do "what we can do." The narrator apparently believes that this triad could be the start of something big. Others may join in, creating a vast family of love and peace and sexuality.

It's all too beautiful.

I needn't go into detail about how Charles Manson, who made headlines less than two years after this song was recorded, was nothing less than the nightmare manifestation of such sappy communitarian California dreams. He and his pathological parody of a family signaled the beginning of the end of hippiedom, a slaughter of the intellectual and moral innocents. As for "Triad," call it a fossil from a time when naiveté was both a virtue and a stock fuel for record sales, when young romantics—or at least the ones who didn't regularly express their disdain for gay people by calling them "fags"—seemed to consider bisexuality less a sexual orientation than a would-be political ideology that might also serve as a conveniently trendy means of getting laid twice as often.

▪ JETHRO TULL ▪ "MOTHER GOOSE" ▪

Songwriter:	Ian Anderson
Year of Release:	1971
Original Album:	*Aqualung*
Chart Performance:	Not released as a single, but the album reached #7
Availability:	CD, CS (Chrysalis 21044)

The group Jethro Tull can be held accountable for some of the most achingly pretentious, wildly imaginative, lyrically crude, and surprisingly tuneful music of the 1970s. Leader-songwriter-flutist-vocalist Ian Anderson (who essentially *was* Jethro Tull and, in fact, still is) would often create fascinating musical constructs that dallied simultaneously with rock, jazz, and old English folk traditions. The only things that rivaled the music in its sheer baroqueness were some of the arcane lyrical references that I doubt whether anyone other than Anderson himself fully understood.

Consider, for example, the song "Mother Goose" from one of Tull's most popular LPs, *Aqualung*. It appears to be a recollection of a youthful stroll through a village inhabited by rather colorful characters, including a bearded lady and the "Mother Goose" of the title. He also mentions two other locals who are of special interest to us: a "chicken-fancier" and his "weird" sister, who "drives a lorry." Now, not a whole lot of people outside the gay community would know what's meant by "chicken-fancier" —that is, a man who's attracted to much younger men or boys. An unfortunate reference nonetheless. But then it gets even worse and far more obvious. The "weird sister" (shades of *Macbeth*!) drives a truck—what an *original* concept! Chalk it up to what you might call "heterosexist semiotics," a shorthand method of saying precisely what you want about certain types of people without actually coming right out and saying it.

▪ JOBRIATH ▪ "BLOW AWAY" ▪

Songwriters:	Bruce Campbell – Jerome Brandt
Year of Release:	1973
Original Album:	*Jobriath*
Chart Performance:	Not released as a single, and the album didn't chart
Availability:	Out of print (Elektra 75070)

It took me *years* to find this record. You've probably never heard of Jobriath, but *The Rolling Stone Encyclopedia of Rock & Roll* cites him for his "historical importance as one of the few openly gay rock 'stars.'" They were right to put "stars" in quotes: he never attained anything even remotely resembling stardom. A brief phenomenon of the glitter-rock era, Jobriath (whose real name, according to the U.S. Copyright Office, was Bruce Campbell) had a fondness for telling interviewers that he was "a true fairy." Not surprisingly, his career went nowhere. Still, the *Rolling Stone* people thought enough of him to insert his dazzling if kitschy photo in their encyclopedia, which is a lot more than the Captain and Tennille got.

Jobriath released two albums before vanishing into the ether of failed rock stardom. The first one, named after himself, attracted attention primarily for its gatefold cover photo of the discreetly nude singer done up to resemble a broken statue with subtly pointed ears. That right there should tip you off that the Bowie influence permeates this album, most notably in its conceit that gayness is the stuff of science fiction. To be fair, I can suggest that this metaphorical whimsy may have been born of a misguided attempt to defuse gayness of its "queerness" by couching it in something even queerer. That is, if you can accept the premise of rock star as extraterrestrial, you shouldn't have much trouble accepting a rock star as a gay earthling.

The *Jobriath* album opens with a hazy S&M fantasy titled "Take Me I'm Yours," moves through the likes of "Space Clown" and "Morning Starship," and concludes with "Blow Away," a mini-epic in which the title phrase refers to both oral sex and the sands of time. This final cut features dissonant piano, mellotron, and guitar, while flighty falsetto vocals of unknown gender back up Jobriath himself, who sounds as though he learned to sing at the feet of David Bowie and Mick Jagger. At least "Blow Away" is extremely interesting, which easily makes it the best track on the album.

If you happen to have this record tucked away somewhere, gathering dust among other seventies oddities—the uproarious Disco-Tex and the Sex-o-lettes, perhaps—consider yourself very lucky; you have a collector's item. Meanwhile, I'd *love* to know whatever happened to Jobriath. If nothing else, he was a pioneer.

Elton John, 1992. (Photo: Patrick Demarchelier. Courtesy MCA Records.)

▪ ELTON JOHN ▪ "DANIEL" ▪

Songwriters:	Elton John – Bernie Taupin
Year of Release:	1972
Original Album:	*Don't Shoot Me—I'm Only the Piano Player*
Chart Performance:	The single reached #2
Availability:	CD, CS (MCA 31077)

I remember when this pretty little song was a big hit. People were falling all over themselves trying to figure out why one man would be singing such a loving song about another man. One popular story held that Daniel was Elton John's or Bernie Taupin's older brother who was killed in a plane crash. Of course, when the initial supporters of this theory dug into the matter, they learned that there was no such dead sibling in either songwriter's life. Mind you, this was several years before Elton's much-publicized "coming out" as a bisexual in the pages of *Rolling Stone*—publicly revised in the early nineties to full-fledged gayness. It was even before he started to get *really* bizarre with his on-stage costumes. But with Elton on the verge of becoming the biggest thing in rock since the Beatles, nobody wanted to admit that "Daniel" might just be a love song to a male non-relative.

When once pressed on the matter—since people *had* to know—Bernie Taupin told how "Daniel" was inspired by the haunting visage of a stranger, a blind veteran, whom he saw at an airport. So, OK, "Daniel" isn't necessarily about a gay relationship. But with lyrics like

> *Lord, I miss Daniel*
> *Oh, I miss him so much*

it's easy to see how a whole generation of gay rock music fans might claim this song as one of their own.

Remember, any work of art is a collaboration between the artist who creates it and the audience that brings their own experience to their enjoyment of it. Any man who has seen his lover off at the airport and eagerly awaits his return knows exactly the kind of deep, personal meaning lyrics like these convey. Given that, "Daniel" is indeed a gay song—despite the way in which one of Elton's biographers, Philip Norman, took pains to emphasize that the lyrics are "platonic" and even "hetero." But if there weren't something there to deny, he wouldn't bother denying it, now would he?

▪ ELTON JOHN ▪ "ALL THE GIRLS LOVE ALICE" ▪

Songwriters:	Elton John – Bernie Taupin
Year of Release:	1973
Original Album:	*Goodbye Yellow Brick Road*
Chart Performance:	Not released as a single, but the album reached #1
Availability:	CD, CS (MCA 6894)

Although this book focuses on depictions of gay men in popular music of the rock era, I'm going to devote some time to "All the Girls Love Alice"—a song that claims female homosexuality as its theme—because it speaks volumes about one of the most prominent openly gay men in popular culture, Elton John, and where his head was at when he recorded it.

I hope that nowadays, many years and many changes later, Elton John has grown to regret ever co-writing and recording this singularly nasty piece of work. And double-shame on Bernie Taupin for writing such hateful lyrics. They both should have known better. Because of Elton's mid-seventies megastar status (nobody, but *nobody* was bigger), "All the Girls Love Alice" was almost certainly heard by more listeners than any other song in the rock era with obvious lesbian-related subject matter.

Early in the song, Taupin engages in some amateur psychoanalyzing, facilely suggesting that at least part of Alice's supposed problem (an inability to "get it on with the boys") stems from her "blues" at feeling unloved by her mother. But, then again, "What do you expect from a chick who's just sixteen?" Winking, condescending, sexist tripe.

Harsh, dissonant, distorted guitars punctuate the instrumental accompaniment, creating an air of danger. This is clearly meant to be taken as rough, scary stuff. The chorus features the come-on lines of Alice's female paramours as they try to persuade her to give them a call—but "wait 'til my husband's away." OK, I'll admit, that's funny. But then the song really nose-dives as it describes how Alice was recently found dead in the subway. The equation is brazenly simple: girl sleeps with girls, girl winds up dead. And if you think that's bad, there's more. It seems that the only "friends" poor Alice had were "one or two middle-aged dykes in a Go-Go." But then Alice *was* just "a sixteen-year-old yo-yo." Insulting the dead, even if she is only the fictional dead. How low can you go?

Well, still lower. The printed lyrics that come with the album are accompanied by a picture of a blonde nymphet, presumably Alice herself, sandwiched between two stereotypical "middle-aged dykes"—with short, "mannish" haircuts, wearing coats and ties, no less—*who are mirror-images of each other.* Are they improbable twins or simply unindividualized, depersonalized carbon-copy facsimiles? Whichever the case, both of them leer and smirk at poor, sexy, fawn-like Alice.

This was, of course, well before Elton John's public statements about his sexual orientation. His words and actions since, especially in very recent years, have revealed him to be anything but homophobic. Therefore I suspect that we can chalk up this horrid piece of work to pre-coming-out internalized homophobia and the gross insecurities that go along with it. Although Elton didn't write the words themselves, he surely could have refused to use Taupin's lyrics had he found them offensive. But perhaps his willingness to record "All the Girls Love Alice" was a closet-inspired defense mechanism. After all, Elton had to go through quite a bit—including a significant dip in his popularity, alcoholism, a failed marriage, and witnessing friends and colleagues die of AIDS—before he was willing to publicly state that he was gay (as opposed to his much earlier admission of bisexuality, which now appears to have been another defense mechanism). Still, it would be very nice if at some point Elton could address the issues surrounding this song (if he hasn't already), perhaps even apologizing for having granted to posterity one of the vilest anti-gay album cuts in the history of rock music.

■ ELTON JOHN ■ "BIG DIPPER" ■

Songwriters:	Elton John – Gary Osborne
Year of Release:	1978
Original Album:	*A Single Man*
Chart Performance:	Not released as a single, but the album reached #15
Availability:	CD, CS (MCA 31181)

A Single Man, with its telling title, was the first album released by Elton John after his late-seventies statements to the press regarding his "bisexuality." It also became his first LP of new material that failed to hit the Top Ten since 1971's *Friends* and *11–17–70*. And it was his first album since *Madman Across the Water* (also from 1971) that failed to generate a Top Ten single in the U.S. While by no means a flop (it eventually racked up sufficient sales to be certified platinum), *A Single Man*'s comparatively disappointing performance suggested that Elton's openness had indeed hurt his career. In fact, while he would continue to produce successful singles throughout the eighties (if at a less spectacular pace than he had in the seventies), it wasn't until *The One* in 1992 that Elton would earn another Top Ten album.

Because *A Single Man* coincided almost precisely with the early phases of my own coming out period, I quickly listened to it for indications of sexuality other than of the hetero variety. And I found them in "Big Dipper." To be sure, they could hardly be missed, what with an opening-line reference to "a cute little slip of a sailor." Elton had never sung anything quite like *that* before!

Elton's new lyricist, Gary Osborne, was weaving a spicy male-to-male pickup tale, heavy with obvious double-entendre. The narrator looks on and describes the action as a friend goes about seducing a handsome seaman. The end of each verse summarizes the seducer's progress. At first the sailor doesn't seem interested. But our friend's friend is persistent, so the swabbie eventually begins to relent. Finally, sailor-boy sounds downright eager to explore new waters:

> *He's got his own big dipper*
> *But he's got his eye on yours*

That's pretty much all we're told, aside from the fact that the narrator's friend and his seafaring conquest go off to a private room together. The moral to the story is quite simple: "Everybody's got to do their thing." A dreadful cliché, even in the seventies, but *apropos*, to say the least.

I wonder what all of Elton's teenybopper fans, who bought his previous records by the truckload—hell, by the oil-tanker load—thought of *that*!

Well, *A Single Man* was Elton John's final platinum album for more than a decade thereafter. That's what they thought of it.

▪ ELTON JOHN ▪ "ELTON'S SONG" ▪

Songwriters:	Elton John – Tom Robinson
Year of Release:	1981
Original Album:	*The Fox*
Chart Performance:	Not released as a single, but the album reached #21
Availability:	CD, CS (MCA 10497)

As just about everybody knows, Elton John's first big hit was "Your Song." Needless to say, it occupies a place of tremendous importance in his career. Therefore, if he comes along more than a decade later and records a new number titled "Elton's Song"—*Elton's* as opposed to *Your*—you might think that that song may be pretty important, too, at least to Elton himself. And so I believe it is.

Tom Robinson is a musical gay activist (or activist gay musician) who enjoyed a brief blaze of glory in the late seventies—a rarity indeed. And, as you know, Elton John had identified himself as bisexual. It's an overstatement, of course, to say that it was only natural that these two British subjects should get together at some point to write songs, but that's precisely what they did. "Elton's Song" is, if you'll pardon the expression, among the fruits of that collaboration.

116

"Elton's Song" is a gay love song, although nowhere in the lyric does it come out, in a manner of speaking, and say that. The gender of the loved one is discreetly avoided, which frankly surprises me in light of the fact that the usually outspoken Robinson was the lyricist. On the other hand, perhaps his whole point was to create what was fully intended to be a gay love song—what many if not most listeners would fully realize was a gay love song—yet to make it universal in such a way that non-gay as well as gay listeners could identify with it, thus making a subtle point about the universality of love, be it gay or not. Mind you, I'm just speculating here, but I'm going to proceed with that speculation.

Accompanied only by his piano and later by string synthesizers, Elton sings the somber but attractive melody that he composed for Robinson's lyrics of adolescent love. His youthful persona muses on the "razor-blade smile" of another boy, noting that, "It's all around the school that I love you." But this is no fantasy world in which homoerotic attachments come to the young free of anguish and difficulty:

> If you only knew what I'm going through
> Time and again I get ashamed

Again, these are words that could describe many if not most adolescent heterosexual infatuations, but they bear special poignance for gay listeners, for whom the experience of suppressing their true feelings is all too familiar. "They say it isn't real"—I've heard that one before; haven't you? Society at large tries over and over to suggest that the love that gay people feel for each other is somehow less real, less viable than the love of heterosexuals.

By song's end, we've been treated to a deeply moving expression of unrequited love, the lyrics conveying a painfully desperate sense of longing. Keep in mind that, if we're to trust the song's title, the narrator is probably meant to be taken as Elton himself. Indeed, he sings these words with an unmistakable ache in his voice, yet he manages to avoid any expression of self-pity. As a result, "Elton's Song" stands as one of his most moving performances on record.

And just in case anyone doubts whether "Elton's Song" is *truly* gay, all you have to do is see the video, which has been rarely shown on American television. But if you can find Elton's compilation *Visions* at your local video store, you can see it for yourself. Set in a typical English boarding school, it shows a youngster longingly watching an older boy shooting pool, playing cricket, performing gymnastics, and—most torturous of all —kissing a girl. Our lonely young protagonist is teased by the other boys and sometimes cries himself to sleep. Heaven forbid that MTV, which seldom has qualms about showing all manner of misogyny, simulated violence, disrespect for reasonable and legitimate authority, and other forms of sociopathology, should allow anything so subversive as that.

■ ELTON JOHN ■ "NIKITA" ■

Songwriters: Elton John – Bernie Taupin
Year of Release: 1985
Original Album: *Ice on Fire*
Chart Performance: The single reached #7
Availability: CD, CS, LP (MCA 10500)

Yes, I'm well aware that the video for this song makes it perfectly clear that "Nikita" is a Russian soldier of the female gender, so that Elton's song of love is indeed a song of love for a *her*. But we have to remember the commercial realities of the marketplace. Do you suppose MTV or VH-1 would have played the video if Nikita had been a man? Yet, before they saw the video, what gender would most listeners have assigned to Nikita? The lyrics always refer to Nikita in the second person ("you"), so we never hear whether Nikita is a he or a she. Because of Nikita Khrushchev, the decidedly male former premier of the Soviet Union, most Americans would have regarded Nikita as a man's name. And keep in mind that any rock fan worthy of that epithet almost certainly knew of Elton's avowed "bisexuality." In light of all that—and in spite of the video—"Nikita" deserves noting here.

I think the Beach Boys' Mike Love would agree. While serving as a guest veejay on VH-1 several years ago, he capped a showing of the "Nikita" video by affecting a conspicuously "effeminate" voice and referring with seeming disapproval to Elton's apparent infatuation with "that Russian *minx*." Whatever else you might think of it, you have to admit that it was perceptive of him.

■ ELTON JOHN ■ "THE LAST SONG" ■

Songwriters: Elton John – Bernie Taupin
Year of Release: 1992
Original Album: *The One*
Chart Performance: The single reached #23
Availability: CD, CS (MCA 10614)

One of the finest songs yet to emerge from the AIDS nightmare. Against the backdrop of an understated, even stark musical accompaniment, Elton assumes the role of a dying young man expressing bittersweet wonder and joy inspired by his father's love. He sings of his sense of liberation and relief upon confiding in his father the "hidden truth" of his sexuality, and he confesses his own weakness and mortality—so hard for a young person to accept, yet so very necessary in the midst of such an epidemic. "I can't believe you'd love me," he cries to his father, "I never thought you'd come." But he did. Almost too late, but he did. And that counts for a lot. Far too many gay men dying of AIDS don't even get that much from their parents.

At least in this one musical instance—and, no doubt, in a great many real-life situations as well—there's still "love between a father and his son." Now, if only all of us could *always* count on such love, even when terminal illness isn't a mitigating factor.

Incidentally, I should note that shortly before he released this record, Elton announced that his share of the proceeds from all future singles sold in the United States would be donated to AIDS-related charities. Given his track record, that should prove a hefty sum of steadily flowing cash. "Bravo" doesn't suffice, Elton. May you shine on brightly as long as people continue to listen to rock music, and hopefully beyond.

▪ KING CRIMSON ▪ "THE GREAT DECEIVER" ▪

Songwriters:	John Wetton – Robert Fripp – Richard W. Palmer-James
Year of Release:	1974
Original Album:	*Starless and Bible Black*
Chart Performance:	Not released as a single, but the album reached #64
Availability:	CD, CS (Editions EG 12)

I can say with justification that King Crimson, led by the highly innovative guitarist Robert Fripp, was the quirkiest, most musically adventuresome of the progressive rock groups of the 1970s. At least one of their compositions (I would call only a few of them mere "songs") is of interest here. "The Great Deceiver," with lyrics by Richard W. Palmer-James, is a bitter warning against some unnamed person. Whether this is any actual, particular person is uncertain; I've heard speculation as to who it might be, but I won't repeat it here. So nasty a rebuke is this song that I'd hate to mistakenly link any innocent person's name to it.

The opening line makes reference to a "health-food faggot with a bartered bride." This may or may not be intended to mean that the object of the stream of insults to follow is a homosexual, since "health-food faggot" can be construed to mean that this person is, to use an exactly parallel metaphor, "queer for" health food. The mention, however, of a "bartered bride" leads me to doubt this. It suggests a false, illusory marriage, with sexuality being one of the things that the Great Deceiver is deceptive about. Besides, later lines seem to draw upon that tired old Freudian warhorse about unhealthy mother-son relationships, stating that the Deceiver's mom "canonized the ground that he walked upon."

The music is fast, frantic, imaginative—amusing yet technically impressive. And when the words aren't being homophobic (for even if the lyricist doesn't intend for the Great Deceiver to be viewed as a homosexual, the "faggot" reference is still despicable), they're extremely clever. I especially like the line "Sing hymns make love get high fall dead"—as cynical a summation of life as I've ever heard. It's regrettable that a few offensive lines almost (note, *almost*) ruin my enjoyment of what is in every other way a brilliant piece of work.

▪ KINKS ▪ "SEE MY FRIENDS" ▪

Songwriter:	Ray Davies
Year of Release:	1965
Original Album:	*Kinks Kinkdom*
Chart Performance:	The single failed to chart, but the album reached #47
Availability:	CD, CS (Rhino 75769, combined with the album *Kinks-Size* to create *Kinks-Size Kinkdom*)

Unlike nearly all of the other songs in this book, this track all but required the songwriter's acknowledgment of its homoerotic content. In other words, if lead singer and songwriter Ray Davies hadn't been so forthright in his public statements (and if the Kinks' "official" biographer, Jon Savage, hadn't been so diligent in repeating them), I wouldn't have noticed anything "gay" about "See My Friends" at all.

This droning, repetitive song finds its narrator confessing that his female lover has gone "way across the river," leaving him with "no one else to love except my friends." There's not much else to it. But then we have what Davies has said about the song: "It's about being a youth who is not sure of his sexuality. I remember I said to Rasa [his wife] one night, 'If it wasn't for you, I'd be queer.'"

If I were a woman, I'm not sure how I'd take that. At any rate, if Ray Davies says that "See My Friends" is about a young man uncertain about his sexuality, then I guess that's what it's about.

120

The Kinks: Lead "Kink" Ray Davies is third from the left. (Photo: Michael Ochs Archives.)

▪ KINKS ▪
▪ "DEDICATED FOLLOWER OF FASHION" ▪

Songwriter:	Ray Davies
Year of Release:	1966
Original Album:	*The Kinks' Greatest Hits*
Chart Performance:	The single reached #36
Availability:	Original album out of print; available on *Kinks-Size Kinkdom*, CD, CS (Rhino 75769)

Years before "Lola," Ray Davies was honing his satirical skills on relatively easy targets, as well as some idiotic ones, as in "A Well Respected Man," myopic in its criticism of a young man for being so respectable. But the heterosexual victim of Davies' ire in that song doesn't concern us here. Rather, we should consider the protagonist of "Dedicated Follower of Fashion," recorded during the same period.

Nowhere, mind you, is the fashionplate subject of this song identified as homosexual. In 1966 that would have been most unlikely, regardless of Davies' intentions. But this sixties Beau Brummell does seem unduly concerned with clothes as "he flits from shop to shop just like a butterfly." And perhaps Davies couldn't come right out and say that this guy was queer, but he could refer to him pulling "his frilly nylon panties right up tight." What do you suppose his listeners thought of *that*? Would a self-respecting girl want to date this guy? More to the point, would he care to date her? If you ask me, this "Dedicated Follower of Fashion" is more than just one of Davies' satiric straw horses. He's a *gay* straw horse.

▪ KINKS ▪ "DAVID WATTS" ▪

Songwriter:	Ray Davies
Year of Release:	1967
Original Album:	*Something Else*
Chart Performance:	As the flipside of the unsuccessful "Autumn Almanac" single, it didn't chart; the album reached #153
Availability:	CD (Reprise 6279)

Davies plays the role of a self-confessed "dull and simple lad" whose limitless admiration for the title character serves as the *raison d'être* for this excuse in backhanded sardonicism. With its rough, almost amateurish sound, which parallels the narrator's own lack of sophistication, the song contains line after line extolling David Watts' advantages and virtues.

These include, among other things, his material wealth, his leadership qualities, and his marvelous skills both athletic and academic. Our young protagonist can scarcely conceal his envy ("I wish I could have all he has got"), repeating over and over how he would like to be like David Watts.

Davies is, of course, far less naive than his persona here, and he can't resist dropping a little hint along the way as he inserts "He is so gay and fancy-free" within the catalog of Watts' attributes. And he comes dangerously close to giving it all away in the final stanza, when he describes how "all the girls in the neighborhood" try—unsuccessfully—to make it with the "pure" David Watts. If irony were raindrops, we'd be bailing out the basement.

To confirm our suspicions, Davies (via biographer Jon Savage) has provided an account of the song's origins. It seems that David Watts is based on a real person, a wealthy concert promoter who had the hots for Davies' brother and fellow-Kink, Dave Davies. Ray tells of a party at this fellow's home in which pink champagne was flowing like water: "I said to David Watts, 'Don't you fancy that big hunky drummer?' He said, 'Get lost, sweetie, it's your brother I'm after.' . . . But Dave didn't fancy him, it's as simple as that." Apparently there were no hard feelings, for Davies reports that he remained friends with Mr. Watts long after this incident, and even after he wrote and recorded this song.

In light of all this, the ambivalent feelings Ray Davies expresses about gay people in his music can be awfully confusing. I suppose people who are as confused about their sexuality as Davies has admitted to being can't help but confuse others with the mixed signals they send.

▪ KINKS ▪ "LOLA" ▪

Songwriter:	Ray Davies
Year of Release:	1970
Original Album:	*Lola Versus Powerman and the Moneygoround, Part One*
Chart Performance:	The single reached #9
Availability:	CD, CS (Reprise 6423)

One shouldn't be surprised that a delightfully kinky little song like this would come from a group called the Kinks. They've made a career out of recording satirical music that rubbed just about everybody's nose in their own excrement. As for "Lola," the phrase "kinky little song" is an understatement. This one's a *monument*.

Ray Davies invites us to join his persona in a reminiscence about an evening that changed his life. It started in "a club down in old Soho, where they drink champagne and it tastes just like Coca-Cola." From the start, the song is fraught with ambiguities. Is it champagne or cola? A feminine figure walks up to the narrator and asks for a dance. He asks her what her name is,

> *And in a dark brown voice she said, "Lola"*
> *L-O-L-A, Lola*

The "dark brown voice"—a superb application of a visual image to an audio concept—tips us off right away. There's something different about Lola; she's not your typical girl. And, besides, what else is dark brown? Cola, for one thing. So maybe, just as the champagne may not really be champagne, maybe Lola—but I get ahead of our narrator, who can't quite understand why Lola "walked like a woman and talked like a man." He also notes that Lola's embrace seems a tad stronger than one would expect from the average woman. Get the picture?

Our hero is having a good time under decidedly unusual circumstances, dancing "under electric candlelight." Ambiguities again. Or, more accurately, sheer falseness. But he has ambivalent feelings about it all. Simultaneously repelled and attracted, he admits that he finds himself falling for Lola, but he nevertheless tries to escape. Something from within, however, pulls him back. He realizes that, for all of the uncertainty and confusion he sees around him, there's something perfectly natural about Lola. In an absolutely classic line, we're informed that "Girls will be boys and boys will be girls." Everything seems confused—everything, that is, " 'cept for Lola." We then learn a little more about our naive narrator. He's just off the farm, so to speak, and he's a virgin, never having kissed a woman. But what Lola wants, Lola gets.

Davies caps this amazing story with one of the most audacious, most cleverly executed double-entendres in the history of popular music:

> *Well, I'm not the world's most masculine man*
> *But I know what I am and I'm glad I'm a man*
> *And so is Lola*

So is Lola him/herself glad to be a man or merely glad that the narrator is? Is our hero gay or isn't he? Personally, I have no doubt in my mind, but if you doubt it, that's OK. I told you that this song was fraught with ambiguities, which leave room for loads of different interpretations. But the very fact that Davies and the Kinks were willing to write and record such a song in 1970 is remarkable. I mean, it's one of the *gayest* things ever to play on U.S. Top 40 radio. And the fact that it made the Top Ten, for goshsakes, is simply remarkable. It makes you wonder whether anyone was actually *listening* to the lyrics! Or maybe they were and they merely thought it was—well, kinky.

Songwriter:	Ray Davies
Year of Release:	1978
Original Album:	*Misfits*
Chart Performance:	Not released as a single, but the album reached #40
Availability:	CD (Arista 8069)

I just don't know what Ray Davies was thinking of when he wrote this song. It seems thoroughly ambivalent about gay people, sounding half supportive and half oppressive. Maybe Davies *is* ambivalent about gay people. But it doesn't sound as though it came from the same pen that wrote "Lola."

Recorded with a mildly countrified instrumental track, "Out of the Wardrobe" tells the story of "a chick called Dick," who is, by the way, quite hairy and burly. Davies delights in frustrating expectations by juxtaposing seemingly incongruous elements; thus a "burly chick." As in his earlier, vastly superior "Lola," Davies is setting us up for a tale of cracked conventions. It seems that Dick married a girl named Betty Lou back in the sixties, "when you had to be butch to survive." But of late he's been viewing his wife "with mixed emotions." As Davies puts it, "he's not a commonplace closet queen." As it turns out, Dick's a transvestite who "feels just like a princess" when he gets all dolled up.

But is he gay? Well, we're later told that he's *not* a "faggot." He just likes wearing "women's" clothing. Furthermore, "he's not a pansy—he's only being what he wants to be." And I suppose "faggots" and "pansies" *aren't* being what they want to be—or *have* to be, for that matter? What kind of double standard is this, anyway? It's almost as if Davies is saying that Dick may have odd tastes in clothes, but that he's still cool because, after all, he's not queer. Maybe that's precisely what he's saying. But the Kinks are so neck-deep in satire that you can never be completely sure when, if ever, you can take them seriously.

Davies goes on to tell us that Betty Lou had a lot of trouble accepting these changes in her husband at first—that she was angry and contemplated a trial separation—but she learns to adjust. In fact, she learns to thrive. She starts wearing conventional male attire and smoking a pipe. The couple's traditional gender roles become completely reversed. The marriage is saved by adapting heterosexuality to the husband's crossdressing fantasies, with the wife's accommodating attitude ultimately working to her benefit as well.

Is this a "gay" song? No. It dabbles its toes in queer waters, but refuses to get wet. Every reference to homosexuality is a denial: he's not a queen, a faggot, or a pansy. What he *is* is a heterosexual transvestite, which is probably why the song is titled "Out of the *Wardrobe*" rather than "Out of the *Closet*." And that's perfectly fine, but why does Davies have to use insulting terms like "faggot" and "pansy" to make his point that simply wearing a dress doesn't make a man gay? Does his support for "unconventional" behavior end when the people involved *are* gay? Was "Lola" indeed nothing but a farce? Despite his much-vaunted ridicule of social conventions and criticisms of hypocrisy and narrow-mindedness, is Davies nevertheless a homophobe? Are you tired of my rhetorical questions yet?

■ KITCHENS OF DISTINCTION ■
■ "4 MEN" and "BREATHING FEAR" ■

Songwriters:	Kitchens of Distinction (Patrick Fitzgerald – Julian Swales – Dan Goodwin) (both songs)
Year of Release:	1992
Original Album:	*The Death of Cool*
Chart Performance:	Not released as singles, and the album didn't chart
Availability:	CD, CS (A&M 5402)

The name of this band is a thoroughly camp creation, a satirical evocation of the kind of *Better Homes and Gardens* mentality that, depending on their socioeconomic aspirations, gay people often either embrace fanatically or disdain utterly. But the music itself isn't campy. Rather, it gets downright intense. In fact, Kitchens of Distinction makes some of the most intense music I've ever heard. To listen to them is to be awash in guitars —a virtual orchestra of Julian Swales' strummed, multi-tracked electric and acoustic guitars, augmented by the frequent and strategic use of feedback. It's an angry, eerily beautiful soundscape of alternating consonance and dissonance, tugging you back and forth between aesthetic pain and pleasure. And we haven't even touched upon the lyrics.

Take, for instance, the internalized struggle of "4 Men," in which bassist-vocalist Patrick Fitzgerald poetically muses about the ramifications of loving another man. He starts off singing in the third person, describing how some unnamed "he" had never dreamed "that he would ever want this much from a man." But as the song progresses Fitzgerald moves into the first person, as if his narrator had initially been trying to disassociate himself from his true feelings but has now given up trying to do so. Simultaneously, he stops fighting his sexual urges and admits to himself that he longs to lie between the thighs of the man he loves. He continues, however, to wonder whether his desires are really "allowed," and he recognizes how difficult it is initially to put one's gayness into action when there's so much cultural disapproval to overcome, much of it internalized:

126

Kitchens of Distinction, 1992: (l-r) Dan Goodwin, Patrick Fitzgerald, and Julian Swales. (Photo: Colin Bell. Courtesy A&M Records.)

Fear rules me easily
It takes lust and strength to turn to you and say
"I want you and I need you"

It's not made clear whether he gets to make love to the object of his passion, but that's not the point. It's the internal struggle that matters, not its physical resolution. The narrator asserts, at least to himself, that he will indeed have this other man, eventually "crushing" him in his arms and "melting" inside him.

Incidentally, the song's title, which until the very last line seems an enigma, refers to the circumstances under which this situation has evolved; four men together in a room, probably some "non-gay" social function, where two of them had gravitated toward each other in mutual attraction. It only adds to the ironic power of the music, with love manifesting itself as a glorious accident waiting to happen.

Another astonishing track from the same album, *The Death of Cool*, is "Breathing Fear," which again focuses on a type of struggle—this time the struggle of living a semi-closeted life in a homophobic society. The main character is a young man who's been gay-bashed "by the lads who plague us outside." When he goes to work the next day, his co-workers inquire about his bruises. Instead of speaking the truth, he "mumbles excuses" and tells lies, which are only "half-believed." The Kitchens disapprove of this deception, but they remain understanding and sympathetic, suggesting that if this young man were to tell the full truth to his heterosexual colleagues, he could open himself to further attacks, in which they might "finish him off," psychologically or otherwise. In a fury (further intensified by the harshness of the music) they accuse "straight" society of

Giving us grief for centuries now
Can you never rest?

Though heterosexuals "breathe this fear" (of beatings? of social disapproval? of gayness itself?) only on rare occasions, "we suffocate every day"—"we" surely meaning gay people. This just might be one of the most forceful indictments of heterosexism that you're likely to hear in more or less "mainstream" popular music.

The Death of Cool and other records by Kitchens of Distinction provide additional examples of "gay" songs, such as "On Tooting Broadway Station," a strangely lovely tune about trying to get over a lost same-sex lover and finally doing so through anger, which seems the chief emotion in the Kitchens' repertoire. To be sure, they include "straight" as well as "gay" lyrics in their work, so much so that a *Rolling Stone* reviewer once adroitly described them as "promosexual." But the gay angle has probably been more than enough to limit their success so far with the music media. Consider the music, too. Though a little intensity and dissonance goes a long way, too much of it taxes the sensibilities of most folks. Still, the Kitchens seem to be slowly garnering a well-deserved audience among "alternative" rock fans (mostly college students listening to college radio stations), and that's just fine. After all, look where it got R.E.M.

• CYNDI LAUPER • "SHE BOP" •

Songwriters:	Cyndi Lauper – Steve Lunt – G. Corbett – Rick Chertoff
Year of Release:	1983
Original Album:	*She's So Unusual*
Chart Performance:	The single reached #3
Availability:	CD, CS (Portrait 38930)

Rock has given us a number of odes to masturbation—the Who's "Pictures of Lily" and Jackson Browne's "Rosie" immediately spring to mind —but nowhere else does autoeroticism assume such epic proportions as in "She Bop." With its thunderous fuzztones, synth-trumpet fanfares, and Cyndi Lauper's comic-defiant disposition, you'd think that sexual self-gratification hovered in the moral structure of the universe somewhere between a violent revolutionary act and a profound religious experience. Frankly, I'm surprised it wasn't written by Prince. The song's inclusion here may be somewhat tenuous, but its significance lies in the fact that the lyrics prove conclusively, by Cyndi's own admission, that gay men aren't the only ones who can derive intense pleasure from *Blueboy* magazine. Chalk up another contribution to the culture at large.

• CYNDI LAUPER • "BOY BLUE" •

Songwriters:	Cyndi Lauper – Stephen Broughton Lunt – Jeff Bova
Year of Release:	1986
Original Album:	*True Colors*
Chart Performance:	Not released as a single, but the album reached #4
Availability:	CD, CS (Portrait 40313)

Cyndi Lauper has been laudibly forthright in her support for gay rights and AIDS-related causes. In fact, the song "Boy Blue" from her second album, *True Colors*, reportedly originated with the loss of a close friend to AIDS. One especially touching verse describes, it would seem, how a young man has been thrown out of his parents' home. And now he's dead. Though singing to a surprisingly bouncy track for a song of grief (a celebration of life in the midst of sorrow, perhaps?), Lauper obviously misses her friend. She cries, "It's just the pain that never disappears," and asks— later, all but shrieks—"Tell me, where is boy blue?"

Ultimately, in the midst of her loss, Lauper summarizes how best to cope with such pain in life: "Dance a little, cry a little." Sounds like a fairly significant little piece of philosophy for someone who spent the first several years of her big-time career developing a conspicuously "daffy" persona. (That was her singing the theme song to the dearly departed *Pee Wee's Playhouse*, you know.) How do you pull yourself through? "Dance a little, cry a little."

It's intriguing that a song dedicated to Lauper's gay friend should be called "Boy Blue." After all, three years earlier Lauper had referred to *Blueboy* in a major hit. A coincidence? I don't think so.

And while we're on the subject of Cyndi Lauper, her song "True Colors" (written by Tom Kelly and Billy Steinberg) deserves at least a short note, too. While it doesn't appear to have any direct relation to gay people, its core message about allowing one's "true colors" to come "shining through" should be taken to heart by everybody, not just gay people. I'd say it's a prime candidate for adoption by the gay community, if it hasn't been claimed already.

▪ LAVENDER COUNTRY ▪ "WALTZING WILL TRILOGY" AND "LAVENDER COUNTRY" ▪

Songwriters: Patrick Haggerty ("Waltzing Will Trilogy);
                      Robert Hammerstrom – Patrick Haggerty
                      ("Lavender Country")
Year of Release: 1973
Original Album: *Lavender Country*
Chart Performance: Not released as singles, and the album didn't chart
Availability: Out of print (Gay Community Services of Seattle
                      PC-160)

Everyone knows that country-western music has become a very big thing in gay circles over the past few years. On any given night, hordes of gay men and lesbians flock to select bars across the country and kick up their heels two-steppin' and line-dancin'. Commentators have attributed this phenomenon to a number of different factors: a reaction to the AIDS crisis, manifesting itself as a largely unconscious rejection of the seventies-style disco culture associated with its genesis; a laying claim, for psychosexual or sociological reasons, to the rural-traditional and/or "macho" ideals embedded within country music; a Baby-Boom rebellion against musical and lyrical styles (house, hip-hop, rap, techno, heavy metal, etc.) favored by the younger generation; an assertion of romanticism given a particularly campy twist. Whatever the cause(s), country-western music and dance has become as much a part of gay culture as disco ever was—which is to say it's entrenched.

Those of my readers who, as a part of this cultural paradigm-shift, only recently discovered country music may be surprised to learn that a gay country album was released as long ago as 1973. *Lavender Country* served multiple purposes as the name of a group, an album, and a song on that album, all of which were sponsored by Gay Community Social Services of Seattle. Singer-songwriter Patrick Haggerty led the three-man, one-woman band. Their album is an eye-opener.

We who have grown accustomed to the modern "young urban country" music of Garth Brooks, Wynonna Judd, Clint Black, and Roseanne Cash may find *Lavender Country* a jarring experience. Decidedly in the acoustic, folk-country mold, bearing a strong influence of bluegrass, it sounds dated and unsophisticated. It is. Haggerty's high-pitched, Appalachian-accented vocals give new meaning to the term "nasal twang"—something that most nineties country stars are scrupulous to avoid. The instrumentation consists almost exclusively of acoustic guitars, fiddle, piano, and dobro. (If you don't know what a dobro is, it's the metallic guitar-like thing that's shown on the cover of Dire Straits' *Brothers in Arms* album, and which Eric Clapton plays with a bottleneck slide during his famous *Unplugged* performance of "Running on Faith.") By current standards, even by the "countrypolitan" standards that were evolving in Nashville at the time it was recorded, *Lavender Country* sounds primitive. But at the same time it has a markedly *authentic* feel to it, though not without an eye to parody and camp. Gay people performing country music *cannot* do so without at least some nod to the intensely camp ramifications of what they're doing.

Keeping the aforementioned reservations in mind, let me say that every song on *Lavender Country* has something to recommend it. I especially like the "Waltzing Will Trilogy," an uptempo dose of country boogie-woogie, the angry lyrics of which (about various injustices heaped upon gay people, ranging from electroshock therapy to prison gang-rapes) remind us of a time when talk of revolution tripped off the tongues of disenchanted youth like one-liners at a comedy club.

> *Rise up and rip this goddamn system down*
> *'Cause there ain't no hope till it tumbles to the ground!*

If you feel like shouting, "Right on, brother," go right ahead.

The album closer, "Lavender Country," seems like something that might have played at the Grand Ol' Opry in the late 1940s. Musically, that is. Lyrically, it's another matter altogether.

131

You all come out, come out, my dears
To Lavender Country
You all come out and make yourselves at home
It don't matter here who you love or what you wear

The effectiveness of this song, like the entire album, hinges upon the performers' and the listeners' awareness of the apparent contrast between the traditional, "down-home" sentiments usually associated with the musical style and the very nontraditional sentiments articulated by the lyrics. Gayness becomes part of the natural landscape of the hills. In fact, it always has been. There have been gay "hillbillies" just as surely as there are gay urbanites; rural America is just as much home to homosexuality as the big cities. In essence, *Lavender Country* proclaims that the separation of gay people from the countryside is at root a lie, only forced in the direction of truthfulness by a culture that has always driven its sexually "deviant" citizens toward urban areas to seek safety and solace in anonymity and numbers. But that's not as it should be, and since not all gay people have fled the rural heartland, that's not as it is, either. *Lavender Country* asserts this fact, doing so with just the right balance of anger and humor.

I can't leave *Lavender Country* without mentioning one other highlight: a rewrite of the Gene Autry standard "Back in the Saddle Again" as "Back in the *Closet* Again," which satirizes the mindset that urges gay people back toward greater discretion and secretiveness in times of increased oppression. Hilariously biting.

Unfortunately, since *Lavender Country* is now out of print, it now seems less a viable musical statement than an historic document. But what a document it is! It's all but impossible to find now, except as I did by borrowing it from Winston Leyland who's had it for almost twenty years. Hold on to your gay artifacts, my friends. You never know when today's *commonalia* will become tomorrow's treasures. Of course, anybody into antiques already knows that.

▪ PAUL LEKAKIS ▪
▪ "BOOM BOOM (LET'S GO BACK TO MY ROOM)" ▪

Songwriters: M. Chieregato – R. Ballerini – S. Montin –
                       R. Turatti – T. Hooker
Year of Release: 1987
Original Album: *Tattoo It* (1990)
Chart Performance: The single reached #43
Availability: CD, CS (Sire 26312)

Here's a guy with actor-model-waiter good looks and a hilarious song that reminds us how much fun sex and/or being young can be. The first time I heard "Boom Boom (Let's Go Back to My Room)," I could've sworn it was by those masters of fey dance-pop, Dead or Alive, fronted by the gender-bending Pete Burns. But it wasn't. And it took me months to find out who *was* responsible. Personally, I think laws should be passed requiring radio stations to say the names of the artists whose records they play.

If you've never had the pleasure of hearing "Boom Boom," you're missing a treat. The chorus, especially, is a hoot:

> *Boom boom boom*
> *Let's go back to my room*
> *So we can do it all night*
> *And you can make me feel right*

Actually, there's nothing necessarily "gay" about these and the other lyrics in the song. But one listen to *how* they're sung and it's undeniable. For instance, when Lekakis (who's been known to perform in gay establishments for very enthusiastic audiences) intones, "How's about comin' back to my room for a little boom-boom?" in a voice that would sound blasé if it weren't backed by an audible (and seductive) smile, you just *know* they don't come much gayer than this. The overused but essential term "camp" doesn't quite do it justice.

Incidentally, you might want to check out another Lekakis dance track (on the same album—what a deal!) with the winking title "You Blow Me Away." One notch below "Boom Boom" in the fun factor, but still utterly shameless.

■ *LET MY PEOPLE COME* (ORIGINAL CAST) ■
■ "I'M GAY" ■

Songwriter:	Earl Wilson, Jr.
Year of Release:	1974
Original Album:	*Let My People Come* (original cast recording)
Chart Performance:	Not released as a single, and the album didn't chart
Availability:	Out of print (Libra 1060)

"I'm Gay" is one of the most tasteful songs in the self-proclaimed "sexual musical" *Let My People Come*—in my opinion one of the *least* tasteful shows ever to grace a stage. Not that I've ever seen it; just listening to the music is enough. "How tasteless is it?" you ask? Let it suffice to say that one of the big, climactic (no pun intended) numbers is titled "Come in My Mouth." John Waters has nothing on *that*.

By contrast, "I'm Gay" seems the very portrait of decorum. The song takes the form of a letter written by a young man to "Dear Mom and Pop" in which he comes out to them. His words throughout are echoed by another young man, apparently also writing to his folks, thus poignantly expressing the irony of gay people feeling isolated despite the fact that they're far from alone. The lyrics sound naive and bittersweet by modern standards, but the culminating message is as valid today as it was in 1974:

> *Maybe one day*
> *It won't be such a hard thing to say—*
> *I'm gay*

As the chief narrator repeats the final "I'm gay" over and over, he's joined by more voices, both men and women, a few at first, but then still more, all chanting "I'm gay" in unison, until an entire chorus is singing those two little words. A powerful musical image. Too bad the rest of the show, for all of its taboo-breaking qualities, embarrasses me to listen to it. Maybe it's my Southern Baptist upbringing.

▪ LITTLE RICHARD ▪ "TUTTI-FRUTTI," "GOOD GOLLY MISS MOLLY," AND "LONG TALL SALLY" ▪

Songwriters:	"Tutti-Frutti" — Richard Penniman – Dorothy LaBestrie – Joe Lubin; "Good Golly Miss Molly" — Robert A. Blackwell – John Marascalco; "Long Tall Sally" — Enotris Johnson – Richard Penniman – Robert A. Blackwell
Year of Release:	1956 ("Tutti" and "Sally") and 1958 ("Molly")
Original Album:	*Here's Little Richard* ("Tutti" and "Sally") and *Little Richard* ("Molly")
Chart Performance:	The three singles reached #17, #6, and #10, respectively
Availability:	Original albums out of print; available on *Little Richards' 18 Greatest Hits*, CD, CS, LP (Rhino 75899)

With his swept-up pompadour, obvious makeup, high-pitched squeals, loads of glitter, and all-around flamboyance years before anybody even dreamed of glam-rock, nobody had ever seen anyone or anything like Little Richard. He boldly proclaimed himself "The King of Rock and Roll," and with good reason: in his prime, few could match him as a performer, and none could surpass him. And say what you want about Elvis Presley and Chuck Berry, but no one has had a greater stylistic influence on rock vocals than Richard Wayne Penniman.

Little Richard had a string of pull-out-the-stops hit singles during the early years of rock and roll, but after a religious experience in the late fifties, he temporarily quit show business and turned to preaching. In his sermons (as reported in Charles White's amazing 1984 biography, *The Life and Times of Little Richard: The Quasar of Rock*, and elsewhere), Richard would frequently refer to his former life of drugs and homosexuality, joyfully declaring that he'd been saved from his past life of sin. Yet in interviews he also maintained, "I don't have anything against gays. Jesus loves gay people." Nevertheless, no matter what you may think of all this, his importance remains indisputable as a pioneer and major force in the history of rock music.

A number of tunes from Little Richard's early, pre-evangelism days invite consideration as possibly "gay" in their subtexts. Most notable among them are his first big smash, "Tutti-Frutti"—a testament to the cathartic power of purposeful foolishness whose title alone makes it suspect—and the subsequent hits "Long Tall Sally" and "Good Golly Miss Molly," which some people believe to be about drag queens. Did you ever wonder why Sally was so long and tall? And the title "Good Golly Miss Molly" is indeed the kind of tight rhyming line that was typical of African-American gay slang of the pre-Stonewall era, and perhaps to a lesser extent still today. The "Miss" business is itself suggestive.

Maybe. The only trouble is, if these songs had been done by anyone but Little Richard, I doubt whether anyone would make the possible connection. But they *were* done by Little Richard. And that alone demands attention.

▪ JOHNNY MATHIS ▪ "LOVE THEME FROM *ROMEO AND JULIET* (A TIME FOR US)" ▪

Songwriters:	Larry Kusick – Eddie Snyder – Nino Rota
Year of Release:	1969
Original Album:	*Love Theme from "Romeo and Juliet"*
Chart Performance:	The single reached #96
Availability:	Original album out of print; available on *16 Most Requested Songs*, CD, CS (Columbia 40217)

How, by any stretch of the imagination, can a lyrical rendition of the love theme from the 1968 film version of William Shakespeare's classic tragedy of young heterosexual love, *Romeo and Juliet*, be a "gay song"? Here's how:

1. The singer, Johnny Mathis, is an openly gay man. While he doesn't shout it from the rooftops—which leaves many of his fans "in the dark," so to speak—he came out in the pages of *Us* magazine during the early eighties and has been open about his gayness in other publications as well.
2. Consider the lyrics, which include lines expressing a desire for
   A time when dreams so long denied can flourish
   As we unveil the love we now must hide
   The relevance of these words to gay people could not have been lost to Mathis as he recorded this song in the late sixties—to be sure, before Stonewall, before Mathis himself was "out," but no less deeply relevant to him and countless other gay people.
3. Besides, who's to say that the tale of forbidden heterosexual love so evocatively told in *Romeo and Juliet* wasn't considered an apt metaphor for another type of forbidden love by Franco Zefferelli, the gay producer/director of the film—and, if some scholars are correct in their speculations about Shakespeare's possible bisexual proclivities, by the Bard himself?

Johnny Mathis in the mid-1970s. (Photo: Michael Ochs Archives.)

Songwriters: Barry Manilow – Marty Panzer
Year of Release: 1976
Original Album: *This One's for You*
Chart Performance: Not released as a single, but the album reached #6
Availability: CD, CS (Arista 8331)

As everyone knows, just because a person writes and/or performs a song that can readily be interpreted as gay-related, it doesn't necessarily mean that he or she is gay. And Barry Manilow—former accompanist and musical director for Bette Midler back in her days at the Continental Baths—has never, to my knowledge, made any public statements indicating that he may be gay. Keeping that in mind, I humbly suggest the lyrics of this song for your consideration. I can't quote them at length, but Manilow sings (either in his own voice or in that of a narrative persona) about having once felt alone in the world, fearing that he was "crazy in a way that no one else could be." Then he describes how much he longed for someone, anyone, to tell him, "You're not alone," and the joy he felt upon discovering that he truly wasn't.

The rest of the song is in precisely the same vein. These words express feelings that virtually every gay man and lesbian in modern western civilization (and surely in many if not most other civilizations as well) have experienced, particularly in their youth. Of course, it expresses feelings felt by other people who perceive themselves as "different" somehow, so this song isn't necessarily "gay." But it has nevertheless been adopted by a number of gay choruses across the country (along with some other poignant Barry Manilow songs, such as "I Made It Through the Rain") and has often been sung in their concerts.

In the unlikely case that Barry and any other persons involved in the creation and production of "All the Time" are offended by its inclusion in this book, I would hope that they could take satisfaction in the fact that a song like this has such wide appeal that many different types of people—gay people included—can closely identify with it. That's in the unlikely case.

▪ GEORGE MICHAEL ▪ "TOO FUNKY" AND "DO YOU REALLY WANT TO KNOW" ▪

Songwriter:	George Michael (both songs)
Year of Release:	1992
Original Album:	*Red Hot + Dance*
Chart Performance:	"Too Funky" reached #10, but "Do You Really Want to Know" wasn't released as a single
Availability:	CD, CS (Columbia 52826)

So far George Michael has had an amazing career, to say the least. Emerging seemingly out of nowhere as the dominant half of the multi-platinum duo Wham!, he leapt quickly to even greater success by himself, his first solo LP *Faith* selling zillions of copies, spawning *six* Top Five hits (four of them reaching Number One), and winning a Grammy Award as Album of the Year. Not bad for a guy who wasn't even born when Beatle-mania first struck his native Great Britain. Adding to his aura is the fact that he has repeatedly lent his considerable talents to a wide variety of charitable causes. One of the causes most frequently benefiting from his work is AIDS relief and research.

The *Red Hot + Dance* album is one such project, with all artist and producer royalties plus record company net profits (kudos to Columbia) going to AIDS-related charities. Fully one-quarter of that album consists of songs by George Michael, including the big hit single "Too Funky." There's nothing especially "gay" about the song itself. But then there's the video, with all of those female models walking up and down the runway, some of them adorned in terrifically campy creations. And that's not even the clincher. Part of the fun is trying to figure out which of those models are actually drag queens. Then again, just between you and me, I didn't find it too terribly difficult.

Reportedly, in the initial version of the video, the drag queens were more numerous and even more obvious. But (so the story goes) Michael backed off from the original, fearing that such a blatant display of drag would offend a lot of his fans—not to mention hurt the single's chance of success, thus reducing the amount of money it would earn on behalf of AIDS research. He reshot parts of the video and re-edited it to make the drag angle much less acute. I don't know how much of this story is true; I'm only relating what I've read elsewhere.

Video aside, a far more interesting song from *Red Hot + Dance* is Michael's "Do You Really Want to Know," a sizzling house-music track that demonstrates our hero's knack for keeping up with the Madonnas and Pet Shop Boys of the world in borrowing musical styles from gay African-American pop culture. Sometime when you're not dancing, pay close atten-tion to the lyrics, in which Michael may be playing a clever metaphorical game with his audience. At the most readily apparent level, the song concerns a heterosexual couple's gnawing interest in each other's past sex lives, an extremely pertinent subject in the context of AIDS. During the first rendition of the bridge, Michael's narrator states that "if you knew every woman and I knew every man"—that is, the people with whom they had each been previously involved—their love might never have survived its earliest stages. But when he repeats the bridge a little later, he subtly shifts the pronouns: "If I knew every woman and you knew every man." You can draw your own conclusions as to what that implies.

As other music journalists have pointed out, "Do You Really Want to Know" may even refer to the burning question among gay pop music fans—and perhaps in the world of pop music in general—about George Michael himself: namely, "Is he or isn't he?" Depending on how one interprets the lines quoted above, he may have already provided an answer.

▪ MICKEY'S 7 ▪ "DO IT ALL OVER YOU" AND "I GOT MY RIGHT HAND" ▪

Songwriters:	("Do It All Over You") Roy C. Ames – C. Holzhaus; ("I Got My Right Hand") J. Hoyer
Year of Release:	1975
Original Album:	*Rocket to Stardom*
Chart Performance:	Not released as singles, and the album didn't chart
Availability:	Out of print (Home Cooking 101)

I was quite prepared to hate these songs. Everything about Mickey's 7 and *Rocket to Stardom* points toward musical disaster. The album is surely one of the most obscure I've ever run across. The band was named for its lead singer, Mickey Brewster, who in the 70s was featured in erotic gay magazines. (The "7" reportedly referred to his endowment.) The album cover features a drawing of several shirtless young men riding through a starry sky astride an unmistakably phallic rocket, which is gripped by a hand that has morphed out of the young men's legs. The song list includes such titles as "Rock Around the Crotch," "Funk-y Butt," and "Stroke My Spoke," and the liner notes speak of "hard sex-rock." In short, the situation doesn't look promising, at least musically speaking.

So I reluctantly played the album. The first song, a failed single titled "(Maybe I Need Him, Maybe I Need) Medi-Care" *(beg pardon?)*, reveals a strong James Gang influence. Sure enough, what with the fuzz-toned, wah-wahed guitar, "hard sex-rock" is an apt description. And, surprisingly, it isn't half bad. Nothing to pin one's Grammy hopes on, but not bad at all.

Love & Peace,
Mickey.

Mickey Brewster, openly gay lead singer of the band Mickey's 7, 1975.

Then comes a nervy but passable remake of the Nat King Cole standard, "Nature Boy," which sounds a bit like one of Emerson, Lake and Palmer's "soft" songs, in the mold of "Lucky Man." Continuing, "Rock Around the Crotch" reminds me of a Bachman-Turner Overdrive outtake. "Uranus (Space Butt Hole)" takes the Bowie-Jobriath astro-queer metaphor to the lewd extreme. The badly sung "Don't Let Go" bears a marked similarity to early Steely Dan, but without the polish. And "Stroke My Spoke" recalls, of all things, Southern rock *à la* Lynyrd Skynyrd. In other words, *Rocket to Stardom* is a veritable *mélange* of mid-seventies rock stylings, performed by what sounds like a group of crack session players—plus the fair-to-middlin' vocals of lead singer Mickey. Which makes me think, *"Is this somebody's idea of a joke?"*

Joke or not, the album's lyrics are forthrightly gay, though usually tending toward the, shall we say, "unrefined" side. Two songs deserve particular mention here. "Do It All Over You" is a blues-structured uptempo number with damn fine lead guitar work, again resembling pre-*Aja* Steely Dan. A lusty song of sexual passion, its lyrics include the crude but thoroughly delightful line (probably inspired by Mickey's "other" career), "If I had to do it all over again, I'd do it all over you."

The other track of special note is the album closer, "I Got My Right Hand," a comic, seemingly impromptu, blatantly masturbatory ditty that starts off with studio banter, passes through a snatch of Scott Joplin's "The Entertainer," and turns into a New Orleans-style rinky-tink tune. Mickey, who has proven himself a versatile if inconsistent vocalist throughout the album, sings in gravelly tones,

> *I got only one love*
> *And she fits inside a glove*

Given the indisputably "gay" nature of the rest of the album, I don't know why they bother with the "she" pronoun. But it matters little. Following a chorus consisting solely of the repeated title, there's more talk, more studio tomfoolery, and a drum-machine solo accompanied by moans and gasps, clearly designed to provide an aural simulation of the subject— ahem—at hand. The chorus returns and the song fades out. Fun stuff, if on a decidedly unsophisticated level.

Regrettably, the title *Rocket to Stardom* proved overly optimistic. Mickey Brewster's musical career went nowhere. It makes me wonder what happened to ol' Mickey. Although he was undoubtedly backed up by some significant anonymous talent, he himself also showed some real potential. And if you've got what it takes, stardom in music remains a definite possibility years after it's inconceivable in certain other fields.

▪ BETTE MIDLER ▪ "FRIENDS" ▪

Songwriters: Mark Klingman – Buzzy Linhart
Year of Release: 1973
Original Album: *The Divine Miss M*
Chart Performance: The single reached #40
Availability: CD, CS (Atlantic 7238)

This selection from her debut album is the closest thing to a theme song that The Divine Miss M has. That alone probably qualifies it for inclusion here, considering that gay men gave Bette her start (in New York's Continental Baths), gay men have remained her always-faithful core audience, and gay men have supplied her chief source of inspiration. I mean, how do you think her stage persona originated except as a "real" woman's impersonation of a drag queen? And a damn good impersonation at that.

Anyway, "Friends" is an important Midler-gay song because of its central repeated message: "You've got to have friends." And while that's true for everybody—at least for anybody who wants to have a life worth living—it's especially true for gay people, for whom their closest friends often form a kind of surrogate family. Bette has always known that messages of this sort are close to the hearts of gay people, which is one of the chief reasons for Bette herself staying close to their hearts as well.

▪ JONI MITCHELL ▪ "TAX FREE" ▪

Songwriters: Joni Mitchell – Larry Klein
Year of Release: 1985
Original Album: *Dog Eat Dog*
Chart Performance: Not released as a single, but the album reached #63
Availability: CD, CS, LP (Geffen 24074)

Joni Mitchell—with the possible exception of Carole King the single most important female singer-songwriter of the rock era—vents her rage and frustration at television evangelists who rake in nontaxable cash while advocating militarism and other tenets of right-wing ideology. She regards this as more than merely hypocritical; it's an outright threat. Fortunately, when one isn't actively opposing this menace, one can cry "Fuck it!" (as she does) and temporarily escape from it: "Tonight I'm going dancing with the drag queens and punks." Thus Mitchell seeks deliverance from "sanctimonious skunks." Then again, I suppose dancing with drag queens is an even *more* active way of opposing the religious right, only having fun while doing it.

▪ MOE AND JOE ▪ "WHERE'S THE DRESS?" ▪

Songwriters: Tony Stampley – B. Lindsey – G. Cummings
Year of Release: 1984
Original Album: *The Good Ol' Boys—Alive and Well*
Chart Performance: The single failed to make the pop chart, but it
                        reached #8 on the country chart
Availability: CS (Columbia 39426)

To prove just how big a pop-culture phenomenon Boy George was circa 1984, I offer this startling record. And what's so startling about it? The fact that the mere existence of homosexuality or something like it was acknowledged in a big hit on the country music charts during the Reagan era —*that's* what's startling.

Moe and Joe are Moe Bandy and Joe Stampley, a successful pair of solo country stars who made a series of albums and singles together in the 1980s. They cultivated a rough-housin', hard-drinkin', truck-drivin', good ol' boy image (male bonding, you know, country-style) that's carried over into "Where's the Dress?" The track starts off with the instantly recognizable opening riff from Culture Club's "Karma Chameleon," but quickly moves into a song of its own with Joe describing his first glimpse of Boy George on television. What's more, he's amazed and—as we shall soon see—quite impressed that this "man dressed like a woman" is "makin' a million bucks."

Now this is intensely interesting. In passing, Stampley uses the term "ol' boy" to refer to Boy George, which could be significant. It possibly indicates that Moe and Joe consider him something of a peer, not altogether unworthy of respect. And with the assertion that he's making a fortune, we see not only the likely source of that respect but also a hint that Moe and Joe doubt that Boy George could be "for real." In other words, they suspect it's all an act to make money. Setting aside the fact that they are of course at least partially correct, isn't this fascinating? Obviously even the most backward hicks must know in the late twentieth century that such things as drag queens and cross-dressing really do exist. That's not the question here. Rather, it's whether they could be "for real" in a person who's making a million dollars, a tremendous success. It's like when I was in college and one of the guys in the dorm room next to mine insisted that David Bowie's glam image was "just an act." My friend knew damn well that "androgyny," however you define it, was for real, but in such a public figure as David Bowie—nah, it was an act. As I've said before, yes, it was an act, but it was *more* than an act, too.

How can one cope with this?

At any rate, confronted with the fact that Boy George seems to be rolling in dough, Moe admits to his buddy that they'll never get rich "drivin' trucks" (how butch). Rather, why not get a piece of the action?

Where's the dress?

We'll be money-makin' fools

So with their own willingness, even in the context of a country novelty song, to become cross-dressers for the sake of cash, Moe and Joe confirm their own doubts about Boy George's homosexuality. High-heels and a little makeup wouldn't make *them* queer, no sirree. And they're sure to tell us that they'll still have girls around, even if one of them is there to tease their hair. They'll still drink beer and go fishing, but "when it comes to show time," proclaim Moe and Joe, "we'll be country queens."

Well, if that don't beat all. And you'd think that a coupla good ol' boys would never stoop to such, not even for a million bucks. But the whole point is that by joshing around about their own readiness to put on a drag show for money, they suggest that Boy George is putting on a similar act. Why, maybe when he gets home from a hard day on stage, he takes off his makeup, puts on a pair of jeans, and downs a few brews. Maybe the Boy is one of the boys after all.

"Where's the Dress?" is nothing less than a country-music exorcism of the psychosexual demons unleashed upon American culture by Boy George in the early 1980s. David Bowie was a profound influence in the world of rock music in the early 1970s, but he was a ripple in the larger cultural current compared to Boy George. Bowie didn't do American talk shows dressed as Ziggy Stardust. Bowie didn't make the cover of major news magazines in his Aladdin Sane guise. Bowie didn't appear on the Grammy Awards show thanking America for "knowing a good drag queen when it saw one." Boy George did all of these things in his cuddly, androgynous glory and not even the fans of *Hee Haw* could ignore it.

If you can't ignore it, you have to explain it. And how do you explain it?

- Option A: Androgyny and homosexuality are perfectly natural.
  Analysis: Unacceptable. Next option.
- Option B: Western civilization is crumbling around us.
  Analysis: Perhaps, but awfully depressing. Can't you do better?
- Option C: The Boy is nothing more than a crass money-making act.
  Analysis: *Bingo!*

Denial, denial, denial. Just because there's a shard of truth in it doesn't make it any less a denial of the basic reality: that Boy George was *queer*, an outlandishly successful queer, and a talented, respected, apparently comfortable queer, one who had become *the* pop culture icon of the early 1980s with innumerable legions of adoring fans. Small wonder that Moe and Joe had such a big country hit in "Where's the Dress?" It explained Boy George in a manner wholly acceptable to much of their audience. It made him utterly nonthreatening.

Before I move on, I should recommend that if you can finagle some way of watching the "Where's the Dress?" video, do. It's a scream seeing the heavily bearded Moe Bandy and Joe Stampley cavorting in their Boy George drag. And they seem to be having a good ol' time doing it, too.

▪ GEOF MORGAN ▪ "HOMOPHOBIA" ▪

Songwriter:	Geof Morgan
Year of Release:	1980
Original Album:	*It Comes with the Plumbing*
Chart Performance:	Not released as a single, and the album didn't chart
Availability:	Out of print (Nexus 102449)

With several albums to his credit, Geof Morgan is something of a pioneer, if not the patron saint, of a "men's music" movement that roughly parallels and complements "women's music." It springs from a steadfastly anti-sexist empathy for feminism that manifests itself as a supportive "masculinism," if you will, that seeks to be both strong and gentle, closely in touch with what it means to be a man without in any way devaluating women. It opposes the oppression and exploitation of women and children, campaigning against rape and domestic violence. It means being pro-choice, supporting a woman's right to choose whether to have an abortion or, for that matter, to decide any other personal issue involving her body. And, because homophobia is rooted in sexism as well as in a pervasive anti-choice worldview, it means being gay-supportive, regardless of whether you're gay, straight, bisexual, or whatever. It's extremely "politically correct," but only in the best sense of that oft-abused term.

Morgan's song "Homophobia" comes across as an honest, sincere catharsis *qua* confession by a "straight" man. (At least Morgan *seems* "straight" to me, if I may say so without being insulting. A number of his songs talk about romantic relationships with women and being a father.) He speaks of homophobia as if it were a miserable old friend of whom he's terribly ashamed and would just as soon be rid of, but can't quite shake. It's a deeply ingrained part of him, despite his every intention of overcoming it, because of his growing up in a homophobic culture.

What's most interesting about this song, however, is that it so clearly describes how homophobia screws up the lives of heterosexuals as well as gay people. Homophobia causes a lot of men, gay and non-gay alike, to

146

feel tremendous anxiety over their masculinity, judging themselves and their "maleness" according to how well they perform in sports, in business, in bed, etc. It divorces them from their innermost feelings and prevents them from taking part in activities that they might otherwise enjoy. And, as Morgan repeats in his chorus, "it keeps me from touchin' my friends." It all adds up to a powerful indictment, and provides excellent reasons (as if any more were needed) for people to get over their homophobia—*because it's in their own best interest, even if they themselves aren't gay.*

Contributing to the effectiveness of Morgan's message is its musical setting. "Homophobia" is a fast-paced number in the country-folk vein, almost but not quite bluegrass. Morgan sings with an appropriately down-home style that at first seems to clash with his "progressive" ideas, but ultimately serves to lend them credence (again, as if any more were needed), making an anti-heterosexist stance sound as folksy and natural as a Sunday picnic in the valley after church. And why *shouldn't* it be? The Appalachian region of North America, from which both country and folk music can trace most of their roots, was largely settled by people with somewhat libertarian goals in mind, though they would hardly have articulated them as such. They were seeking political, social, and economic freedom and opportunity for themselves, far from the crowds and oppression of Europe and even the East Coast of colonial America. A lot of people refuse to see it in this light, but gay rights is a perfectly natural outgrowth of the basic birthright of every American: freedom of opportunity, pursuit of happiness, liberty from oppressive government, and political equality.

Damn, get me off on an Americana kick and I won't shut up. But as for Geof Morgan, "Homophobia" is only one of several delights from *It Comes with the Plumbing.* I especially like "Goodbye, John Wayne" (a moving post-mortem to traditional concepts of masculinity), "The Penis Song" (no comment necessary), and title track. I think you'd like the album too—if you can find it—even if you don't care much for folk music. Neither do I. But I like this.

• MORRISSEY •
• "(I'M) THE END OF THE FAMILY LINE" •

Songwriters:	Morrissey – Mark E. Nevin
Year of Release:	1991
Original Album:	*Kill Uncle*
Chart Performance:	Not released as a single, but the album reached #52
Availability:	CD, CS (Sire 26514)

From one of the driest wits in rock—and from an album the title of which is probably a sly, cynical reference to the ways in which heterosexuals often teach their children to feel about gay people, including (knowingly or unknowingly) their own close relatives—we have this somber but brilliant track. In that unmistakable voice of his, Morrissey drones to a mid-tempo backdrop about "fifteen generations . . . all honoring Nature." That is, as Morrissey puts it, "until I arrive (with incredible style)." And this means that his family line ends with him.

There's a complex blend of emotions underlying these words—a mixture of sadness and pride, thoroughly stirred by irony. With Morrissey, that irony can be infuriatingly relentless. But even at his most frustrating he remains supremely interesting. And in songs like this he provides tremendous insight into the bewildering, often humorous machinations of the human mind when confronted by the inherent absurdities of life. Not that gayness itself is absurd, but rather the feelings it sometimes inspires in a heterosexist culture such as ours.

As a solo artist Morrissey has written and recorded a number of songs of special interest to gay people, such as "Lucky Lisp" and "He Knows I'd Love to See Him." If you're not familiar with his work, you may want to check him out, though his voice and style can take some getting used to. Meanwhile, I refer you to the Smiths, a band in which he served an extremely productive apprenticeship.

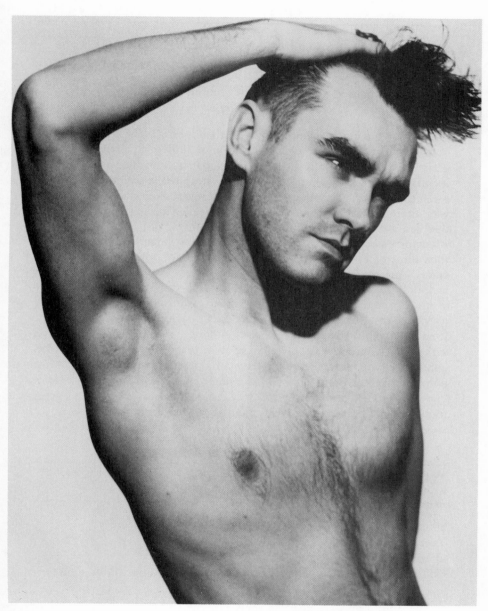

Morrissey. (Photo: Courtesy Sire Records.)

▪ ELTON MOTELLO ▪ "JET BOY JET GIRL" ▪

Songwriters:	Lou Deprijck – Yves Lacomblez – Alan Ward
Year of Release:	1978
Original Album:	*Victim of Time*
Chart Performance:	Both the single and the album failed to chart
Availability:	Out of print (Pinball 6-23650)

Sung-spoken in a near-monotone over a hopping New Wave beat, this quasi-hit (a very loose English translation of a major Belgian-French single) turned out to be quite a success in gay dance clubs. But nary a note of it could be heard anywhere else. You see, despite the seeming equal time given to both sexes in the title, which is repeated over and over again, it was another recurring line that both propelled its gay popularity and doomed it to commercial limbo: "He gives me head." And unlike 1973, when most people apparently didn't know what "giving head" referred to, thus allowing Lou Reed's "Walk on the Wild Side" onto Top Forty radio, enough people knew what it meant just five years later to guarantee a lack of radio airplay.

Aside from that brazen, oft-repeated line and its terrific dance beat (swell to "pogo" to), "Jet Boy Jet Girl" really didn't have much to recommend it. It had no melody to speak of, it was numbingly repetitious, and its lyrics articulated a rather sexist, exploitive view of gender expectations: "I'm gonna treat you like a girl," complete with references to penetration. Most unfortunate. Still, though it failed as a single in terms of "Top Forty" radio, "Jet Boy Jet Girl" became a gay dance classic. I mean, it really *was* great to pogo to! Who needs art when records can be this much fun?

▪ ELTON MOTELLO ▪
▪ "WHEN ALL THE BOYS ARE ENGLISH" ▪

Songwriters:	Andrew Goldberg – Alan Ward
Year of Release:	1980
Original Album:	*Pop Art*
Chart Performance:	Not released as a single, and the album didn't chart
Availability:	Out of print (Passport 9846)

Well, maybe Elton Motello needed art. Within two years of having scored a minor triumph with "Jet Boy Jet Girl," he released an album titled *Pop Art*—a ponderous tag for any record to bear. For all the stiff competition, this simply *must* be one of the worst LPs in my collection. Among its many low points are a Devo-ish, criminally mutilated version of the Who's "I Can't Explain" (the real Devo would've done it *much* better) and a tune with the promising title "Queen," but which I can't make sense of, so grating is its music, so unintelligible its lyrics. (I think I figured out the line "My brain is out of tune.") With its irritating saxophone, crashing guitars, and wailing vocals, "Queen" sounds as though Motello were trying hard to mimic David Bowie on a bad day, but succeeded only in approximating the musical quality of a badly malfunctioning garbage disposal.

Also betraying the unmistakable influence of Bowie is the immediately preceding track, "When All the Boys Are English," which Motello deeply croons like an Anthony Newley on phenobarbital. Fortunately, this time you can understand most of the words. They seem to focus on a young man who discovered early on that he liked looking at pictures of athletes on the sports pages. He confesses that he "tried hard to be male" but doesn't know where he "failed," and that he later experienced a "Cambridge affair," which taught him the pleasure of being made love to by other young men but left him devoid of any genuine human warmth. He warns his listeners again and again not to trust anything, "especially love." If this is the way one's emotional life turns out "when all the boys are English," one should fraternize with some other nationality with all due haste.

You can't escape the fact that this is a terribly bleak portrait of a homosexual male, compounded by murky electronic music. For all of the narrator's negativity, he steadfastly maintains, "I don't want to be straight again," whatever *that* means, yet there's no air of comfort or satisfaction about such an assertion. It just sounds hopeless.

This is not gay music. I'm not sure it was *meant* to be. But it does make me wonder why people bother to record things like this. If the performer isn't gay, then the music is a lie created to capitalize on and profit by the fears and prejudices of others. If the performer *is* gay, then the music expresses the self-pity and self-hatred that arises from an inability to transcend homophobia. In such cases the artist is probably much better off remaining in the closet—which may also provide the fringe benefit of sparing gay and non-gay people alike the pointlessness of such unpleasant songs.

As for Mr. Motello, we've heard nary a peep from him after the commercial failure of *Pop Art*. For that I suppose we should be grateful. Unless, of course, he's managed to get his act together so that he stands a better chance of producing something worth listening to.

▪ MOTT THE HOOPLE ▪
▪ "ALL THE YOUNG DUDES" ▪

Songwriter:	David Bowie
Year of Release:	1972
Original Album:	*All the Young Dudes*
Chart Performance:	The single reached #37
Availability:	CD, CS (Columbia 31750)

Personally, I think this is one of the funniest songs ever played on Top Forty radio. David Bowie took a frustrated, relatively unsuccessful, ready-to-disband group of (presumably) heterosexual boys, gave them a camped-up glam image, and handed them a song that became a virtual anthem for the glitter rock movement as well as for certain segments of the early-seventies gay community. And it was all incredibly tongue-in-cheek.

Ian Hunter's performance as the lead vocalist is perhaps the very epitome of punk-queendom in rock. With a voice that somehow manages simultaneously to sound bitchy, bored, stupid, and strident, he satirically bemoans society's misunderstanding of him (his persona, that is) and his allegedly "juvenile delinquent" peers, glam-rock devotees of T-Rex that they are. In the course of his lament, he tells us about his friend Billy, who "dresses like a queen." And then there's the chorus—an unforgettable hook as well as a call to arms: "All the young dudes, carry the news." Of course, in addition to a revolutionary cry, it's also a call to party on: "boogaloo, too." This, it would seem, is a social movement that *moves*.

The very best lines of the song sum up both the rebelliousness and the confusion of this young man even as it spells out his sexual interests:

> *Gonna race some cat to bed*
> *Is the concrete all around or is it in my head?*

As the song nears its fade-out conclusion and the chorus is repeated over and over again, Hunter continues to camp it up, crying out to all the young dudes who may be listening. At one point he declares that he wants to "relate" to them—and the exaggerated way in which he intones the word "relate" leaves absolutely no doubt about the kind of "relating" he has in mind. But just in case, he adds, "I wanna kiss you." It's barely discernible, however, beneath the repeating chorus; otherwise the song probably wouldn't have gotten any airplay.

It's all too much. Yet judging by the record's success, it's doubtful whether most listeners really understood what was going on, and most of the ones who did understand probably just thought it was funny—largely because it *was* funny, and still is. Really, I'm surprised that the ever commercially minded Bowie didn't decide to keep this delicious, decadent pop pastry for himself.

Mott the Hoople's subsequent singles weren't as popular and they soon left the glitter scene behind. They managed to crank out a few more things —such as the noteworthy "All the Way from Memphis"—but their finest day in the sun would remain "All the Young Dudes." Credit Bowie for writing and producing a great record and Hunter for a brilliant vocal. It proved an impossible act to follow.

■ MARTIN MULL ■ "MEN" (AND A FEW OTHERS) ■

Songwriters:	Martin Mull – Steve Martin ("Men"); Martin Mull (the others)
Year of Release:	1976
Original Album:	*I'm Everyone I've Ever Loved*
Chart Performance:	Not released as a single, but the album reached #184
Availability:	Out of print (ABC 997)

I have a lot of respect for Martin Mull. You've got to admire a man who's been slugging away at big-time stardom for more than two decades but has only managed to carve out a niche as a competent, reliable second-stringer. He has a talent for recording comic-satirical music and has released a number of albums, none of which has broken into the Top 100. He's managed to produce one Top 100 hit (just barely—#92), the bizarre novelty-parody instrumental "Dueling Tubas." He's had the good humor to make fun of his own lack of commercial success, such as when he titled his "best of" album *No Hits, Four Errors*. An accomplished comic actor, he's starred in several syndicated television shows that have achieved cult status— *Mary Hartman, Mary Hartman* and its spinoffs *Fernwood 2-Night* and *America 2-Night*— as well as other, more "mainstream" programs that have bombed miserably. He's also appeared in a number of films (such as *Mr. Mom*), always as a supporting player. And he wins big bonus points for his former recurring role on the *Roseanne* TV show as Roseanne's boss, who happened to be gay but whose gayness only occasionally had any overt mention or plot relevance—which, in my opinion, is exactly the way it should have been for a peripheral character. Mull has perfected his cynical, egotistical, too-smart-for-his-own-good terribly-white-guy jerk act to the point that nobody, except perhaps Steve Martin, does it better. All of this, plus the fact that he's as cute as a button. As I said, I respect the man.

Speaking of Steve Martin, he's the co-writer with Mull of "Men," an absolute gem of a novelty number. Probably inspired by Monty Python's classic lumberjack song, "Men" goes a few steps further. Whereas the Python number is basically just a delightfully silly parody of transvestism, "Men" both exposes and pokes fun at the homoerotic implications of traditional male bonding, serving the dual function of humor and social critique. And it does so in a completely disarming, almost affectionate manner.

Singing *a cappella* with a male chorus in a full-bodied but not exaggeratedly "masculine" voice (exaggeration would have reduced the satire to a cartoon), Mull tells us how great it is to be out at sea with a ship full of men. In just the first eight lines of the song, Mull and/or Martin (whoever is primarily responsible for the lyrics) summarizes one of the prime forces behind male bonding—namely, a rejection of what men have traditionally considered to be the stifling, "civilizing" influence of women. According to this notion, men can be Men (with a capital M) only around other men, whereas around women they're forced to be something other than (less than?) Men. Mind you, I'm not saying this notion is true; I'm only saying that it's part of the subconscious male psyche.

What's more, Mull gives robust voice to the often hinted-at but seldom fully explored ramifications of the traditionally all-male environment of naval crews. For instance, it has been suggested in some examinations of gay history that pirate ships of the seventeenth and eighteenth centuries were largely manned (pun intended) by homosexual or bisexual men. These men saw the "pirate lifestyle," so to speak, as a good way to enter a virtually all-male universe while simultaneously escaping the heterosexual expectations of "conventional" society. I consider this an intriguing albeit unattractive theory (pirates don't exactly make for ideal role models) for which I would love to see more evidence.

Where was I? As "Men" continues, Mull's persona positively exults in the totally masculine atmosphere of the ship and the complete absence of women, repeating the word "men" over and over again. Then he really starts to show his hand. He tells the names of some of his comrades, including Butch and Spike "and one guy we call Sally." Mull's character knows that his fondness for maleness might easily be mistaken, so he assures us that there's nothing "queer" going on:

> None of us are sissies
> At night we sleep in separate beds

—but the underlying truth will out—

> And blow each other kissies

And then comes the *coup de grace*, a brilliantly funny double-entendre that functions as a shorthand means of indicating precisely what's going on without actually spelling it out. Ironically, the double meaning was possible only in the pre-AIDS era of the 1970s. "Throw your rubbers overboard," he cries out, "there's no one here but men!" Are condoms unnecessary because there's no sex at all, or only because there's no sex with women? (Ah, the nostalgia.) So, with a resounding "A*men*," the song ends.

Various gay choruses across the country have discovered the butch-camp potential of "Men" and have performed it in concert. Realizing that "Men" may prove to be one of the most enduring things he's ever recorded, Mull has performed it on television himself, and always without the slightest shade of homophobia—although, one might argue, low-key homophobia provides the basis of the humor for "straight" audiences. But for gay listeners it's just good, clean fun.

An added attraction: the album on which "Men" appears, *I'm Everyone I've Ever Loved*, features several other songs of special note to gay men. In the title song, the egomaniacal narrator describes how he himself has all of the qualities he's ever loved in a woman. At one point, after cataloguing the traits he shares with the many women he's loved, he reveals, "And as far as that time in the bus station goes, I'm everything that he was."

In the track titled "Artist Relations (or Don't Write Me at Home)," Mull chastises an extramarital lover for mailing letters to him at home where his wife can see them. Among his complaints are, "Whatever could have possessed you to sign it, 'Love, Maurice'?" Yet another cut, "The Humming Song," includes a list of unusual sex practices, with the presumably naughty parts "hummed" out, such as "Hmmmmm jars of Vaseline, hmmmmm pick up the soap," and "Hmmmmm your wife." So he's obviously humming it to another man.

Now, I imagine there might be some gay people out there who find these things offensive, considering them examples of humor at our expense. But I would have to disagree. I find nothing offensive in Mull's good-natured songs, and it's refreshing to find a presumably heterosexual man (gee, I don't know!) who's willing to raise eyebrows with allusions to homosexuality in his own life, or at least in the lives of his musical personae. Between songs like these and his former character on *Roseanne*, Martin Mull just may wind up adding significant numbers of gay people to his cult following, if he hasn't already. And he *is* cute.

• CHARLIE MURPHY • "GAY SPIRIT" •

Songwriter:	Charlie Murphy
Year of Release:	1981
Original Album:	*Catch the Fire*
Chart Performance:	Not released as a single, and the album didn't chart
Availability:	CS, LP (Icebergg 5103)

"Gay Spirit" stands as one of the authentic anthems of the gay rights movement, a song you're liable to hear performed at any gay pride rally. In its original rendition by its writer, Charlie Murphy, it's a driving, rousing number—is there such a thing as "hard folk"?—with a message familiar to gay men and lesbians but which our society at large just can't seem to understand. "When we were born they tried to cover our eyes," Murphy sings, describing how our culture seeks to deny our true selves, trying "to tell us what to see." Feel free to join in on the chorus. Most of you know the words:

> *There's a gay spirit singing in our hearts*
> *Leading us through these troubled times*
> *There's a gay spirit moving 'round this land*
> *Calling us to a time of open love*

This is not a time for subtlety. When have you ever heard a subtle anthem?

"Gay Spirit" is a decidedly political creature. It's meant to stir people to action and to shake the foundations of a system of ignorance and oppression. Still, it moves beyond the realm of the merely political in the final verse—my favorite—where Murphy describes how difficult it can be to feel "gay" (in the more traditional sense of that word) "in the face of all the pain we see." Yet, he assures us, we can look into our hearts, find the gay spirit there, and heal each other. That's even more important to remember today than it was more than a decade ago, when this song was written.

As wonderful as "Gay Spirit" is, I have some personal difficulties with some other parts of Murphy's *Catch the Fire* album, which is characterized by some pretty facile pantheistic sentiments. I find the chants to Pan, Wodin, Isis, Astarte, Demeter, Hecate, Osiris, Diana, and other lesser-known deities a bit hard to swallow, and one track suggests that the erect penis is the emblem of a goat-godling. I get the willies when heavy-metal bands howl about "the Horned One," and I'm certainly no fonder of it when gay troubadours do similar things. And, wouldn't you know it, *Catch the Fire* even has a whale song (I *hate* whale songs) and another that decries nuclear power plants, which I believe to be far less dangerous to the environment (at least when they're built and run properly) than the ones that burn fossil fuels, which pump untold tons of carbon monoxide, nitric oxides, and sulfur oxides into the atmosphere every year. But these are debates for another time and place, aren't they? Let's just say that Charlie Murphy's "Gay Spirit," both the song and the album, are extremely important musical contributions to the lives of lesbians and gay men everywhere, and leave it at that.

As for Murphy, he has resurfaced through the years with periodic musical output, most notably the excellent 12-inch single "Fierce Love" (which also includes two other tracks, "Mean Spirit" and "Fool for the Cause"), released in 1985. While none of these three songs featured "gay-specific" lyrics, they did boast a totally revamped sound for Murphy—a hot, percussive, electric sound which seemed to come from a different artist altogether. The heightened social awareness, however, was still intact, with two of the songs warning of government conspiracies, declining tolerance, the threat of pollution, and other issues that demand attention. With "Gay

156

Spirit" and these later songs, Charlie Murphy proved himself a musician who demands attention as well.

▪ RANDY NEWMAN ▪ "LOVE STORY' ▪

Songwriter: Randy Newman
Year of Release: 1968
Original Album: *Randy Newman*
Chart Performance: Not released as a single, and the album failed to chart
Availability: Out of print (Reprise 6286)

This much-too-idealized-to-be-for-real depiction of a heterosexual romance appears on Randy Newman's eponymous first album of vocal music (an instrumental LP preceded it) and was one of the first songs to attract attention to his uniquely peculiar songwriting talent. In the course of the narrator's description to his beloved of the life he envisions for them together, he notes that the child they'll have (a son, of course) has "got to be straight—we don't want a bent one."

The narrator's insistence on having a "straight" child may seem offensive, but we shouldn't assume that Newman considers his narrator a paragon of ideal attitudes. I don't think I've ever heard a Randy Newman song that wasn't in some way satirical, although he can be so subtle about it that the satire escapes people who aren't familiar with his technique, and they sometimes wind up being offended. I only wonder whether Newman was aware when he wrote this song that "bent" is a common British equivalent of "queer."

▪ RANDY NEWMAN ▪ "HALF A MAN" ▪

Songwriter: Randy Newman
Year of Release: 1979
Original Album: *Born Again*
Chart Performance: Not released as a single, but the album reached #41
Availability: CD (Warner Brothers 3346)

Warning: Severe Satire Alert!

No, not *my* satire—Randy Newman's. As I've already suggested, Newman is responsible for some of the most devastating, controversial, yet often eerily beautiful satire in the history of American popular music. Take, for instance, his sole big hit, "Short People." It was widely misinterpreted as a nasty joke at the expense of people of small stature, when anybody with a good lick of sense realized that it was actually a wry put-down of bigotry. Sometimes Newman even creates satires within satires—rich layers of irony that can't readily be consumed at only one or two sittings—using narrators who are speaking satirically while they themselves are being satirized. Consider "Rednecks," a song that you'll probably never, ever hear on the radio. It's a blisteringly accurate depiction of racism, but it's also easy to misunderstand, not only because it repeatedly uses the word "niggers" but also because, even as it castigates its racist Southern narrator, it allows him to sarcastically berate hypocritical Northern liberals who are equally worthy of condemnation. A satiric *tour de force*, but a tough pill to swallow.

One of the things that makes Newman's satire so powerful (aside from his sheer tunefulness and astounding sense of harmonic progression) is the fact that he consistently refuses to see the targets of his ironic barbs as mere monsters. More often than not, they're people who, for all of their awfulness, are themselves victims of cultural circumstances beyond their control, victims even as they victimize others. To this day most listeners —critics included—aren't quite sure what to make of Newman's classic *Good Old Boys* album, on which the aforementioned "Rednecks" appears. One moment it's ridiculing and excoriating racist Southerners, and the next moment it seems to sympathize with them, even painting them with faintly heroic colors. But Newman knows that it's too pat, too easy to self-righteously detest the monster. It's far more challenging and productive to acknowledge the common, flawed humanity of people, ourselves included, and to try to deal honestly with it, to change it for the better. You don't *change* monsters, you kill them. People you try to avoid killing.

Which brings us to "Half a Man," another easy song to misunderstand. To be sure, it's not on a par with such Newman masterworks as "Sail Away," "Mama Told Me Not to Come" (the satire of which is barely detectable in the hit Three Dog Night version), or the rarely heard but lovely, totally affecting "Marie." But "Half a Man" very cleverly satirizes the stupid notion that homosexuality is somehow contagious, that it spreads infectiously from one potentially or formerly "straight" person to another. An unwary gay or gay-supportive listener might hear it and be shocked at its apparent crudeness and malevolence. An equally unwary homophobe hearing it might have high regard for the cautionary tale it seemingly tells. But you and I, we're now smart enough to know better, aren't we?

The story is told from the viewpoint of a stereotypical trucker who encounters an equally stereotypical homosexual in some generic urban venue:

> *This big old queen was standing*
> *On the corner of the street*
> *He waved his hanky at me*
> *As I went rolling by*

The trucker pulls his rig over, gets out of his cab, and grabs his handy tire-chain and knife, manfully ready to teach this pansy a lesson he'll never forget—should he be lucky enough to survive at all. But just as he's about to land his first pulverizing blow, his victim, "trembling like a bird," pleads to be granted "one final word":

> *"I am but half a man, half a man*
> *I'd like to be a dancer*
> *But I'm much too large*
> *Half a man, half a man*
> *I'm an object for your pity*
> *Not your rage"*

Now, if I didn't know better, I'd be furious at this point. These references to an "old queen," his groveling pleas for pity, and this "half a man" stuff are almost too much to take. But remember—we're in satirical territory.

To continue with the story, listening to the gay man speak of his struggles in life has an immediate effect on the trucker, who begins to experience "the strangest feeling." Much to his dismay, his speech and manner start to become "much more refined." The speed with which his "refining" transformation takes place is so ridiculous that anybody but the most ignorant or inattentive listener must be grasping the irony by now. By merely talking to a homosexual, perhaps even by staying the righteous, violent hand of retribution, one risks becoming one of those dreaded objects of loathing and pity himself. Heightening the irony is the fact that, at least to any sensible person, the superficial manifestations of this change would seem a definite improvement—described, after all, as "refinement."

To the trucker's fearful question, "What is wrong with me?" the "old queen" replies in the final lines of the song,

> *"Girl, it happens all the time*
> *And you are half a man, half a man*
> *Look, you're walking and you're talking*

Like a fag
Half a man, I am half a man
Holy Jesus, what a drag"

The homophobe's worst fears are confirmed. Just coming into contact with a queer makes you one. Or is Newman actually implying that only deeply repressed homosexuals would feel so threatened by openly gay people that they might threaten them with violence? Whichever the case, we're told "it happens all the time." In fact, the stereotypically gay hero has scored a "victory," not only saving his own life but also transforming the enemy into a "sister" ("Girl . . ."). The tables have been turned: the would-be gay-basher has been figuratively "bashed" by his own gayness. As a result, the man who was openly gay to begin with positively crows with simultaneous recognition and triumph.

See what I meant by layers of satire? Newman knows perfectly well how broadly he has painted his stereotypes of both the trucker and the "fag." He knows how absurd the transformation scene is. And he probably knows how offensive the words that he puts into the gay man's mouth sound. But he uses these outrageous devices to emphasize the sheer lunacy of the whole situation and the culture that makes it conceivable. That anyone would consider jumping out of a truck to kill someone just because he looked like an "old queen" and waved a handkerchief—ridiculous. That anyone might fear turning gay because of the mere presence of a queer—ludicrous. That anyone could be considered only "half a man" because he's gay—preposterous. But still, to a great extent, that's the way the world is. Too many people really do think and act that way. And that, my friends, is the bitter, bitter real-life joke that Randy Newman dares us to laugh at.

▪ PANSY DIVISION ▪ "BUNNIES" ▪

Songwriter:	Jon Ginoli
Year of Release:	1993
Original Album:	*Undressed*
Chart Performance:	Not released as a single, and the album failed to chart
Availability:	CD, CS (Lookout 70)

On the cover you see a nude young man, his long hair flowing around his neck and shoulders, lying in a field of lavender blossoms. You open the package and examine the liner notes, which provide instructions on how to use a condom. You skim through the lyric sheet, which features frank talk about various aspects of gay culture and being gay, including lots and lots of sex. And when you listen to the music, you note that it's right up

160

the "alternate rock" alley, with simple, guitar-dominated instrumentation, simple, uncomplicated song structures, and simple, unaffected vocals.

I could easily write about any of the thirteen songs on *Undressed* by Pansy Division (whose name, I suspect, is a camp take-off on the German Panzer Divisions of World War II). Each and every one of them brandishes its gayness like a rainbow flag at a Gay Pride parade. And they do so without making any concessions to polite society or general concepts of good taste. This is *raw material*, people. Among the song titles you'll find "Versatile," "Fem in a Black Leather Jacket," "Boyfriend Wanted," "The Cocksucker Club," and "Rock & Roll Queer Bar." And the album's closing tune, "Anthem" (for which the liner notes provide the Beastie Boys–spinoff epigraph "You've got to fight for your right to buttfuck"), is so aggressively gay that it would scare the living daylights out of any heterosexual who hears it.

But of all the songs on the album, I especially like the fast, furious, and funny "Bunnies" (as in "we fuck like —"). Get ready for the blunt truth of contemporary gay youth:

> *Hearing you knock on my door gets me hard*
> *You drive me rough like a pick-up truck*
> *It's a never-ending nonstop boy fuck*

There's lots more where that came from, but let's leave it at that.

To be honest, the music of Pansy Division isn't exactly my style. I think it helps if you're 22 or younger. Maybe even 18 or younger. I can, however, appreciate it. If I were a comfortably gay high-school or college student right now, I could go for this stuff in a big way. But I wouldn't let my *parents* hear it. They'd be just getting used to Kitchens of Distinction.

▪ LARRY PAULETTE ▪ "OUR DAY WILL COME" ▪

Songwriters:	Bob Hilliard – Mort Garson
Year of Release:	1977
Original Album:	*What Makes a Man a Man?*
Chart Performance:	Not released as a single, and the album didn't chart
Availability:	Out of print (Vanguard 79386)

Larry Paulette, an alumnus of the *Let My People Come* original cast, has a great baritone voice. It's a pity the way he mires it in oily MOR stylings that were already dated in 1977, the year of his album *What Makes a Man a Man?* His choice of material could have been a lot better, too, featuring as it does "Freakin' at the Freaker's Ball," "Triad," and the especially loathsome "What Makes a Man."

But then, unexpectedly—epiphany. He converts Ruby and the Romantics' 1963 love-song smash "Our Day Will Come" into a confident assertion of eventual triumph over bigotry. And suddenly, for one shining moment, the badness of the thing in every other respect doesn't matter. Inspiration. A rip in the time-space continuum. Ruby and company gave life to the original just so that Larry Paulette could do *this* to it. Human civilization evolved solely for the purpose of recording this fabulous, little-known, badly arranged album track. Yes, our day will come.

If for no other reason (though the amusingly gender-tweaking cover photos provide another), this makes Larry Paulette's album worth seeking out and owning.

▪ TOM PAXTON ▪ "ANITA O.J." ▪

Songwriter:	Tom Paxton
Year of Release:	1978
Original Album:	*Heroes*
Chart Performance:	Not released as a single, and the album didn't chart
Availability:	CD, CS, LP (Vanguard 79411)

You probably recognize the name Tom Paxton even if you don't know much about him. He's a politically oriented folkie from 'way back (gee, aren't most folkies politically oriented from 'way back?) whose songs have been covered by scads of more prominent artists, including Judy Collins, John Denver, the Kingston Trio, and Peter, Paul and Mary. He has many albums to his credit, including *Heroes* from 1978, when folk music was hardly at its peak of popularity. But as that album's "Anita O.J." demonstrates, he was still waxing political.

Gay people of my generation and older certainly don't need to be told to whom "Anita O.J." refers. But for the youngsters among my readers (those of you under the age of, say, 23) I'll reiterate the tale of Anita Bryant, the former beauty-queen-turned-singer-turned-has-been (if indeed you can describe anyone who never really "was" as a "has-been") who made national headlines in the late seventies with her prominent stance against gay rights in Florida, where she was also employed as the commercial spokesperson for the citrus growers. The aftermath: gay rights were overturned in Dade County, gay activists organized a nationwide boycott of Florida orange juice, and Anita became a worldwide symbol of homophobic bigotry cloaked in religious zealotry. We've heard barely a peep from her in more than a decade now. It would be nice to think that she has reversed her opinions about gay people, but I'm not aware of any such divine miracle taking place.

The first verse of Tom Paxton's pun-laden commentary on this affair focuses on Anita's willingness to "squeeze fruits for heavy bread"—a reference to her contract with Florida citrus growers as well as her religious fundraising. Then comes the chorus, a Caribbean-styled reprimand that warns, "You squeeze mine, Anita, I'll squeeze yours." Paxton's puns get even more outrageous as his criticism of Ms. Bryant becomes more direct. While accusing her of hatemongering, he also slyly hints at the possibility of sexual frustration on her part:

> One wonders, dear Anita
> If you'll ever get ahead

If you don't get that one, don't ask me to explain it to you.

Too bad I don't like folk music any more than I do. If there were a lot more stuff like this, it might grow on me.

▪ FREDA PAYNE ▪ "BAND OF GOLD" ▪

Songwriters:	Ronald Dunbar – Edythe Wayne
Year of Release:	1970
Original Album:	*Band of Gold*
Chart Performance:	The single reached #3
Availability:	Original album out of print; available on *Freda Payne's Greatest Hits*, CD, CS, (HDH 3905)

Even at the tender age of fifteen, I figured there was something funny going on in this tragedy of a young bride's humiliation and frustration at being neglected by her husband on her wedding night. The most common explanation I've heard for the groom's refusal to make love to her, going so far as to sequester himself behind locked doors in a separate room, is impotence. Call me cynical, but I've always suspected something else.

Of course, being a fiction, this song needn't have any "explanation." Nothing exists outside the story that we're actually told, and in any case it's not the cause of the female narrator's heartache but the heartache itself that matters here. Nevertheless, gay disco star Sylvester knew exactly what he was doing when, more than a decade later, he took this thing and remade it into one of the finest examples of camp dance music you may ever have the pleasure of hearing. The real twist in all of this is that camp dance music may well have been what Ms. Payne had in mind all along. That is, I can't imagine many people not seeing something funny—and this time I mean humorous—in this record, even in 1970. And that includes the people who made it.

▪ PET SHOP BOYS ▪ "RENT" ▪

Songwriters:	Neil Tennant – Chris Lowe
Year of Release:	1987
Original Album:	*Actually*
Chart Performance:	The single didn't chart, but the album reached #25
Availability:	CD, CS (EMI 46972)

Allow me to say that the British duo known as the Pet Shop Boys makes *the* most thoughtful, lyrically interesting dance music on earth. No exceptions.

According to *The Faber Companion to 20th-Century Popular Music*, the Boys' song "Rent" is regarded by some to be "a reference to homosexual prostitution." It's easy to see why. The narrator's frankly mercenary refrain, "I love you—you pay my rent," could be viewed as the assertion of a heterosexual gigolo. But then you have vocalist Neil Tennant's blasé, languid reading of the lyrics and the campy exaggeration of it all. He's heavily into fine dining and Broadway. And when he proclaims, "I'm your puppet, and I *love* it!"—well, it's just too much.

Besides, in British slang a male homosexual prostitute *is* a "rent boy."

▪ PET SHOP BOYS ▪ "LEFT TO MY OWN DEVICES" ▪

Songwriters:	Neil Tennant – Chris Lowe
Year of Release:	1988
Original Album:	*Introspective*
Chart Performance:	The single reached #84
Availability:	CD, CS (EMI 90868)

I once read some silly reviewer's comment that this song expressed "the desperation of the gay lifestyle," or some such rot, as if there were a single lifestyle that constituted the gay one. For goshsakes, I know a lot of gay people whose own particular styles of living more closely resemble the stereotypically "heterosexual" lifestyle of familial domesticity than those of a lot of non-gay folks I know. And I'm one of the most boring people I know.

That having been said, I'll grant that "Left to My Own Devices" does describe a sort of T.S. Eliot-esque quiet desperation that can readily, though not necessarily, be interpreted as "gay." It's all that business about tea and shopping and staying out late and non-competitiveness as a child. You know the story. And all set to a marvelously brooding dance beat. The Pet Shop Boys are, as I suggested earlier, the thinking person's dance band,

The Pet Shop Boys: (l-r) Chris Lowe and Neil Tennant as they appear in a 1993 video. (Photo: Chris Nash. Courtesy EMI Records.)

producers of synth-pop that stimulates your brain as it shakes your booty. They obviate any guilt that you in your hedonistic pleasure may feel, almost like sacrificial lambs as they assume the collective neuroses of their generation and exorcise them under the strobe lights and glitter balls.

Another case in point—

▪ PET SHOP BOYS ▪ "BEING BORING" ▪

Songwriters:	Neil Tennant – Chris Lowe
Year of Release:	1990
Original Album:	*Behavior*
Chart Performance:	The single didn't chart, but the album reached #45
Availability:	CD, CS (EMI 94310)

When was the last time you heard dance music described as "wistful"? Yet that's precisely the word that summarizes "Being Boring," a track that I'm absolutely sure was inspired by the AIDS crisis. In essence, this song deals with the narrator's reflection upon his life, decades characterized by hope, anticipation, and pleasure among friends. As he says with understated pride, "We were never being boring." But beneath it all is a pervasive sense of melancholy, not because of any failures on his part, but rather because he's unable to share his latter-day success with certain persons who have played important roles in his life.

> *All the people I was kissing—*
> *Some are here and some are missing*
> *In the nineteen-nineties*

One person in particular is the most sorely missed of all, and his absence prevents the narrator from fully enjoying the various triumphs of his life. The sauntering music, far from distracting us from what's going on lyrically, serves to underscore the fundamental ambiguity of life: joy tempered by sorrow, upbeat rhythms peppered with shifting major and minor harmonies.

For those of you relatively unfamiliar with the Pet Shop Boys (whose name, by the way, has nothing to do with unconventional sexuality, as once was rumored; rather, it's a nod to some friends who indeed own a pet shop), I heartily recommend their *Discography* "best of" collection. Along with "Rent," "Left to My Own Devices," and "Being Boring," it offers all their big international hits, such as "West End Girls" and "What Have I Done to Deserve This?" plus a fine selection of other jewels, many of which have pronounced gay overtones. For instance, there's the trenchant, marvelously overblown "It's a Sin" and, most significantly, the defiant "Was It Worth It?" (the answer is a resounding "Yes," adding "I resolve to live my life the way I choose"). It even has the Boys' inexplicable, brilliantly quirky medley of U2's "Where the Streets Have No Name" and Frankie Valli's "Can't Take My Eyes Off You," as ingenious a musical *non sequitur* as ever conceived by the mind of gay man. As audio dance parties go, this is about as intelligent as it gets.

• PET SHOP BOYS •
• "LIBERATION" (AMONG OTHERS) •

Songwriters: Neil Tennant – Chris Lowe
Year of Release: 1993
Original Album: *Very*
Chart Performance: Not released as a single (as of this writing), but the album reached #20
Availability: CD, CS (EMI 89721)

In late 1993 the Pet Shop Boys released *Very*, the finest album of their career thus far. And it also contains their "gayest" music yet.

It's tough focusing on any one song on such a good album, but if I had to choose, it would be "Liberation." In this gentle, beautifully melodic dance song, Neil Tennant adopts the role of an ex-cynic who had thought he was immune to love. But after a long drive home in which his friend had fallen asleep on his shoulder, he drops all of his defenses and revels in his new feelings. Much to his surprise, the personal relationship that he had feared would confine him instead gives him a powerful sense of freedom. "Now, right now," Tennant sings, "your love is liberation." And as he sings the word "liberation," Tennant's voice enters into multi-tracked harmonies, the music swooping upward in a contagious expression of sheer joy.

While this sense of exhilaration can come from love of either the hetero-sexual or homosexual variety, a song about the liberating power of love has special poignance for gay people. The Pet Shop Boys play with this poignancy by punning on the dual nature of the freedom they're celebrat-ing. For "straight" people love can indeed be a liberating experience, but only for gay people is love in and of itself a veritable political statement. Rightly or wrongly, it is in their expressions of love that gay people are dis-tinguished from non-gay people. By falling in love with a person of the same sex, gay men and women become freedom-fighters, whether they intend to or not. For what, after all, is gay liberation but the freedom to love whom we please? Yes, our love *is* liberation.

Very contains a number of other pertinent songs as well. Neil Tennant has stated in interviews that "Can You Forgive Her?" (a Number One dance-club hit) concerns a man who has trouble accepting his gayness and must contend with a girlfriend who's aware of this fact and uses it against him. The dense, haunting "Dreaming of the Queen" employs the figure of Princess Di (punning again, this time with the word "die") in a night-sweat-drenched AIDS nightmare in which "there are no more lovers left alive," the narrator himself having lost his partner to the disease. "To Speak Is a Sin" is a melancholy but tuneful depiction of the bar scene. And in their grand tradition of truly inspired remakes, Tennant and Lowe excavate the Village People's "Go West" to convey the gay California social milieu just before the onset of AIDS. As the Boys do it (with the help of a male chorus), "Go West" becomes an eerily uplifting disco dirge, both happy and sad at the same time. Extraordinary.

Am I overstating my case to say that *Very* is one of the best albums of 1993? Perhaps. But already I can't wait for the *next* Pet Shop Boys CD. These guys just keep getting better.

▪ PIRATES OF THE MISSISSIPPI ▪ "FEED JAKE" ▪

Songwriter:	Danny Bear Mayo
Year of Release:	1990
Original Album:	*Pirates of the Mississippi*
Chart Performance:	The single didn't hit the pop charts, but on the country chart it reached #15
Availability:	CD, CS (Liberty 94389)

Here's an example of that rare species, a country song with the word "gay" (meaning you-know-what) in it. And if that's not enough to surprise you, just wait 'til you hear how it's used.

The Pirates of the Mississippi is a *nouveau*-C&W band that released its eponymous debut album in 1990, in the process earning themselves recognition as the Top New Group by the Academy of Country Music. "Feed Jake," one of the singles from that album, is a slow, somewhat curious number, the chorus of which takes a highly sentimental approach to devotion to one's dog. But the individual verses seem to have little or nothing to do with a canine. For example, the narrator describes the bums, hookers, and winos on city streets and bemoans their fate. Socially conscious country at its best.

It's the third and final verse, however, that most interests us here. Would you have thought that you'd ever hear lyrics like these on a country radio station?

If you get an ear pierced some will call you gay
But if you drive a pickup
They'll say no, you must be straight

At which point the narrator concludes, "What we are and what we ain't,
. . . does it really matter?" It's a first-rate debunking of gay/straight stereotypes, plus a lesson in putting things in their proper perspective. With all
of the problems facing us (such as the urban ills cited in the previous verse),
the stupidity of categorizing and judging people according to earrings and
pickup trucks seems obvious. "Does it really matter?" the narrator asks,
essentially demanding "No" for an answer.

And then there's the dog connection. In the video, the narrator is jour-
neying back to his home town, reminiscing about his lifelong friendship
with another young man. A dog plays a prominent role in these poignant
memories. As it turns out, the narrator is going home to attend the funeral
of his friend, whose old dog Jake is still alive and now needs someone else
to care for him. The narrator will be that someone else.

The mentioning of gayness in the song raises the distinct possibility that
one or more of the characters in the video are meant to be viewed as gay.
While the "gay part" is being sung, the video's protagonist and a handsome young good ol' boy appear to be exchanging long, cruisey looks. And
with the spectre of death hanging over the video, perhaps AIDS has something to do with the overall plot.

All such speculations aside, it's enough for me to know that we've finally come to a point when gayness can be mentioned at all in a country hit.
What's more, it can be mentioned in a fairly positive light. There *is* such
a thing as progress.

▪ POLICE ▪ "ON ANY OTHER DAY" ▪

Songwriter:	Stewart Copeland
Year of Release:	1979
Original Album:	*Reggatta de Blanc*
Chart Performance:	Not released as a single, but the album reached #25
Availability:	CD, CS (A&M 3312)

Let me tell you about a certain computer screen-saving program. One
of the things it does is run allegedly humorous statements across an idle
screen. I once saw this scrolling across a colleague's screen: "You know it's
going to be a bad day when your son says he'd wish Anita Bryant would
mind her own business." Never mind the fact that it's badly outdated. What
matters is that it's a vicious, homophobic insult on two counts. First of all,

it's an example of the majority heterosexist culture's unending war of intellectual terrorism against pro-gay sentiment, falsely implying that anyone who supports gay rights is probably themselves gay, thus actively discouraging pro-gay feelings (or at least their public expression) among heterosexuals. Secondly, even if you assume that "your son" *is* gay, it maintains that that alone makes it "a bad day." Sorry, all you sexually repressed nerds who author such computerized effluvia, but any day in which someone freely affirms his or her gayness or expresses support for gay people in general is a damn *good* day.

Now here's a song that offers the precise musical equivalent of that computer slur. In fact, the Police's "On Any Other Day" may even have served as the computer program's source of inspiration. It's ostensibly about just how awfully bad life can get. As one of many examples, the narrator whines, "My son just said he's gay—it's been a terrible day." Now, maybe the Police intend for us to consider this guy a jerk. But even if that's the case, most listeners probably wouldn't get the message. They'd just chuckle at the plight of such a sad-sack narrator. After all, what a rotten thing it must be to have a faggot son—but funny as long as it's happening to somebody else.

Who needs this kind of shit from a peroxidized trio that spent three-fifths of its career as a group specializing in watered-down quasi-reggae?

Fortunately, lead singer Sting has in recent years come out unabashedly for gay rights. For a far more gratifying image of gay people—or at least of one gay person in particular—I refer you to Sting's solo number "Englishman in New York."

■ ELVIS PRESLEY ■ "JAILHOUSE ROCK" ■

Songwriters: Jerry Leiber – Mike Stoller
Year of Release: 1957
Original Album: *Elvis' Golden Records*
Chart Performance: The single was #1 for seven weeks
Availability: CD, CS, LP (RCA 5196, retitled *Elvis' Golden Records, Vol. 1*)

What?! 1957?! Elvis?!

Well, given the jailhouse setting of this song, what else can you make of lyrics in which one convict says to another, "You're the cutest jailbird I ever did see," and then asks to "do the jailhouse rock" with him? In fact, the whole cell block winds up "dancin' to the jailhouse rock."

Of course, 1957 was a more innocent time. Not many people knew about the original sexual connotations of the word "rock," as in "rock and roll." And few thought about what went on behind prison walls—about the rampant situational homosexuality, commonly of a violent, coercive nature. So "Jailhouse Rock" received plenty of airplay, enough to propel it to #1 and keep it there for nearly two months. Lyrics like these, when they were really listened to at all, could be brushed aside as part of the sheer silliness of rock and roll, that passing teenage fad. I even doubt whether Elvis himself, when he recorded this song, was conscious of the ramifications of what he was singing.

But you can hardly miss it now.

▪ DORY PREVIN ▪ "THE MIDGET'S LAMENT" ▪

Songwriter:	Dory Previn
Year of Release:	1972
Original Album:	*Mary C. Brown and the Hollywood Sign*
Chart Performance:	Not released as a single, and the album didn't chart
Availability:	Out of print (United Artists 5657)

Dory Previn—known for composing music for films and TV shows, for marrying and then splitting with conductor Andre Previn (after he skedaddled with Mia Farrow), and for writing Dionne Warwick's big hit "Theme from *Valley of the Dolls*"—garnered a reputation for herself in the 1970s as a producer of what one critic has called "angry, intimate confessional songs set to a rough folk-rock backup." While "The Midget's Lament" doesn't appear to be confessional or even intimate, it's certainly angry. Previn assumes the voice of a midget—or, in the most reasonable modern politically correct terminology, a "little person." (I refuse to dignify euphemistic nonsense like "height-challenged"—and, as I understand it, so do most of the people meant to be the beneficiaries of such linguistic revisionism.) She caustically describes her lot in life at "knee level," bemoaning the way in which others judge her in terms of her height and nothing else.

A potent indictment of bigotry of every stripe, "The Midget's Lament" notes the difficulties little people must face as they put up with the world's relentless stereotyping of them. The narrator reminds us that midgets are much more than just small, and in the course of her catalog of all the things little people can be in addition to little, she cites gay midgets. She's right: it had never occurred to me. I'm reminded of my youthful amazement—in retrospect, my incredibly *stupid* amazement—upon first discovering that blind people could be gay, too.

This passing reference to gayness is completely overshadowed, however, by the song's bitterly comic, brutally frank final line: "So don't tell me about minorities. . . . I wish to Christ I was black." A shocking reminder of how pervasive and crippling bigotry is in human culture.

▪ DORY PREVIN ▪ "MICHAEL MICHAEL" ▪

Songwriter:	Dory Previn
Year of Release:	1973
Original Album:	*On My Way to Where*
Chart Performance:	Not released as a single, and the album didn't chart
Availability:	Out of print (Mediarts 41)

Now for a bit of anger that hits a little closer to home. You wouldn't know it from what some other gay writers have said about it, but "Michael Michael" is one of the most insidious pieces of music I have ever run across.

"Michael Michael" might be described as fast-paced folk-rock with a harpsichord as lead instrument. (Simon and Garfunkel did a similar sort of thing early in their career with "Leaves That Are Green.") Keep that harpsichord in mind; it's important. You could say the song is light, airy, even frivolous in mood. That too is significant. Previn's lyrical portrait of a gay man named Michael starts off surprisingly for so early as 1973— very butch at a time when most common image of gay people in popular culture was anything but. Michael, it seems, is a virtual "superman":

Muscle-bound and super-tan,
Leather jacket, denim pants

Then Previn states bluntly, "Michael makes it best with men." Remember, this is a good half-decade before the widespread popularization of the ultra-butch "clone look" and its most notorious pop-culture manifestation, the Village People. But being part of the Hollywood crowd, Previn may have been in on the latest trends long before the rest of us. Anyway, lines like these sound wonderful on first hearing: a *positive* image of gay men, set to a springy, happy beat. Hallelujah!

Things are going along so nicely, in fact, that you almost miss the ominous note that begins to creep in. As Previn describes it, every move that Michael makes, every word he speaks, is thoroughly calculated, as though he's always trying to prove something to himself and the world. Well, so what? After all, gay men *do* have something to prove in our heterosexist culture, don't they? Maybe they shouldn't have to, but they do. Unfortunately, Previn's portrayal of Michael becomes increasingly unflattering as the song progresses. For one thing, Michael is a dope-pusher. Admittedly, that didn't quite carry the onus in the early seventies that it does today, but in the larger context of the words that follow, I still don't believe Previn approves. And when she gets to Michael's occasional switch-hitting behavior, her use of a particular verb is telling: "And if he wants to he can con any bird he's turning on." The verb is "con." Michael's a con, at least when it comes to certain aspects of his sexual behavior. Now I *know* Previn disapproves. "So what again?" you may ask. "Why shouldn't she disapprove? Knowingly deceiving women in that way is reprehensible." Yes, I agree. Michael *is* reprehensible.

But not nearly so reprehensible as Previn's final verse, where she conjures up one of the lamest of all homophobic myths: that gay men are drones to their domineering mothers. In Michael's dreams, his mother calls him "Maryjane." Then some heavy-handed musical symbolism: when Previn sings "Maryjane," the music suddenly dips down into previously unheard minor chords. How clever. How profound. Michael answers, "I am coming, mother dear." Oh, please, I just ate.

Now we know what that harpsichord and that light, airy, frivolous mood is all about. For all of his butch exterior and self-conscious attempts at proving himself, poor Michael is Tinkerbell inside. He's a *girlie*—Maryjane, no less. He's fixated on mama. He's a silly joke with a macho façade, as baroque, light, and frivolous as the musical backdrop to his story. As I said, insidious.

I know I shouldn't read such things into songs, but I suspect Previn must've really been burned by someone like Michael. I mean, what else could account for such nastiness? Either that or simply blissful ignorance.

▪ PRINCE ▪ "UPTOWN" ▪

Songwriter:	Prince
Year of Release:	1980
Original Album:	*Dirty Mind*
Chart Performance:	The single didn't hit the pop chart, but it reached #6 on the "Black Singles" chart; the album reached #45 pop
Availability:	CD, CS (Warner Brothers 3478)

The first time Prince dealt with homosexuality in his music, it was in the form of "Bambi," a heavy-metal funk-punk grind from his second, self-titled album that lyrically attempts to seduce a lesbian Lolita. "It's better with men," he assures her (though he doesn't say how he knows *that* for a fact). Interestingly, the song doesn't leave us with the impression that he succeeds in his efforts to get this young woman in bed.

The following year Prince released his revolutionary, amazingly lascivious album *Dirty Mind*. One of its tracks, "Uptown," starts off with Prince walking down the street, perhaps near Lake and Hennepin, the well-known Uptown of his native Minneapolis. He's minding his own business when he's suddenly confronted by a young woman who asks, "Are you gay?" To which he replies, "No, are you?"

This is probably Prince's way of addressing the frequent rumors about his sexual orientation that were widely circulating early in his career. These rumors were perhaps understandable given his penchant at the time for brandishing more mascara than any male African-American performer since Little Richard, not to mention his fondness for wearing little more than black bikini briefs on stage. It was also around this time, if you recall, that he was booed off the stage as opening act for the Rolling Stones, with some members of the audience shouting "Faggot!" at him.

One of the things I like best about "Uptown" is that, when Prince denies being gay, he does so without the slightest hint of anger or indignation. His response isn't self-righteous or defensive; it's matter-of-fact and inoffensively humorous. And then he goes on to extol the virtues of "Uptown," his utopian vision of a place where social and sexual freedom is the norm, where "we don't let society tell us how we're supposed to be."

Amen to that.

▪ PRINCE ▪ "WHEN YOU WERE MINE" ▪

Songwriter:	Prince
Year of Release:	1980
Original Album:	*Dirty Mind*
Chart Performance:	Not released as a single (except as the flip side to "Controversy"), but the album reached #45
Availability:	CD, CS (Warner Brothers 3478)

It should've been a hit, but it wasn't. Proclaimed by one critic to be among the most perfect pop songs ever recorded, "When You Were Mine" may not be as immediately stunning as Prince's later "When Doves Cry" (one of the four or five most radically innovative Number One songs in rock history), but it nonetheless demonstrates the Purple One's mastery of deceptively simple but unforgettable melodic structures. But it's not because of the melody that I'm writing about it.

In lyrics addressed to an ex-lover, the bit about how the narrator "used to let you wear all of my clothes" seems only mildly interesting—unless you start considering whether Prince's falsetto "oh girl" ejaculations here are less literal than camp. But the subsequent line about "when he was there sleeping in between the two of us" is inescapably bisexual, not to mention scandalously titillating. It's mild by comparison, however, on an album that features songs blatantly celebrating oral sex and incest. Still, "When You Were Mine" (which probably missed being titled "When U Were Mine" by only a year or two) has managed to retain its kinky edge in remakes by both Mitch Ryder and Cyndi Lauper, such being the inherent quality of a *ménage à trois*. But nobody does it better than Prince.

▪ PRINCE ▪ "CONTROVERSY" ▪

Songwriter:	Prince
Year of Release:	1981
Original Album:	*Controversy*
Chart Performance:	The single reached #70
Availability:	CD, CS (Warner Brothers 3601)

Shortly before he achieved superstardom, His Royal Badness once again addressed rumors and speculations about his sexual orientation. He expresses wonderment and confusion at the public's curiosity about his personal traits and habits, and, in so doing, cites some of the key questions being asked about him: "Am I black or white? Am I straight or gay?"

Of course, these questions are purely rhetorical. Prince has no intention of answering them. They were largely moot points when he recorded this song, anyway. Prince was already a critic's darling by this time and had acquired a fairly large following, but he wasn't yet the household name and face that would captivate the whole world of popular culture just three years later with the huge success of *Purple Rain*. In short, not many people really cared, and even reciting the Lord's Prayer to a thudding synthbass disco beat couldn't generate the commercial sparks that Prince was so transparently seeking when he publicly resorted to asking such questions of himself. Sometimes there's a fine line between exploiting oneself and exploiting others.

▪ PRINCE AND THE NEW POWER GENERATION ▪
▪ "DIAMONDS AND PEARLS" ▪

Songwriters:	Prince and the New Power Generation
Year of Release:	1991
Original Album:	*Diamonds and Pearls*
Chart Performance:	The single reached #3
Availability:	CD, CS (Paisley Park 25379)

A bisexual tease if there ever was one, primarily because of the first two lines in the chorus:

> *If I gave u diamonds and pearls*
> *Would u be a happy boy or a girl?*

The Material Bi, perhaps? I've heard suggestions that this question is totally nonsexual in nature, maybe even caringly addressed to a theoretical child, but what do children care about gemstones? Are jewels liable to make kids happy?

I do, however, have some trouble with that video. Like most by Prince, it's so obsessively heterosexual that the bi-tease seems gratuitous and out of place. In fact, the male-male-female bisexual element of the lyric is all but lost under a relentless heterosexual veneer—which may of course be precisely what Prince wants so as not to offend homophobic segments of his audience. But then why fool around with the "boy or a girl" business in the first place? Mere titillation? Controversy for the sake of publicity? Confusion?

Actually, the heterosexuality of the video isn't totally relentless. The bi-tease is there, all right. It's just that it's quasi-lesbian in nature. The gorgeous women who serve as the objects of Prince's video desires also seem somewhat desirous of each other, lightly nuzzling and fondling each other as they stare provocatively at the camera. Prince has used this device before—in his "1999" video, in which two female backup singer-musicians pull the same stunt while sharing a keyboard. While this kind of behavior isn't exactly commonplace in music videos, it's hardly unique to Prince. Take, for example, the original, uncensored version of Duran Duran's "Girls on Film" video, with its obsessive bitch-goddess imagery, complete with beautiful pseudo-dykes.

Isn't it interesting that you never see two men cuddling like this in music videos?—not even in those by openly gay or bisexual artists. Maybe such videos are made, but they're never shown, at least not on MTV or VH-1. What it all boils down to is a sexist double-standard that permits the exploitation of alleged "lesbianism" for the purpose of exciting the collective libido of the rock video audience, presumably composed mostly of young heterosexual males.

And they have the nerve to call *us* sick.

I couldn't possibly leave the subject of Prince without addressing one other aspect of his remarkable career. Always one to toy around with gender ambiguity, Prince took his longstanding androgyny thing to new, onomastic heights in June 1993. No longer content to construct sexual guessing games with his lyrics and personal appearance, he announced that from thenceforth his name would cease being "Prince" and would instead consist of the unpronounceable, unalphabetizable symbol that had already served as the title of his fourteenth album. This symbol, reproduced above, a stylized blending of the traditional signs for female and male, has widely been interpreted as signifying androgyny and/or bisexuality, though some people stick their heads in the psychosexual sand and refer to it as the "Love Symbol."

Some may view this change in handle as a bold statement—or, alternatively, as a brazen eccentricity—but, personally, I suspect that it's akin to his declaration a few weeks earlier that he would stop recording new "routine" material, issuing older but previously unreleased music or "special projects" in its place. That is, it strongly suggests a major change of direction in his already phenomenal career. The former Prince's new nomenclature may be unpronounceable, but it has all the hallmarks of a major pronouncement: that we should continue to expect the unexpected, perhaps even things more unexpected than before, from an artist whose restless creativity and playfulness has continually kept music critics and the public in general guessing as to what he would do next.

▪ PUBLIC ENEMY ▪
▪ "MEET THE G THAT KILLED ME" ▪

Songwriters:	Keith Shocklee – Eric Sadler – Carlton Ridenhour
Year of Release:	1990
Original Album:	*Fear of a Black Planet*
Chart Performance:	Not released as a single, but the album reached #10
Availability:	CD, CS (Def Jam 45413)

The most critically acclaimed, artistically innovative, and overtly political of rap acts, Public Enemy has unfortunately been unable to transcend the homophobia that mars so much rap music and, to be sure, rock music in general. Consider "Meet the G That Killed Me"—a stark, cautionary tale that condemns an irresponsible character who has promiscuous unsafe sex and shares needles. That's cool. But right off the bat we're told that "man to man . . . the parts don't fit." Not only uncool, but not even terribly original. When asked about this in an interview, Public Enemy leader Chuck D (Carlton Ridenhour) commented, "Love between men shouldn't involve sex." Easy for him to say; I assume he's heterosexual.

Incidentally, "G" doesn't stand for "gay." "G" is apparently hip-hop lingo for a "homeboy"—a reliable friend. Only in this case he doesn't seem so reliable.

It's too easy to parody the album title and wonder whether Public Enemy has any fear of a *gay* planet. That's a stupid notion, isn't it? (Besides, somebody else has already done it.) Still, stupidity hasn't stopped people from saying things like, "But what if everyone were gay? Where would we all be then?" When faced with such deep questions, simply point out that good heterosexual sex is too much fun to be given up wholesale, and no "straight" person is going to "convert" from innate heterosexuality. On the other hand, you could gasp, "Well, I don't know about *you*, but *I'd* be down at the bar seducing that *divine* ex-football coach of mine!" And then scamper off to saner pastures.

▪ PUBLIC ENEMY ▪
▪ "A LETTER TO THE NEW YORK *POST*" ▪

Songwriters:	William Drayton – Gary G-Wiz – Stuart Robertz
Year of Release:	1991
Original Album:	*Apocalypse 91 . . . The Enemy Strikes Back*
Chart Performance:	Not released as a single, but the album reached #4
Availability:	CD, CS, LP (Def Jam 47374)

Public Enemy has built much of its reputation on controversy. Witness the ruckus over their video for "By the Time I Get to Arizona," a revenge fantasy in which an African-American paramilitary unit assassinates a gaggle of white politicians whose chief offense is opposition to a holiday honoring the outspokenly non-violent Dr. Martin Luther King, Jr. His widow, Coretta Scott King, called the video "misguided." I should say. Then again, I can think of lots of other videos that I find more offensive, such as that nadir of sleazy female objectification, Robert Palmer's "Addicted to Love." That, however, is another story.

Getting back to the matter at hand, a bit of controversy has also been stirred up by "A Letter to the New York *Post*," with lyrics by Public Enemy's resident court jester, the clock-wielding Flavor Flav (William Drayton). Flav suggests that we follow the example of one of his apparent heroes, James Cagney, who allegedly "beat up on a guy when he found he was a fagney."

"Fagney"?

When questioned by *Musician* magazine about this cachet of bigotry, Chuck D said that we "shouldn't take it that seriously" because Flavor Flav "just found something that rhymes."

OK, I'll buy that. I used to coin mean-spirited rhymes like that, too— back in junior high. Then I grew up.

▪ QUEEN ▪ "KILLER QUEEN" ▪

Songwriter:	Freddie Mercury
Year of Release:	1974
Original Album:	*Sheer Heart Attack*
Chart Performance:	The single reached #12
Availability:	CD, CS (Hollywood 61036)

One had every reason to expect great things from a band called Queen. In its early years, lead singer Freddie Mercury (who died of AIDS-related pneumonia in November 1991) out-glittered the best of them during the heyday of glam rock, with makeup, mascara, sequins, and skin-tight body suits that left little to the imagination. In interviews he would drop more "darlings" than a Gabor sister. He strutted and posed on the stage, one moment martial, the next mincing. It was incredibly queer and incredibly calculated as well. But as glitter became passé in the late seventies, Mercury embraced the butch drag that gay men had themselves embraced only slightly earlier. He wore jeans or leather pants, T-shirts, tanktops, or no shirt at all, his extremely hairy chest sometimes clothed only with a chain. He cut his hair short and grew a thick moustache. Do you think he was trying to tell us something?

"Killer Queen" was the group's first American hit (they'd had previous hits in their native Britain) back in the glitter rock days. Mercury sang the lyrics in his feyest voice, clueing those "in the know," as it were, to the true subject matter—although it's terribly difficult to decipher words like these without them written down in front of you. Take the chorus, which opens with the line, "She's a killer queen," and then elaborates the point with such ammunition-metaphor puns as "gunpowder gelatine" and "guaranteed to blow your mind." If you can hack your way through the explosive imagery and the traditional, closet-born inverted pronouns, there's plenty of eyebrow-raising material, such as in the second verse: "She spoke just like a baroness," which is of interest "if you're that way inclined." Her "perfume came naturally from Paris"—after which the campy, overly har-

Queen during their early glitter-rock days of 1974: (l-r) Roger Taylor, Brian May, Freddie Mercury (1946–1991), John Deacon. (Photo: Mick Rock.)

monized background vocals respond, "Naturally." And in case anyone still hadn't figured it out, following the final repetition of the chorus, Mercury sighs, "What a drag!"

Which all boils down to the fact that, unless you count the Kinks' slightly ambiguous "Lola," "Killer Queen" is the only panegyric to a drag queen to make it into the Top Twenty.

▪ QUEEN ▪ "BOHEMIAN RHAPSODY" ▪

Songwriter:	Freddie Mercury
Year of Release:	1975
Original Album:	*A Night at the Opera*
Chart Performance:	The single reached #9 the first time around in 1975, but upon its re-release in 1992 (spurred by the double-barrel impetus of its appearance in the movie *Wayne's World* and Freddie Mercury's death) it went all the way up to #2
Availability:	CD, CS (Hollywood 61065)

This two-time, record-breaking international hit is actually not so much a coherent song as a jumble of pretentious but often amusing lowbrow pseudo-operatic bosh. It wouldn't even be worth writing about in the context of this book if it weren't recorded by Queen.

"Bohemian Rhapsody" seems to be the story of "just a poor boy" who is, by his own admission, "easy come easy go" and whose motto is "Any way the wind blows, doesn't really matter to me." When sung by Freddie Mercury, lines like that are loaded. Besides, our hero has a confession to make to his "Mama" about how he's just committed a murder, sung to a very pretty little melody:

> Put a gun against his head
> Pulled my trigger, now he's dead

Not *the* trigger, mind you, but "*my* trigger," playing off the phallic metaphor of the gun and adding a clear male-male sexual component to the alleged killing. You have to expect these kinds of things from a band called Queen.

Just in case you suspect I'm reading too much into these lines, consider the full implications of the title. With its central European reference point, "Bohemian" certainly plays into the grand operatic pretense. But it also calls to mind the sort of brazenly unconventional, "artistic" lifestyle that the word is more commonly associated with today. And we know what *that* can mean, don't we?

After a second verse employing the same pretty melody, things rapidly

181

deteriorate into a mishmash of multi-tracked Scaramouches, Fandangos, Galileos, Figaros, Bismillahs, Beelzebubs, and Mama-mias. Near the conclusion there's a nifty hard rock passage of defiance, but overall you just have to take it for the blatant nonsense that it is. Smile at the vast silliness of it all, which probably is exactly what Queen wanted you to do in the first place.

▪ QUEEN ▪
▪ "DEATH ON TWO LEGS (DEDICATED TO . . .)" ▪

Songwriter:	Freddie Mercury
Year of Release:	1975
Original Album:	*A Night at the Opera*
Chart Performance:	Not released as a single, but the album reached #4
Availability:	CD, CS (Hollywood 61065)

This is just about the most blistering, scathing collection of bitchy accusations and insults ever committed to vinyl, boasting such lines as "You suck my blood like a leech" and "Screw my brain till it hurts"—words that certainly carry sexual connotations. And the lyrics make absolutely clear that the miserable soul to whom Freddie Mercury (or his persona) is addressing this vitriol is a male. The song continues to describe his antagonist as a "dog," a "sleaze," a "sewer rat," and the "death on two legs" of the title. Such touching sentiments, such lovely imagery. There's more acid here than in a lemon plantation.

Do you get the feeling Freddie was angry at someone when he wrote this? And wouldn't you just *love* to know the name discreetly omitted from the dedication? Probably no one we've ever heard of. Besides, unknowns can sue for libel as easily as the famous—perhaps more easily.

Of course, tirades like this don't do much for one's image in the eyes of the general public. Then again, Queen always did seem to consider bad P.R. to be good P.R., if you know what I mean. If they didn't, they would never have done such things as sponsor a nude female bicycle race to promote their *Jazz* album. Nor would they have recorded songs like this.

Songwriter:	Freddie Mercury
Year of Release:	1977
Original Album:	*News of the World*
Chart Performance:	The single reached #4
Availability:	CD, CS (Hollywood 61037)

In their religio-fanatical diatribe against rock music, *Why Knock Rock?* Dan Peters and Steve Peters write that one of Queen's biggest hits, "We Are the Champions," is "the widely-accepted anthem of gay liberation." Gosh, that's news to me. Have *you* accepted it as an anthem of gay liberation? Do you know anybody who *has?* And all this time I could've sworn it was just an egomaniacal rant by a self-important rock band. Shows how much I know.

By the way, who would've thought that a song based on the melody (and sentiment) of the familiar, near-universal childhood "na-na-na-na-na" taunt—

—could be such a big hit? Could the use of this melody be Queen's tip-off that "We Are the Champions" is all a joke? That really wouldn't be surprising considering that nearly everything these guys recorded is at root a joke, anyway. The most serious thing they ever did was their truly profound collaboration with David Bowie, "Under Pressure," a masterful single best known today for providing the riff upon which Vanilla Ice's repulsive vanilla rap "Ice Ice Baby" was structured. And "Under Pressure" probably derived its seriousness from Bowie himself. For here's one of the essential differences between Queen and Bowie: Queen is joking even when they're serious (as when they conclude their hard-rock hymn "One Vision" with the deflating exclamation "Fried chicken!"), whereas Bowie is dead serious even when he's joking (listen to "Fame" or "Golden Years" in the dark sometime and just *tell* me that it doesn't give you the creeps). Could that be the difference between low camp and high camp?

I digress. I guess you could say that if the members of Queen were the champions of anything, it was tongue-in-cheek rock, as "We Are the Champions" aptly demonstrates. And we mustn't forget the album track that segues directly into it: "We Will Rock You." No, these aren't gay liberation anthems. Throngs of beer-guzzling sports fans don't mimic gay liberation anthems in arena stands before the big event. On the contrary, as rock critic Paul Williams has succinctly stated, these songs are both "'fuck you!' anthems."

But I don't suppose the Peters brothers would appreciate that.

▪ QUEEN ▪ "I WANT TO BREAK FREE" ▪

Songwriter:	John Deacon
Year of Release:	1984
Original Album:	*The Works*
Chart Performance:	The single reached #45
Availability:	CD, CS (Hollywood 61233)

There's nothing in the lyrics of this song, written by Queen's bassist, John Deacon, to suggest that it has anything to do with gay-related subject matter. Lyrically, it simply concerns the narrator's desire to break away from a relationship with someone whom he describes as a self-satisfied liar. Nothing uniquely gay about that.

But, as I've said before, you ought to see the video.

The first minute or so features all of the members of Queen gotten up in dowdy, housewifely drag. Freddie Mercury is especially outrageous, vacuuming a carpet while dressed in a poofy wig, a too-tight black leather miniskirt, and an even tighter top with huge false breasts underneath—while sporting his heavy, dark moustache along with his makeup. After that, the video switches to Mercury romping around in masculine gear again—short hair, tight pants, no shirt, remarkably hairy chest—but it hardly mattered anymore. As the group's guitarist, Brian May, suggested while hosting a retrospective of Queen videos on VH-1, that sequence probably did more than anything else to all but demolish Queen's career in the United States in the mid-eighties.

With this video, "I Want to Break Free" comes across as one big double-entendre: a surface plea to end an unhealthy relationship and a more generalized underlying wish to put an end to the lies and self-satisfaction that underlie sexual stereotypes. I'm not sure whether the members of Queen would have put it in quite those terms. But whether they intended it or not, it's there. Take one gander at that video, baby, and you *know* it's there.

■ RAMONES ■ "53RD & 3RD" ■

Songwriters:	Joey Ramone (Jeffrey Hyman) – Johnny Ramone (John Cummings) – Dee Dee Ramone (Douglas Colvin) – Tommy Ramone (Tom Erdelyi)
Year of Release:	1976
Original Album:	*The Ramones*
Chart Performance:	Not released as a single, but the album reached #111
Availability:	CS, LP (Sire 6020)

The Ramones may not have invented punk rock, but they were its earliest and most important evangelists to the world outside New York City. When my friends and I first heard their debut album during my senior year in college, we—deeply immersed in the grandiose virtuoso epics of Yes and Emerson, Lake and Palmer—were amazed at how primitive they sounded. Positively neanderthal. But we immediately grasped and appreciated the humor of the concept: four unkempt, leather-clad guys posing as brothers, playing loud, fast, repetitive, unbelievably amateurish, two-, three-, and (at its most ambitious) four-chord rock, nearly devoid of melody, sing-shouting some of the stupidest, most juvenile-delinquent-oriented lyrics ever committed to vinyl. The songs had titles like "Blitzkrieg Bop," "Today Your Love, Tomorrow the World," "Now I Wanna Sniff Some Glue," and (best of all, despite its violent ramifications) "Beat on the Brat." It couldn't be for real—*could it?* We quickly decided that *The Ramones* was one of the most shrewdly original comedy albums of all time, and it became a cult favorite.

Little did we know. The Ramones would prove a major influence on the growing punk rock scene, not only in New York and elsewhere in the United States but also in Britain. What we were hearing in our senior-year dorms wasn't a comedy album. Or at least it wasn't *just* a comedy album. It was a statement. A crude, inarticulate, loutish statement, to be sure, but a statement nonetheless. Or, to be more precise, the crudeness, inarticulateness, and loutishness of it was the statement itself, a wholly unexpected rock music manifestation of the Marshall McLuhan credo, "The medium is the message." Punk rock was, among other things, an open rebellion against the overblown pretensions of seventies-style art rock, a desperate movement to reclaim rock and roll for the young and unsophisticated. And for all intents and purposes, the Ramones had sounded the opening volley.

All of this brings us to "53rd & 3rd," one of the cuts on the Ramones' first album. The scene is New York City (of course), at a street corner inhabited by our narrator, a hustler looking to get picked up. But he's not gay, mind you. He doesn't want any "more of your fairy stories." He's just doing this to earn a living in the big, mean city. He claims to be a former

Green Beret in Vietnam. In other words, he's a *real* man. Nevertheless, the chorus spells it out with brutal clarity: "I'm trying to turn a trick."

Then comes the *pièce de resistance*, a second verse that's a marvel of ambiguity—hilarious, unconscionable, or both—about using a razor blade to do "what God forbade." As the narrator puts it with a sense of perverse satisfaction:

> Now the cops are after me
> But I proved that I'm no sissy

Pick your interpretation:

Interpretation #1

This punk has just killed someone, probably one of his queer tricks, just to prove to himself that he's not queer, too.

Interpretation #2

The narrator, a bundle of sexual psychoses, has just castrated himself and now takes warped pride in how tough he was to endure such a thing.

I'll grant that the first interpretation is by far the more likely. As such, it's vile. But some friends of mine have interpreted it the second way and, in so doing, consider it terribly amusing—a supreme example of punk camp, if you will. And, I must admit, the ambiguity leads me to think that such confusion may well have been part of the plan. It's not all that far-fetched when you recall that some of the more nihilistic segments of the punk community were heavily into self-defacement, ranging from safety pins through the ears, nostrils, and lips to razor slashes on the arms and—elsewhere.

There's even one other possibility: that "53rd & 3rd" is in fact hateful, homophobic crap, but created with satirical intent as an implicit criticism of homophobia. When the Ramones sang elsewhere, "Now I wanna sniff some glue," did they really mean it? When they sang about beating up a brat with a baseball bat, were they truly advocating such behavior? Maybe they were. I don't know. But the Ramones' music and lyrics were so crude, so primitive that they must have gone to great pains to sound that way. Was it all a joke? Were they making fun of the attitudes they espoused? I mean, we *did* laugh whenever we listened to it.

Then again, these *are* sick jokes. Some jokes are very funny, despite the fact that we immediately reprimand ourselves for laughing at them. Is *that* what's going on here?

To this day, nearly two decades later, I'm still not sure what to make of the Ramones. Or of "53rd & 3rd." I only hope that I'm not rationalizing hatefulness, refusing to see it for what it truly is only because the truth would be so painful. When I laugh, I hope I'm not laughing along with people who'd like to kill me because I'm gay.

▪ LOU REED ▪ "WALK ON THE WILD SIDE" ▪

Songwriter:	Lou Reed
Year of Release:	1972
Original Album:	*Transformer*
Chart Performance:	The single reached #16
Availability:	CD, CS, LP (RCA 4807)

I don't know where to begin.

Lou Reed, former lead singer and chief songwriter for the notorious Velvet Underground, hooked up with the even more notorious David Bowie to create this dark beauty, which has been described as "an ode to the denizens of Andy Warhol's Sixties films." (Some of the characters in the song can even be identified via their first names with such Warhol satellites as Joe Dallesandro, Holly Woodlawn, and Jackie Curtis—the latter two transvestites.) It has also been derided as *the* classic example of "bisexual chic" and cynical commercial exploitation of gayness in rock.

Guided by Bowie, who was at the vanguard of the burgeoning glitter movement of the early seventies, Reed "transformed" himself—putting on lipstick, painting his fingernails black, smearing on the mascara. Then, with Bowie and his guitarist cohort Mick Ronson serving as co-producers, Reed released this, his one and only Top Forty hit to date, to an unsuspecting public. With every refrain he cajoles his listeners, urging them to join him: "Take a walk on the wild side."

As he sings-recites-intones the lyrics over the song's unforgettable sliding bass guitar motif, Reed's deep, dark voice fairly drips with depravity. His inflections waver between those of a bitchy drag queen and a disinterested pimp. But he's ever the seducer, dangling forbidden fruit before our eyes. Each stanza deals with a different character, describing his or her (and sometimes it's not at all clear which pronoun is most fitting) activities "on the wild side." The first verse focuses on "Holly," who, while hitchhiking across the country,

> *Plucked her eyebrows on the way*
> *Shaved her legs and then he was a she*

Another character, "Little Joe," is a hustler. "Sugarplum Fairy" wowed 'em at the Apollo. And don't forget Jackie, a speed-junkie who "thought she was James Dean for a day." Reed goes so far as to prescribe Valium.

If all this weren't enough, he even includes a crude passing reference to oral sex. You see, "Candy" was extremely popular in the back room:

> *But she never lost her head*
> *Even when she was giving head*

Don't you hate it when songwriters can't think of any better rhyme than the same word over again? But that's beside the point. The truly amazing thing is that *those lines didn't even get censored out when the song was*

Lou Reed in 1972, at the height of his "glam" look. (Photo: Mick Rock. Michael Ochs Archives.)

played on the radio in the early seventies, presumably because most radio programmers, deejays, and listeners back then didn't know what "giving head" meant! In fact, when the song was censored at all, what got cut were Reed's repeated references to the "colored girls" who sing backup—which, because of the decadent persona Reed had adopted, comes across not so much as racist as campy-bitchy, like a casual remark tossed off in a comfortably integrated drag bar. But times have changed. Nowadays, when the song is played on the radio, the entire "giving head" stanza is almost invariably deleted but the "colored girls" lines are usually restored.

If it weren't for the fact that it's a *bona fide* "oldie"—and a pretty popular one at that—I doubt that it would be played at all today. A new song of this type wouldn't likely get Top Forty airplay, that's for sure. And as for Reed himself, he's long forsaken the eerie look of *Transformer* (which, to be honest, more closely resembled the living dead from a Grade B movie than any gay people I know), staunchly asserted his heterosexuality both in songs and interviews, and went on record saying that he was finished with the faggot scene. I suppose decadence can only go so far commercially. I mean, once you've exploited the freaky image and it's grown passé, it's time to move on to something else to sell records, right? The irony is that "Walk on the Wild Side" is the most successful thing Reed has ever done in terms of both profit and pop art. *It's brilliant. Period.*

And while we're on the subject, does anybody know for sure whether, as I suspect, the use of "wild side" to describe the "gay life" is somehow linked to Oscar Wilde? Considering that at one time Oscar Wilde was probably the best-known homosexual person—that is, the person best-known to be homosexual—in the whole world, was "wild" ever used as a "code word" of sorts to refer to homosexuality? I've been trying to find out for sure, but so far without luck. Any evidence brought to my attention would be greatly appreciated. For history's sake, you know.

▪ LOU REED ▪
▪ "MAKE UP" AND "GOODNIGHT LADIES" ▪

Songwriter:	Lou Reed
Year of Release:	1972
Original Album:	*Transformer*
Chart Performance:	Neither was released as a single, but the album reached #29
Availability:	CD, CS, LP (RCA 4807)

"Walk on the Wild Side" certainly isn't the only song on *Transformer* that deals with gay people in one way or another. The superb rocker "Vicious," the deservedly obscure "Andy's Chest," and the terribly morose "Goodnight Ladies" all have their, shall we say, queer implications. But none can match "Make Up," a strange cross between a bad joke and a gay liberation anthem.

The song has extremely simple instrumentation: just guitar, bass, drums, and an oom-pah tuba. That oom-pah tuba is the key, I believe, but as for what it unlocks, I'll hold off on that for a bit. Lyrically, at least half of the song is devoted to a detailed description of various types of makeup—pancake powder, rouge, mascara, lipstick, the works—and the process of applying it. "You're a slick little girl," Reed repeatedly assures the person who's putting on the makeup, using that knowing voice of his. And what is this slick little girl getting all made up for? The chorus fills us in:

> *Now we're comin' out*
> *Out of the closets, out on the streets*

Half of me wants to cheer for the transvestites; the other half wants to cry, "No, no, no! Not all gay people wear makeup!" I know that I'm struggling with my own internalized homophobia when I do that, and I know perfectly well which half is politically correct. I'm just not at all sure which half is right and/or wise.

While "Make Up" certainly ranks among my least favorite songs in the "gay corpus," so to speak, one line annoys me in particular: "It'd be so nice to fall in love." Reed seems to think gayness is all about "dressing up" and, if you're lucky, having sex, with love only an impossible dream. In other words, he believes the lies that heterosexist society tells itself—and gay people—about gay people. Homosexuals lead miserable, one-dimensional lives. If you doubt it, I refer you once again to the album closer, "Goodnight Ladies." What with its barroom drinking, TV dinners, going to bed with the 11 p.m. news, and all-encompassing, knock-you-over-the-head loneliness, it's an absolutely wretched depiction of the stereotypical "gay lifestyle," pathetic even by the relatively backward standards of 1972.

And now for the clincher: that fucking oom-pah tuba. What's it doing there in "Make Up"? It sounds comic, like this is slapstick or something.

And that's exactly how it's supposed to sound. This is something the audience is supposed to laugh at! In fact, when Reed describes in loving detail the process of putting on makeup, maybe he's not really talking about a drag queen at all. Perhaps it's a *clown*. After all, clowns wear makeup, too, and they belong in the circus, where you're also liable to hear an oom-pah tuba playing. Maybe "Make Up" is about a bunch of clowns "comin' out on the streets!" Or, more to the point, maybe drag queens, and gay people in general, *are* clowns. Is that what this song is saying?

One more time I suggest comparing "Make Up" to "Goodnight Ladies." The latter song also has a tuba, for cryin' out loud, only this time it's soon joined by a whole Dixieland ensemble playing a background track befitting an old-time New Orleans jazz funeral. Gay life as tragedy *qua* travesty. How liberating.

No thanks. I, for one, am glad that Lou Reed transformed himself right back into a professed heterosexual not long after he recorded these songs. Judging by their content, his life as temporary queer must have been dreadful.

But that, thankfully, isn't the end of Lou Reed's "gay music" saga.

▪ LOU REED ▪
▪ "THE HALLOWEEN PARADE (AIDS)" ▪

Songwriter:	Lou Reed
Year of Release:	1988
Original Album:	*New York*
Chart Performance:	Not released as a single, but the album reached #40
Availability:	CD, CS (Sire 25829)

After queening it up during his *Transformer* phase of the early seventies and then loudly proclaiming his heterosexuality during the late seventies and early eighties, Lou Reed finally came full circle. On *New York*, something of a concept album focusing on his love-hate relationship with his favorite city, Reed includes a vaguely comic yet deeply touching account of a scene he has witnessed: a Halloween drag parade on Christopher Street. Reed's awareness of the AIDS epidemic—how it has decimated the New York community in which he thrived nearly two decades before—darkly colors his perception of the superficially carefree procession. He tells about seeing a "downtown fairy," a brash "Southern Queen," a "Greta Garbo," "five Cinderellas," "some leather drags," "a Crawford, Davis, and a tacky Cary Grant," among others. It's the people he *doesn't* see, however, that make the biggest impression on him. He lists several people who aren't on parade, including "Hairy," "Virgin Mary," "Johnny Rio," and "Rotten Rita."

> *You'll never see those faces again*
> *This Halloween is something to be sure*
> *Especially to be here without you*

Although his coolly detached vocal style may rob these lines of some of their potential power, it's still obvious that Reed (or his persona) painfully misses someone in particular, turning "The Halloween Parade" into a song mourning the loss of a loved one. But in a much wider sense, it mourns the loss of *all* the loved ones, all the precious lives lost to AIDS.

The song continues with its odd, almost countrified arrangement and alternating lines about who is and who isn't in the parade. It's terribly depressing, but depressing in a cathartic way. When Reed sings about not wanting to hear the past as it keeps "knocking on my door," he's expressing emotions felt by millions of people across the country and around the world, gay men in particular—the virtually impotent anger and frustration in the face of a crisis that has no end in sight, the personal losses compounded by the greater communal loss. As he goes on to say, he's overwhelmed with anger and sadness, nearly paralyzed with anguish over AIDS.

And then, out of the depths of fear and despair, a final moment of optimism, half social cement, half prayer: "See you next year—at the Halloween parade." It's almost enough, Lou, to make me sorry I said all of those nasty things about you earlier. But those criticisms were for the jerk you were back then. As for the more sober, more compassionate person you seem to be now, I hope to see you next year, too.

■ R.E.M. ■ "PRETTY PERSUASION" ■

Songwriters:	Bill Berry – Peter Buck – Mike Mills – Michael Stipe
Year of Release:	1984
Original Album:	*Reckoning*
Chart Performance:	Not released as a single, but the album reached #27
Availability:	CD, CS (I.R.S. 44797–0044)

I have a theory about why R.E.M. became the darlings of mid-eighties college radio. Sure, they were correct in their politics, but more importantly they perfectly paralleled the stubborn, not unintelligent inarticulateness of the generation that embraced them. On their first several albums, you have to listen very hard to make any sense out of Michael Stipe's alternately muttered and howled vocals (their first album was appropriately titled *Murmur*), and even then you're lucky if you can glean much more than the chorus. On later LPs, by which time R.E.M. had worked their way up to recording such magnificent tracks as "Fall on Me" and "The One I Love," Stipe had learned to respect his audience enough to sing for them as much as for himself and his bandmates. But until then, they reminded me of some of my former freshman comp students: "What d'ya mean my writing's not clear? *I* can understand it!"

By now my younger readers are surely convinced that I'm a hopeless old fart. No matter. I include "Pretty Persuasion" here because I've seen it cited as an example of unabashed bisexuality in modern rock music. I can see where the chorus,

> *He's got pretty persuasion*
> *She's got pretty persuasion*
> *God damn your confusion*

can lend itself to such an interpretation. But even if this *is* a way cool piece of guitar rock, I prefer a little more meat to my alleged references to bisexuality, thank you. Maybe if I could only figure out the rest of the lyrics.

▪ TOM ROBINSON BAND ▪ "GLAD TO BE GAY" ▪

Songwriter:	Tom Robinson
Year of Release:	1977
Original Album:	*Power in the Darkness*
Chart Performance:	Not released as a single, but the album reached #144
Availability:	CD (Razor & Tie RE 2018)

Whenever anyone has written about British activist-musician Tom Robinson's "Glad to Be Gay," the word "bitter" has been all but unavoidable. It is indeed one of the most caustic songs ever written. It's also perhaps the most outspokenly political gay-related song ever to transcend the "gay and lesbian market" and find a fairly wide audience of non-gay listeners, primarily via college radio stations. Robinson's politics on a variety of issues (including his involvement in Rock Against Racism) endeared him to many critics and college deejays who might otherwise have ignored him. So when he sang-shouted his angry lyrics before a live audience and the performance was recorded for posterity, surprisingly large numbers of people heard the message.

Robinson can barely conceal the sarcasm in his voice when he sings about the British police—"the best in the world"—and their habit of raiding gay bars and abusing the clientele both physically and verbally. The chorus is a scathingly ironic call to sing along:

> Sing if you're glad to be gay
> Sing if you're happy that way, hey

Robinson goes on to tell how "Gay News, our one magazine," is proclaimed obscene despite the fact that it carries far less nudity than many other generally accepted mainstream publications, such as Playboy. He describes how the British press regularly depicts gay people as "disgusting," as "molesters of children, corrupters of youth." And when he gets to the matter of gay-bashing, the anger in his voice is particularly noticeable:

> You don't have to mince or make bitchy remarks
> To get beaten unconscious and left in the dark

He offers as an example a "gentle" friend of his who, while out for a walk one evening, was accosted by queer-bashers. As a result he was hospitalized for a week—to which Robinson parenthetically adds, "And he still bears the scars."

The final verse is aimed directly at gay people themselves, especially those who remain complacent and politically inactive, who lie to their family and colleagues about themselves and their fellow gay people:

> Put down the queens, tell anti-queer jokes
> Gay Lib's ridiculous, join their laughter

By the time Robinson reaches the final chorus of "Sing if you're glad to be gay," it's hard not to be as angry as he.

Before he all but faded from the music scene, Tom Robinson wrote and performed a number of other significant songs, most notably the big British hit "2-4-6-8 Motorway" and the effectively funny and strident call to arms "Power in the Darkness." But none would have the power and impact of "Glad to Be Gay." With this one amazing song, Robinson earned himself a firm place in gay music history. Here was an artist who was willing not only to proclaim himself gay from the very start of his career (getting some positive attention as well as airplay in the process) but also to challenge both gay and non-gay listeners alike with his anger and frustration. He held up a musical mirror and shouted, "Here, look at yourself! And just try to tell me that you like what you see!" It was a tough pill to swallow.

Long out of print, it wasn't until deep into the CD age—not until the Fall of 1993—that the Power in the Darkness album finally became available on compact disc. Now you can hear for yourself this classic burst of righteous anger in crisp digital sound. It's a new world technologically. Regrettably, the anti-gay attitudes that inspired Robinson's fury haven't changed all that much since 1977.

Tom Robinson, ca. 1978. (Photo: Harvest Records. Michael Ochs Archives.)

▪ TOM ROBINSON ▪ "CABIN BOY" ▪

Songwriter:	Tom Robinson
Year of Release:	1984
Original Album:	*Hope and Glory*
Chart Performance:	Not released as a single, and the album didn't chart
Availability:	Out of print (Geffen 20453)

On an album full of notable songs, most of them of special interest to gay people—including a well-publicized remake of Steely Dan's "Rikki, Don't Lose That Number"—one song in particular shows Tom Robinson (at this point in his career a solo artist) at his most playful and gay, in every sense of the latter word. That song is "Cabin Boy," a festival of puns and double-entendres in which the seafaring life becomes an extended metaphor for a man-to-man relationship.

Robinson starts off with the cry, "I wanna go to Frisco Bay," simultaneously invoking the twin iconic status of San Francisco as historic seaport and gay mecca. Then, to a delightfully bouncy post-New Wave rhythm track, he begins to catalog clichéd sea terminology, saying how he wants to do things like "hoist the boat" and "swab the deck." But nothing sounds particularly "gay." That is, not until he adds,

> Hard to starboard, man ahoy
> I wanna be your cabin boy

That's when the song hits its stride, describing how a cabin boy must "go all the way" in his work, all through the day and all through night— "Cook and carry and fetch and hump." Not much doubt about what's going on here, is there?

Robinson sounds as though he's having a great time squeezing every sexual suggestion imaginable out of marine and naval jargon. He wants to "set the sextant, strip the guns, . . . do the hornpipe, jump for joy." Gay music that makes a serious stab for the mainstream market rarely gets as gay (again, in every sense of the word) as this. Of course, I could've told you that "Cabin Boy" and the rest of *Hope and Glory* didn't have a frappé's chance in hell of *real* commercial success. There are just too many layers of homophobia to break through. I only hope neither Tom Robinson nor anybody else connected with *Hope and Glory* lost their shirt over it—in a manner of speaking.

■ ROLLING STONES ■ "HONKY TONK WOMEN" ■

Songwriters:	Mick Jagger – Keith Richards
Year of Release:	1969
Original Album:	*Through the Past, Darkly*
Chart Performance:	The single was #1 for four weeks
Availability:	CD, CS, LP (ABKCO 8003)

As far as I'm concerned, this absolutely essential Rolling Stones song is about as close rock music gets to a Platonic ideal—which is certainly not to say that it's "platonic" in the usual sense of the word. In his entry on music in *The Encyclopedia of Homosexuality*, Stephen Donaldson states that "Honky Tonk Women" contains "references (slightly disguised through the use of British slang) to oral sex by transvestites." Not being up on my British slang, I'm afraid I'll just have to take his word for it, though I suppose the likeliest candidate is the line "She blew my nose and then she blew my mind." I do wonder, however, when Mick Jagger sings about how "a gin-soaked barroom queen in Memphis" had to heave him "right across her shoulder," how many *female* gin-soaked barroom queens would be capable of such a feat of strength? Not many, I'd wager, despite Jagger's less than imposing physique.

Besides, there's also the live version that appears on 1970's *Get Yer YaYa's Out!* to consider. It features an extra verse in which Jagger sings of walking naked down a Paris boulevard (!), taking note of "the sailors, they're so charming." Now, is that a gay tease or what?

■ ROLLING STONES ■ "COCKSUCKER BLUES" ■

Songwriters:	Mick Jagger – Keith Richards
Year of Release:	Not officially released, but recorded in 1970
Original Album:	No appearance on any official album
Chart Performance:	Not released as a single
Availability:	So far available only on bootleg CD, CS, and LP

There are various stories about the genesis of this scandalous but rarely heard song. According to the most plausible version, the Rolling Stones' contract with Decca had already expired and they had signed with a new label. But Decca insisted that they were owed another record and threatened legal action unless the Stones produced one. Just to spite Decca, Jagger and company came up with "Cocksucker Blues," a song with shockingly profane lyrics written from a blatantly homosexual perspective. To be specific, the narrator says that he wants to get his "cock sucked" and his "ass fucked." Needless to say, the record company refused to release the track, thus enabling the Stones to meet their contractual obligation without actually providing Decca with any releasable material.

"Cocksucker Blues" has yet to see the light of day on any official release, which ensures its legendary status in the annals of rock and roll. It has, however, appeared on some hard-to-find bootleg recordings, the most notorious of which featured a cover showing a sweaty Jagger with his head tossed back and mouth wide open (and I do mean *wide* open) as if to— well, you know. This has only served to enhance both the Jagger cult and the reputation of the Stones as the "bad boys" of rock. Of course, that "bad boys" image seems rather quaint and nostalgic in the 1990s, what with the likes of Guns N' Roses and 2 Live Crew out and about.

▪ ROMANOVSKY & PHILLIPS ▪ "WHAT KIND OF SELF-RESPECTING FAGGOT AM I?" ▪

Songwriters: Ron Romanovsky – Paul Phillips
Year of Release: 1986
Original Album: *Trouble in Paradise*
Chart Performance: Not released as a single, and the album didn't chart
Availability: CD, CS (Fresh Fruit 102)

A former friend of mine once accused me of being a "closet heterosexual." His reasoning behind this vicious slur was as follows:
  A) I'm a Baptist;
  B) I don't like Judy Garland;
  C) I enjoy rock music far more than classical music (which of course makes me a hopeless philistine), and even most show tunes leave me cold;
  D) I once flirted with the Republican Party (although, thank God, I've long since gotten over *that*); and
  E) I frequently eat at "chain" restaurants like Bakers Square and Red Lobster.
"Mind you," this person said, "no *one* of these things indicates an inclination toward heterosexuality, nor even just two of them. But *all* of them, honey—well, I can't help but think the worst."

Having been the victim of such gayer-than-thou provincialism, I can readily identify with that wonderful duo, Romanovsky & Phillips, when they open their second album, *Trouble in Paradise*, with "What Kind of Self-Respecting Faggot Am I?" In this delightful parody of a fifties-style doo-wop number (which never becomes heavy-handed, as such parodies

Romanovsky (left: at top & bottom left) & Phillips, 1993. (Photos: Herbert Lotz. Courtesy Fresh Fruit Records.)

often do), Ron Romanovsky laments the plight of being a gay guy "who never really fits in":

> I'm not into disco, and bars intimidate me
> My only can of Crisco is where it's s'posed to be
> What kind of self-respecting faggot am I?

Among the other ways cited in which our protagonist doesn't seem particularly "gay" are the facts that he doesn't even own any records by "Barbra, Bette, or Judy," hasn't seen any Bette Davis movies, doesn't read *GQ*, never goes to brunch on Sundays, and "wouldn't dream of screwing 'til after several dates." In the final verse he confides that, with all these marks against him, "It's so hard to be a homo."

Naturally, what we're witnessing is the playfulness that has made Romanovsky & Phillips favorites in the "gay music scene." Every stanza of the song is a joke on the same theme. But like so many really good jokes, there's an important message underlying it all. "What kind of self-respecting faggot am I?" The repeated question all but answers itself: he's a *self-respecting* faggot. In other words, the kind of gay man who, it is hoped, does indeed respect himself despite the ways in which he fails to fit in with the gay crowd or otherwise doesn't conform to stereotypes.

Ex-lovers but still professional partners, Romanovsky & Phillips have several albums under their belts, such as *I Thought You'd Be Taller, Emotional Rollercoaster,* and *Be Political, Not Polite.* They've recorded so many other superb songs that it's almost silly to focus on just a few of them here. But since we're being silly anyway—

■ ROMANOVSKY & PHILLIPS ■ "HOMOPHOBIA" ■

Songwriters:	Ron Romanovsky – Paul Phillips
Year of Release:	1986
Original Album:	*Trouble in Paradise*
Chart Performance:	Not released as a single, and the album didn't chart
Availability:	CD, CS (Fresh Fruit 102)

Actually, there's nothing silly at all about this track, except perhaps for the prejudice that serves as its subject. On the surface, "Homophobia" is merely a song that describes several real-life incidents of anti-gay bigotry and indicts the social pathologies that make such attitudes not only possible but commonplace. When you listen a little more closely, however, you begin to notice something very strange happening.

Romanovsky & Phillips pull off a remarkable bit of musical legerdemain. They take a very serious subject—the ways in which people are hurt, even killed by homophobia—and turn it inside out, treating it in a tongue-in-cheek manner. But they don't do it as you might expect, using ironic or sarcastic lyrics. No, the lyrics are totally forthright. Instead, with the help of members of the Dick Kramer Gay Men's Chorale, R&P gradually turn the word "homophobia" itself into a chant, and a rather *gleeful* chant at that. It bounces along like the big number from a Broadway musical comedy. In so doing, they *disarm* the dreaded word in exactly the same way that gay men do when they refer to themselves as "queers" and "fags," as lesbians do when they call themselves "dykes," as African-Americans do when they use the word "niggers," as physically handicapped people do when they describe themselves as "gimps." Homophobia needs to be deprived of its power. If only on a symbolic level—and probably on a more substantive level, too—Romanovsky & Phillips help to do just that with this song. And, for that matter, with all their other songs as well.

I've seen Romanovsky & Phillips perform live on a number of occasions and enjoyed it thoroughly each time. If you ever get a chance to attend one of their excellent shows, definitely do so. A good, gay time will be had by all.

- ■ RON ROMANOVSKY ■
- ■ "I LIKE TO POLKA" and "THESE THINGS" ■

Songwriter:	Ron Romanovsky
Year of Release:	1992
Original Album:	*Hopeful Romantic*
Chart Performance:	Not released as singles, and the album didn't chart
Availability:	CD, CS (Fresh Fruit 105)

These are my favorite songs from what has rapidly become one of my two favorite albums by openly gay artists recording on small, independent labels. (The other is John Bucchino's *Solitude Lessons*.) Don't let the fact that they come from a solo recording by Ron Romanovsky dismay you. The performing duo of Romanovsky & Phillips is still intact. It's just that Ron, as he says in his liner notes, needed some "room" to make this album on his own. The results are impressive.

As for these two songs in particular, they range from the ridiculous to the sublime. On the ridiculous side we have "I Like to Polka" (and, yes, it *is* a polka) in which Romanovsky returns to what is obviously one of his pet themes: namely, how he so often feels out of place, even among his fellow gay men. After bemoaning his lack of success and/or comfort at assorted dance styles, including disco, punk slam-dancing, and country clogging, he confesses that, for sheer fun, nothing quite compares to a polka. Hey, with a name like Romanovsky, should we be surprised?

In the course of the song, Romanovsky and his fellow musicians poke gentle fun at what might be described as "polka culture," complete with accordions, sauerkraut, and apple strudel, with Eastern European accents creeping in from time to time. It walks—or rather polkas—a fine line between tribute and parody, succeeding admirably. Of course, Romanovsky does all this while remaining totally gay, as he makes it perfectly clear that he's interested in polkaing with other men. Or, as he puts it,

> But when I meet a guy
> With a sparkle in his eye
> I take out my accordion and polka!

Overall, "I Like to Polka" is a delight, as though Frankie Yankovic had run into "Weird Al" Yankovic in a gay bar. I only wonder what Lawrence Welk would've thought of all this.

By contrast, there's the sublime part: the song "These Things." A softly rolling melody, understated but not simplistic instrumentation, and thoughtful, heartfelt lyrics about the transient nature of romantic love—all combine to create what is perhaps Romanovsky's loveliest recording to date. One quatrain especially stands out, taking a familiar metaphor and expanding it to describe how a different kind of love can emerge from a faded romance:

> A single glance that lit the spark
> A fire that burned for seven years
> And still it flickers in the dark

Listening repeatedly to this song, I sometimes feel that it may have been better served by a stronger singer. But, on the other hand, Romanovsky's pleasant voice seems to fit (maybe he simply resists using echo, reverb, and other studio tricks that so many other singers rely on to augment their vocal skills), adding a general air of peacefulness and vulnerability to the track. In any event, it's a beautiful performance.

Further kudos to the album's producer, Teresa Trull—herself a prominent artist in lesbian-feminist music—for her undoubtedly significant role in the aesthetic success of *Hopeful Romantic*. This is one of the cleanest, crispest-sounding albums I've yet heard in the "gay music" field. Even the superb photographs, taken in the New Mexico desert, contribute to making *Hopeful Romantic* a must for every aficionado. Besides, shouldn't at least *some* of our music dollars go to support performers and businesses that aren't fearfully closeted or even downright antagonistic to gay people?

▪ DIANA ROSS ▪ "I'M COMING OUT" ▪

Songwriters:	Nile Rodgers – Bernard Edwards
Year of Release:	1980
Original Album:	*Diana*
Chart Performance:	The single reached #5
Availability:	CD, CS (Motown 37463-5383)

Songwriter-producers Nile Rodgers and Bernard Edwards (previously of the minimalist disco ensemble Chic) neatly appropriated one of the best-known, most universal bits of gay terminology, itself appropriated with high-camp irony from the high-society debuts of teenage girls from wealthy families, to produce an immortal dance track with an unforgettable refrain:

I'm coming out
I want the world to know
I'm gonna let it show

In this way the Ross-Rodgers-Edwards troika virtually assured massive play for their song in gay dance clubs across the country while simultaneously solidifying Miss Ross' status as a major *doyenne* to the gay community. The fact that it was a dynamite record (I *dare* anyone to tell me that the first 43 seconds don't constitute one of the most electrifying intros ever to grace a pop single) only served to make it a huge across-the-board smash as well.

Besides, when Diana sings, "There is no need to fear!" I believe her.

▪ RuPAUL ▪
▪ "SUPERMODEL (YOU BETTER WORK)" ▪

Songwriters:	RuPaul – Larry Tee – Jimmy Harry
Year of Release:	1993
Original Album:	*Supermodel of the World*
Chart Performance:	The single reached #45
Availability:	CD, CS (Tommy Boy 1058)

As pop-culture drag queen, Boy George only went halfway. RuPaul Andre Charles goes all the way and then some. I imagine a few people don't even realize what's happening before their eyes when they see RuPaul on television. They just think he's a *very* tall woman. At any rate, "Supermodel" didn't get a whole lot of radio airplay, but it became a tremendous dance-club hit, and the video even garnered time on MTV—the latter of which shows just how unpredictable this business can be.

Even setting aside the mere drag angle for a few moments, there are still

RuPaul, 1993. (Photo: Norman Watson. Courtesy World of Wonder/Tommy Boy Records.)

quite a few remarkable things about RuPaul and "Supermodel." First of all, in a subculture in which even the finest drag queens usually perform by lip-synching to other people's hit records, RuPaul actually sings and writes hit records of his own. While, like all first-rate drag performers, RuPaul's looks wouldn't accurately be described as "androgynous"—the masculine element is suppressed as much as possible, leaving an image of arch quasi-femininity—his singing voice, on the other hand, is perhaps the most gender-bending thing about him. The first time I heard "Supermodel," before I had even heard of RuPaul, I figured the vocalist was simply a husky-voiced woman.

Secondly, "Supermodel" is a virtual throwback to the glory days of disco. Though other tracks on *Supermodel of the World* bear the stronger influence of house and other more recent innovations in dance music, "Supermodel" sounds as if it could have been a hit track back in the late seventies. (Don't get me wrong; in my book, that's no criticism.) And, like most disco music, the lyrics aren't terribly important. In fact, they're largely interchangeable from one track to the next. Since one of the chief functions of lyrics in dance music is to serve as a mood-enhancer, that leads us directly to the next remarkable thing about "Supermodel."

Camp. Gobs of camp. Reams of camp. Layers and layers of funky camp. To be sure, "Supermodel" is hardly unique in its campiness. Rather, it's the sheer *depth* of camp that's so phenomenal. Not since the Village People, or perhaps even Tiny Tim himself, has anyone hit the singles charts with such a stratospherically high camp quotient. Of course, there's RuPaul himself, one of the best—not to mention highest-profile—drag queens *ever*. And so tall. So imposing. Illusory woman as figure of intimidation. Which he *is*, and in more ways than one. For all we know, RuPaul may evolve into one of the biggest threats to the mainstream culture's cherished notions about gender constructs since—well, Boy George.

And what about the oft-repeated catch-phrase and subtitle of "Supermodel"—"You better work!"—which RuPaul barks out in a bossy-bitchy yet perversely affectionate manner, sort of like an admonishing mother-figure. (It's no accident that "Supermodel" features a "guest appearance" by LaWanda Page, the comic actress who is herself a major figure in African-American camp sensibilities via her status as mother-figure-from-hell. You might remember her from *Sanford and Son* as Redd Foxx's arch-nemesis.) Most people don't think of what models do for a living as *real* work. To some, the very idea of referring to it as "work" seems ridiculous. I'm not saying that attitude is *correct*; I'm just saying that's the way it is. Therefore RuPaul shouting "You better work!" like a Marine drill-sergeant in chiffon and pumps is inherently campy on multiple levels.

Even "supermodel" itself is a campy appellation, much as "superstar" was until it was rendered virtually meaningless through overuse. Paradoxically, in its *most* meaningless usage, "superstar" reclaims much of its former camp glory, as when I once heard Billy Idol referred to as a "superstar." Billy Idol is many things, but he's *not* a superstar. Let me tell you what a superstar is. A superstar is someone in reference to whom you can use a single name (first, last, or only) and everyone in Western Civilization, plus a fair portion of the rest of the world, will instantly know to whom you are referring. Sinatra. Elvis. (Or Presley.) Streisand. Elton. Madonna. But not "Billy" or "Idol."

But back to the single-named personage at hand. During a "live" performance on MTV, RuPaul shouted out to the dancing audience, "The future belongs to those who can *smell* it comin'!" and after a pregnant pause added, "Can you smell *me*?" Ultimately, despite all there is to behold, camp really isn't the bottom line with RuPaul. It's nothing less than *revolution* —a revolution in popular culture, which now seems close to accepting a major but much-reviled component of gay subculture, drag, as something legitimate. Mind you, drag has long been accepted as a comic device as long as the performer is notoriously (or at least apparently) heterosexual. Countless male entertainers, from Charlie Chaplin and Fatty Arbuckle to Jack Lemmon and Milton Berle, have dressed in drag for laughs, simultaneously making fun of themselves and what they *think* constitutes "femininity" or "womanhood." But that's not what RuPaul does at all. He's not a heterosexual pretending to be something he's not. RuPaul doesn't make fun of himself (well, maybe a little) or of womanhood. If anything—again like all great drag performers—RuPaul satirizes our society's *concepts* of femininity and how it views women. The *culture* is the object of satire, not females themselves. And if RuPaul can get record-buyers of all sexual orientations to appreciate that fact and to accept him as a gay man who chooses drag as a legitimate form of expression, then he will indeed be the agent of cultural revolution.

Then again, maybe RuPaul will only be another curiosity for our pop culture to chew up quickly and spit out as soon as the fruity flavor is gone, in which case he'll simply become the subject of trivia questions—and, if he's lucky, nostalgic shows in small venues—a decade from now. That remains to be seen. All I can say is, "You better work!"

▪ MITCH RYDER ▪ "CHERRY POPPIN'" ▪

Songwriters:	Mitch Ryder – Kimberly Levise
Year of Release:	1978
Original Album:	*How I Spent My Vacation*
Chart Performance:	Not released as a single, and the album didn't chart
Availability:	Out of print (Seeds & Stems 7801)

In the mid-1960s Mitch Ryder had a short string of energetic white-soul hits with his group, the Detroit Wheels. His biggest singles were two-song medleys that included classic Little Richard tunes: "Jenny Take a Ride" incorporated Little Richard's "Jenny Jenny," and "Devil with a Blue Dress On" blended into "Good Golly Miss Molly." The Detroit Wheels' frenetic R&B interpretations were exciting for a while but quickly grew stale. Less than two years after their first hit, Ryder rolled away from the Detroit Wheels and set off on a mediocre solo career. By late 1968 he was a veritable has-been, and in 1970 he declared bankruptcy. In 1973, with no chart success whatsoever, Ryder quit the music business altogether. He remained, however, a fond memory, something of a cult figure among devoted fans and, more significantly, a later generation of rock stars.

What happened during the next five years must have been very interesting. In 1978 Mitch Ryder returned unexpectedly with a solo album aptly titled *How I Spent My Vacation*, which is notable for two things: (1) it's an incredibly obscure, hard-to-find record, and (2) it's the most eye-openingly "gay" album I've ever heard by a sixties star of Ryder's stature, which probably accounts for its obscurity. And it's not a bad album by any means. It's kind of a semi-punk document with lots of R&B influence and periodic hints of Steely Dan-ish instrumental arrangement. Intriguing stuff. But the lyrics are what make *How I Spent My Vacation* really stand out. Not that they're brilliant or anything like that. They're just so—unexpected.

"Cherry Poppin'" is the LP's best song. Now, before I go any further, I should warn those of you with delicate sensibilities who may be offended by the mention of sexual practices which, as of this writing, are illegal in roughly half of the states in the Union—I should warn those people that those things are about to be discussed. OK? "Cherry Poppin'" is a catchy, joyous, and utterly undisguised celebration of the pleasures of anal sex. You were warned.

Although it's occasionally difficult to catch all of the lyrics, some lines come through loud and clear. The introductory chorus features the words, "Cherry poppin', stick it in. . . . cherry poppin', stick it up," with the music literally "poppin'" underneath through the clever use of guitar, bass, and electric keyboards—as cool a translation of verbal meaning to musical metaphor as I've ever heard. Ryder then sings about a "young boy's

dreams" and how one should "recognize the need to satisfy." He also glee-
fully urges his listeners,

> C'mon boys, c'mon men
> Turn around, back up, let's do it again

And just in case anyone should have any theological misgivings about this
activity, Ryder (and/or his persona in the song) assures us that he has just
finished having a talk with God, who allegedly said that "Everything's a
sin." Therefore, why be overly discriminating in your behavior? "We'll be
gay and the band is gonna play." And then it's time for that chorus again.
How he spent his vacation, indeed!

In the second verse, Ryder tells how he's being approached by boys
"wantin' things from me." And in the third stanza he talks about how "all
men live in spite of their longing for each other." But it's the fourth and
final verse that would really shock 'em down on the farm. After asking a
companion to "roll over on your tummy," he cajoles:

> Let me stick it in
> Nothin's queer, just a loss of fear

And back for one last brush with the "cherry poppin'" chorus. *Whew!*

Mitch Ryder's little anal sex jubilee may strike many—even many gay
people—as horribly crude. Yes, it is—and it's also tremendously refreshing compared to all of the other gayish things that were going on in mainstream music in the 1970s. "Cherry Poppin'" isn't ominously decadent like
David Bowie, satirically bombastic like Queen, or cartoonishly coy like the
Village People. For all of its tastelessness, it sounds happy, honest, and
unpretentious; sexy, fun, and as gay as can be. I'd encourage you to scour
the local used and collectors' LP shops in search of *How I Spent My Vacation*. "Cherry Poppin'" alone makes it worth your while. And there are a
few other little bonuses, too—

▪ MITCH RYDER ▪ "POSTER" ▪

Songwriters:	Mitch Ryder – Kimberly Levise
Year of Release:	1978
Original Album:	*How I Spent My Vacation*
Chart Performance:	Not released as a single, and the album didn't chart
Availability:	Out of print (Seeds & Stems 7801)

The final track on Mitch Ryder's *How I Spent My Vacation* album is
also its longest and, in many ways, most curious. An understated midtempo
number highlighted by tastefully rolling, muted guitar runs, "Poster" seems
to be a cross between a confessional autobiography and a description of

a wet dream.

The lyrics do start out dream-like, with disconnected impressionistic phrases, but too quickly they collapse into the lewdly mundane:

> *Dirty underpants*
> *I was dreamin', I started creamin'*

As I said, a wet dream. Then, after singing "Gotta get away from the U.S.A.," Ryder begins to describe an experience (perhaps imaginary) inspired by his dream, by a poster promoting French tourism, and/or by actual overseas events. He becomes a street hustler, "just a piece of meat." It's enough to make you start wondering about Ryder's vacation again. Then we hear more details that, because they refer to the narrator's musical career, smack more than ever of autobiography. He tells of a drunk, "singin' my old songs," who starts "feelin' up my ass."

> *When he hugs me, he said, "Don't you worry son*
> *You don't have to run, I'll tell you what to do"*

As the song moves along, there's some philosophizing—"God will forgive you"—that serves to rationalize all manner of supposedly "low life" behavior in the name of survival. Later, however, the narrator's life seems to take a slight upward turn, no longer hustling on the street but rather sitting on a sugar-daddy's knee on board a cruise ship. And then it's back to the first verse, that business about the French poster and dreaming. Very, very strange stuff.

The position to which Ryder assigns "Poster"—the final song on the album, a traditional place to put an especially important, content-culminating track ever since the Beach Boys and the Beatles set the pattern back in the 1960s with "Caroline, No" and "A Day in the Life," respectively— as well as the sheer length of the song (8:25) makes me believe that he considered it a significant statement. A significant statement of precisely what, I'm not sure. It's not a great song by any means, but it is interesting in the extreme. And one thing's for certain: the narrative persona of this song, which is either Ryder himself or someone he quite closely identifies with, has either availed himself on the street for gay sex or has had erotic dreams about doing just that.

One other song from *How I Spent My Vacation* seems closely related. It's called "The Jon" and, as far as I can tell, Ryder's persona this time is a full-fledged prostitute, male or female, who's in love with one of his or her regular clients. If it's a female prostitute, I can't think of many other rock songs in which a male vocalist sings the part of a female ("Acid Queen" from the Who's *Tommy* springs to mind). And if it's a *male* prostitute who's given such lines as "Honey, I don't need no man that can't make up his mind" and "Take it out, I'm kinda bein' sore," what can I possibly add?

Except that the co-writer of these songs, Kimberly Levise, was Ryder's wife. Go figure.

▪ NEIL SEDAKA ▪ "SOLITAIRE" ▪

Songwriters:	Neil Sedaka – Phil Cody
Year of Release:	1974
Original Album:	*Sedaka's Back* (though it appeared earlier on a U.K. album)
Chart Performance:	Not released as a single, but the album reached #23
Availability:	CD, CS (Polydor 831235)

It might never have occurred to me that this, one of the finest songs Neil Sedaka has ever written, may have gay implications if it weren't for cover versions subsequently made by the Carpenters and Jane Olivor. In Sedaka's original rendition of lyricist Phil Cody's extended card-game metaphor about a lonely man who lost the one he loved "through his indifference," there are absolutely no references to the gender of that lost love. There is, however, an obvious but nonetheless marvelous bit of symbolism. Our protagonist is described as dealing out his cards, "but still the king of hearts is well concealed." Is the king of hearts merely a personification of love itself? Or does it represent the protagonist's own inner self, longing for love? Ah, but there's a third possibility: perhaps the king of hearts refers to the protagonist's potential object of love—another man. I mean, why not the *queen* of hearts, which would be a more apt symbol for a heterosexual male's lost love? Unless, of course, our lonesome hero isn't necessarily heterosexual.

It's what the Carpenters did to "Solitaire" when they recorded it for their *Horizon* album in 1975 (and released it as a single, becoming a minor hit at #17) that's really fascinating. The "king of hearts" line is completely eliminated. In its place is an unequivocal reference to heterosexuality *where none had existed before*. The protagonist cannot win at his game of solitaire because, as the Carpenters put it, "without her love, it always ends the same." Now why do you suppose they did that? Was it because they feared the possible implications of the "king of hearts"? Was it because those implications weren't in keeping with the Carpenters' image? Or did Karen and/or Richard have more personal reasons for avoiding any suggestions, however remote, of gayness in their music?

When Jane Olivor, a somewhat Streisand-esque singer with a large gay following, decided to cover "Solitaire" for herself (on her 1978 *Stay the Night* album), she apparently had no reservations about restoring the original lyrics. There they are again for all to hear and wonder about: "But still the king of hearts is well concealed." A beautiful image, one that's not necessarily "gay"—but close enough, it would seem, for at least some performers to feel uncomfortable about it.

▪ DAVID SEREDA ▪
▪ "MARK" AND "UNDERAGE BLUES" ▪

Songwriter: David Sereda
Year of Release: 1981
Original Album: *Chivalry Lives*
Chart Performance: Neither were released as singles, and the album
                     didn't chart
Availability: LP (Rocky Wednesday 24)

It would be difficult to overestimate the influence of Joni Mitchell on subsequent singer-songwriters. And while that influence has been most obvious among female artists, it would be very wrong to assume that women alone have drawn tremendous inspiration from her. For one thing, there's the Crosby, Stills, and Nash axis. And James Taylor. Perhaps the most *outré* example is Prince, whose affinity for Mitchell's music has been well documented.

Of course, not everyone who has supped at Joni Mitchell's table of inspiration is a household name. For instance, I submit one David Sereda—like Mitchell a native of Canada—whose 1981 album *Chivalry Lives* is without a doubt one of the most obscure discs mentioned in this book. Structurally and harmonically, Sereda's melodies are clearly influenced by Mitchell's (especially her early work, before *Court and Spark*), and his lyrics have the same kind of strongly personal yet effectively detached feel to them. Mitchell is a master of this—"A Case of You" is among the finest of many examples—while Sereda strikes me as a very talented apprentice. Sometimes (such as on the title song) he even plays the dulcimer, a traditional folk instrument that Mitchell did much to popularize beyond the usual boundaries of folk music.

Consider Sereda's song "Mark." Recorded live, like other songs on the album, before an appreciative audience, its debt to Mitchell is immediately apparent. You can hear it in the way Sereda plays piano, as though he'd been taking lessons from Our Lady of the Canyon herself. The chord patterns again sound like classic Mitchell, as do the lyrics, which simultaneously extol and mourn an intense, highly tentative male-male love relationship, now ended. The song's central imagery of two men dancing around each other, a courtship of fearful love, has tremendous power. In my opinion, it's the album's best track.

Another particularly interesting Sereda number—though one I'm personally uncomfortable with—is "Underage Blues." Apparently still a legal minor when he wrote and recorded it (in 1980 or '81, and in the lyrics he states that he was born in '64), Sereda delivers a rousing *a cappella* solo performance (not really very "bluesy" at all) in which he not only celebrates his sexuality but also suggests, with some ambiguity, that he'd like to celebrate it with an older man. Very controversial stuff, even among gay people. While I would unequivocally disapprove if it were an adult seeking the company of a minor, the role-reversal makes me feel a little more ambivalent. It still bothers me, however.

Well, let's not get into the intellectual, emotional, and moral quagmire surrounding *that* whole issue. Rather, I'll simply say that while not all of *Chivalry Lives* is as artful or entertaining as "Mark" and "Underage Blues," it does show remarkable talent and maturity for one so young. I can only hope that David Sereda has been able to develop his skills in the years since—but of that I can't say, since *Chivalry Lives* is the only David Sereda album I know about. If there are others, I trust someone will let me know.

■ SEX PISTOLS ■ "NEW YORK" ■

Songwriters:	Paul Cook – Steve Jones – Glen Matlock – Johnny Rotten
Year of Release:	1977
Original Album:	*Never Mind the Bollocks, Here's the Sex Pistols*
Chart Performance:	Not released as a single, but the album reached #106
Availability:	CD, CS (Warner Brothers 3147)

It opens with power chords and frantic drumming nearly worthy of the Who. From that auspicious beginning it plummets directly downhill. Too bad. "New York," by the short-lived punk sensations the Sex Pistols, is an astoundingly abrasive piece of music. Johnny Rotten's screamed, garbled, audibly sneering vocals render the fragmentary lyrics almost incomprehensible. The lines I've managed to decipher (I don't suppose you can obtain sheet music to Sex Pistols material anywhere) include such pearls as "You're just a pile of shit!" and "You poor little faggot!" Several times, in a clearly mocking tone, Rotten cries, "Kiss me!"—hideously transforming an expression of love into one of hate. He later screams, "Kiss this!" and it's not hard to imagine what "this" refers to. Blessedly, the track lasts for only three minutes and five seconds, although it seems much longer.

To summarize, "New York" is one of the ugliest things upon which vinyl has ever been wasted. It ranks with Lou Reed's legendarily unlistenable *Metal Machine Music*.

An epilogue: Despite the fact that for about a half-year (mid-1977) shrewd hype succeeded in making the Sex Pistols the biggest thing to hit Britain since the Beatles (English teenagers never cease to amaze me) and in convincing a few trendoid critics that they were the most vital, exciting thing to happen to rock and roll since Elvis, their career went nowhere outside their home country and they disbanded shortly after their first American engagements. To his credit, Johnny Rotten disowned his work with the Sex Pistols, reverted to his birth name of John Lydon, and formed another, far better band, Public Image Ltd. Meanwhile, the Pistols' bassist Sid Vicious stayed truer to his reputation by murdering his girlfriend and avoiding prosecution via a fatal heroin overdose. Salt of the fucking earth.

▪ PETE SHELLEY ▪ "HOMOSAPIEN" ▪

Songwriter:	Pete Shelley
Year of Release:	1981
Original Album:	*Homosapien*
Chart Performance:	The single didn't chart, but the album reached #121
Availability:	Out of print (Arista 6602)

On the cover of his *Homosapien* album sits Pete Shelley, the former lead singer of the Buzzcocks (perhaps best known for their notorious "Orgasm Addict"). He fits quite nicely in what appears to be a high-tech office, surrounded by various accoutrements of contemporary taste, knowledge, and affluence, including a computer, a telescope, a trim-line telephone, an Egyptian jackal *objet d'art*, a strange little cubic puzzle, and assorted geometric solids made of stone, metal, and transparent acrylic plastic. Shelley himself is immaculately well-groomed, with his short, dark hair and his slightly off-white suit, pale blue shirt, dark blue necktie, and green carnation. That's right, a green carnation—a largely forgotten but well-documented symbol of homosexuality since the turn of the century, closely associated with Oscar Wilde. In fact, as Shelley lounges there, the very image of tastefulness with a faintly haughty expression on his face, he looks for all the world like a slimmed-down modern-day incarnation (no pun intended) of Wilde himself. This, we are presumably asked to consider, is the *Homosapien* of the title—"wise man."

The title track of this album is a rather noisy, hard-rocking, synthesizer-dominated, dance-pop workout. Aside from its danceability, its chief attraction lies in its unequivocally gay lyrics:

> *I'm the shy boy, you're the coy boy*
> *And you know we're Homosapien, too*

Shelley obviously but cleverly uses the term *Homosapien* to refer simultaneously to humanity *(Homo sapiens)* and gayness (homosexual), the basic implication being that the two are closely linked, if not interchangeable. In other words, gay people are first and foremost human—a fact lost on some not-so-sapient people. In fact, Shelley expresses some discomfort with the very need to "classify" *Homo sapiens* into categories (such as gay and straight?), but he recognizes the inevitability of it in the modern world. The lyrics abound with professions of love for his companion. Shelley's narrator has no illusions about the cruelty of society; he knows that a pair of homosexual *Homo sapiens* face an uphill struggle. Still, he refuses to give up, declaring, "I just hope and pray that the day of our love is at hand."

For all of its cacophony, "Homosapien" deserves praise as one of the most gay-positive tracks in rock music. Besides, you have to like a song that contains the couplet

> *Homo superior*
> *In my interior*

Maybe that's why Shelley looks the way he does on the cover.

▪ SHEL SILVERSTEIN ▪
▪ "FREAKIN' AT THE FREAKERS BALL" ▪

Songwriter: Shel Silverstein
Year of Release: 1973
Original Album: *Freakin' at the Freakers Ball*
Chart Performance: Not released as a single, but the album reached #155
Availability: Out of print (CBS 31119)

Depending on your sense of humor, this song is either liberating or degrading. Depending on your predilections, it may even be both.

Shel Silverstein, a former cartoonist for *Playboy*, started making a name for himself as a satirical songwriter in the late 1960s. He's best known for writing the biggest hit of Johnny Cash's career, "A Boy Named Sue" (which earned brief mention earlier in this tome) as well as early singles for Dr. Hook and the Medicine Show, such as the brilliant but widely misunderstood "Sylvia's Mother." I can't believe that anybody takes that song seriously, but some do. A relative of mine once disdainfully referred to that song's satirical vocal persona as a "whining faggot," missing the humor altogether and apparently ignoring the narrator's heterosexual inclinations. At any rate, one of Silverstein's most frequently covered tunes is the truly novel "Freakin' at the Freakers Ball," which he himself recorded.

"Freakin'" consists of little more than an exuberantly catalogued list of so-called "freaks" who've gotten together for a huge orgiastic party. It sounds as though it's an annual event. Early in the song Silverstein treats us to these lines:

> *Well, all the fags and the dykes are boogeying together*
> *Leather freaks dressed in all kinds of leather*

214

He subsequently refers to S&M devotees, employing the flawed but clever internal rhyme of "greatest" and "sadists." And he has a definite talent for fracturing clichés to good effect ("I'm gonna itch me where it scratches"). Later the narrator observes "hard-hats" and "long-hairs" making out, celebrating the breaking down of barriers (1973 was before a lot of hard-hats *became* long-hairs, and *vice versa*) in this atmosphere of unconventional sexuality. It's a classic of the novelty-tune genre—terrific, lighthearted, nonjudgmental fun.

Or is it? Let's back up a moment. First, I'm not thrilled with the idea of gay men and lesbians, here condescendingly called "fags" and "dykes" by somebody presumably other than one of them, being labeled "freaks" and put on satiric display for the amusement of "non-freaks." Second, I'm quite uncomfortable with some of the company in which Silverstein places gay people. The leather gang is OK. The sadists and masochists are politically incorrect in some circles, but they don't bother me either as long as they're mutually consensual. But Silverstein also includes necrophiliacs and pyromaniacs in his freak show. Just between you and me, I really don't care for that kind of company.

Think about it: gay people on a par with those who have sex with the dead and get their jollies by setting fires.

Sorry, but I'm not playing. I can enjoy the vitality and humor of "Freakin' at the Freakers Ball" only so long as I don't dwell on its wider implications. Having already done so, I think the party's over.

▪ SIMON AND GARFUNKEL ▪
▪ "KEEP THE CUSTOMER SATISFIED" ▪

Songwriter:	Paul Simon
Year of Release:	1970
Original Album:	*Bridge Over Troubled Water*
Chart Performance:	The single (as the oft-played flip side of "Bridge Over Troubled Water") was #1 for six weeks
Availability:	CD, CS (Columbia 9914)

It's been said that this song concerns the difficulties touring musicians face while on the road, but I don't buy it. The protagonist of "Keep the Customer Satisfied" is either a drug dealer or a male prostitute. Nothing else makes any sense whatsoever. You probably know the lyrics well enough that I don't need to repeat them here, but I should remind you about the deputy sheriff who warns the narrator to get out of town. Now, why would an officer of the law concern himself with a mere musician? And why would a performer face the abuse described by Simon in this song, being "slandered," "libeled," and cursed at with words "never heard in the Bible"?

Why? Because he's trying to keep his customers satisfied. See what I mean? Drug dealer or hustler. Between you and me, I suspect the former, but—shades of *Midnight Cowboy*—wouldn't the latter be a stitch?

▪ PAUL SIMON ▪
▪ "ME AND JULIO DOWN BY THE SCHOOLYARD" ▪

Songwriter:	Paul Simon
Year of Release:	1972
Original Album:	*Paul Simon*
Chart Performance:	The single reached #22
Availability:	CD, CS (Warner Brothers 25588)

One of Paul Simon's most famous and popular solo songs, "Me and Julio Down by the Schoolyard" features the narrator's assertion that he's recently been observed doing something unappreciated by society at large: "it was against the law." This time I'd say odds are better than even that illicit sex is involved. Consider the degree to which the teenaged narrator's family is dismayed by his behavior. His mother now spits on the ground whenever she hears his name, and his father threatens to ship him off to reform school. That, plus the "see you, me and Julio" line, the references to "Rosie, the queen of Corona," and even the hilarious bit about the radical priest—all point in the direction of homosexuality.

Mind you, I've never heard or read any Paul Simon explication of this song, not that it would matter much if I had. Artists are no more and often less valid analysts of their own work than any other critic. Of course, I could be totally off base. But if I'm not, what a delightful depiction this song provides of a gay youth—or at least a *curious* one!

Songwriters:	Gary Floyd – Benjamin Cohen
Year of Release:	1991
Original Album:	*Heart and Mind*
Chart Performance:	Neither the single nor album made the charts
Availability:	CD, CS (Reprise 26657)

Gary Floyd, the lead singer and lyricist for the San Francisco-based band Sister Double Happiness, looks as though he'd be more comfortable attending a monster truck-pull than fronting a rock group. Much less hanging out at a gay bar. But such are the misconceptions bred by stereotypes. Floyd is a big, bearded, full-throated bear of a gay man, and he doesn't care who knows it.

Sister Double Happiness trashes stereotypes in other ways as well. Aside from Floyd himself, their most immediately noticeable "difference" is their female drummer, Lynn Perko. You'd think that by now, after the Carpenters and the Velvet Underground (how's that for contrast?), not to mention the Go-Gos and the Bangles, we'd be well accustomed to the sight of a woman behind the drum kit. But women drummers are still the great exception to the rule, especially in groups that include male members. All that aside, Sister Double Happiness plays a brand of what's commonly called "modern rock" or "alternative rock" (like "New Wave," hardly a concrete or even highly descriptive term) that emphasizes the guitar of co-songwriter Ben Cohen, with the influence of country and blues sneaking in every now and then.

Out of commercial considerations (Sister Double Happiness had signed with a major record label, Reprise), gayness doesn't come through *too* strongly on the band's second album, *Heart and Mind*, but it's definitely there. It's most obvious in the hard, semi-metallic rocker "Hey Kids," in which Floyd addresses four different groups of listeners in turn, letting them know what's on his mind as he wrestles with various issues of concern to the gay community.

First he speaks to teenagers in that rough, powerful voice of his. In so many words, he lets us know that he especially wants *gay* teenagers to hear what he has to say, though his message will just as readily appeal to other teens who, for whatever reason, feel repressed and out of place:

> *Hey kids in school*
> *I'm talking to the one whose light's been covered*
> *Having to play by the rules*

Not only does Floyd decry the fact that "different" youngsters are forced to conform to what he considers to be outdated modes of behavior (sexual and otherwise), but he also wonders aloud "why they're messing with you

Sister Double Happiness, with lead singer Gary Floyd out front, 1993. (Photo: Jay Blakesberg. Courtesy Dutch East India Trading.)

in the very same way they messed with me." In short, he's warning kids about the way in which social authorities can do a number on their heads, and he sounds as though he's speaking with the voice of experience.

Next Floyd speaks to "Mr. Businessman . . . every day in your pinstripe running." He, too, is gay, though he denies himself the type of love he needs. The external repression that society imposes on the teenager has become the internalized repression of the adult. But, as too many of us are well aware, that internal pressure can only build up for so long before it starts to do some real damage, when, as Floyd puts it, "those lies start burning." The luckiest among us manage to come out to ourselves before too much damage is done. Is it too late for "Mr. Businessman"?

In the bridge between the second and third verses, Floyd turns his attention to politicians and other people in positions of power, some of whom may be ripe candidates for that phenomenon of great national gay debate, "outing." He warns that, when gay people's lives and freedoms are threatened, anyone and anything is fair game in the battle for survival. Floyd erupts into caustic laughter, relishing the thought of outing some hypocrite who at night enjoys gay sex but by day fights against gay rights. The melodic variation of the bridge gives an extra edge and force to his words. It's a powerful moment.

Finally, in the last verse, Floyd sings to a suffering friend—almost certainly, given the overall context of the song, someone with AIDS: "I know you're sick, but with love you can recover." But as he tries to give comfort to his friend, who clearly symbolizes all of the people with AIDS, Floyd can't conceal his anger. Accusingly, he wonders why his friend hasn't received the help and care he needs, which "should have been done a long long time ago." The end.

If I may sound a bit like a literary critic at this point, let me say that "Hey Kids" is an extremely well structured song, demonstrating a care for parallel narrative construction and a thoughtful use of repetitive but semantically varied phrasing that's rarely found in rock, as well as an apparent awareness of how emotionally effective such literary devices can be. What that all means is this: whether they know it or not, whether they're even aware of how they did it, Floyd and the rest of Sister Double Happiness have a stick of pop dynamite in their hands, and most likely a lot more where that came from. Based on the general high quality of *Heart and Mind*, I suspect there is. Buy this album before, like so much good music by openly gay artists, it quietly goes out of print—which, if enough people buy it, may not happen for a while yet.

Then again, there's good news and bad news. The bad news first. Reprise has dropped Sister Double Happiness from its roster just after the *Heart and Mind* album, which suggests poor sales. Now the good news. Gary Floyd and gang are once again recording on an independent label, which will probably allow them even greater openness and artistic freedom, if less media exposure. I wish them all the luck in the world. It's not so much that they need it, but that they deserve it.

▪ SISTER SLEDGE ▪ "WE ARE FAMILY" ▪

Songwriters:	Nile Rodgers – Bernard Edwards
Year of Release:	1979
Original Album:	*We Are Family*
Chart Performance:	The single reached #3
Availability:	CS (Cotillion 5209)

Nobody can tell me that a couple of canny producer-songwriters like Rodgers and Edwards weren't fully conscious of the impact that a song like this would have in gay dance clubs. To the young women, real-life sisters, who were singing this vibrant piece of music, it may simply have sounded like an exuberant celebration of family. And it is. But in a gay or lesbian crowd, the staccato syllables
> *We are family*
> *I got all my sisters with me*
become a simultaneous statement of camp sensibilities ("sisters" = fellow gay men and/or lesbians) and an assertion of strength through one's substitute "gay family" and even the gay and lesbian pride movement in general. As a result, for several years after this record hit it big, it held near-anthem status in the gay community. And it can still charge a gay crowd like few others.

• THE SMITHS •
• "WILLIAM, IT WAS REALLY NOTHING" •

Songwriters:	Morrissey – Johnny Marr
Year of Release:	1984
Original Album:	*Hatful of Hollow*
Chart Performance:	The single didn't hit the U.S. charts (though it was a big hit in the U.K.), and the album was available in the States only as an import; this song later appeared in the U.S. on the compilation album *Louder Than Bombs*, which reached #62
Availability:	CD, CS (*Louder Than Bombs*, Sire 25569)

The Smiths are a challenge to describe. During their relatively brief career in the mid- and late-1980s, they emerged as perennial critics' pets who achieved a large measure of success in their native Britain but only cult status in the United States. They were led by a pair of rock anomalies. First there was Johnny Marr, a highly talented guitarist who, like U2's The Edge, preferred jangly, layered rhythm passages to the soaring or crunching lead solos favored by his counterparts in other bands. And then there was the outspoken, gay-supportive, but avowedly celibate (sometimes described as "asexual") lyricist-vocalist, Stephen Morrissey, who went only by his last name—a singer of neurotic, self-deprecating, cynical-romantic-ambiguous poetry with a droning voice that some people found endlessly annoying.

Any number of Smiths recordings could find their way onto a list of "gay" songs, but a few in particular stand out. One is "William, It Was Really Nothing." Its fast, almost frantic instrumental track contrasts with Morrissey's trademarked deadpan-evocative vocal as he paints a rather dreary picture of life in "a humdrum town." The narrator directly addresses "William," of whom he asks,

> How can you stay with a fat girl who'll say
> "Would you like to marry me?
> And if you like you can buy the ring"

Morrissey, in his role as William's male lover, then turns those heterosexually oriented propositions around, asking William whether he would like to marry him instead, complete with a wedding ring of their own. Apparently the narrator himself was contemplating a loveless heterosexual marriage. Having rejected that option, however, he now wishes to assure William that "it was really nothing" and that everything can be back to the way it used to be. That includes the narrator's unrelenting solipsism, a common theme in the Smiths' music.

We don't even know how this little drama ends. It's fairly typical of Morrissey to leave us hanging. But, of course, the "ending" (which doesn't

221

really exist) isn't what this song is all about, anyway. "William, It Was Really Nothing" is about the situation at hand, which provides Morrissey with ample opportunity for his standard self-deprecating, cynical-romantic-ambiguous *schtick*. And if you can tolerate his vocals as part of the package, it works quite well. I mean, after hearing songs like "William, It Was Really Nothing," "Heaven Knows I'm Miserable Now," "Please Please Please Let Me Get What I Want," and a dozen others in a similar vein, you really start to feel for these guys—until you've heard about a dozen more, and then you simply start to go numb.

▪ THE SMITHS ▪ "THIS CHARMING MAN" ▪

Songwriters: Morrissey – Johnny Marr
Year of Release: 1984
Original Album: *The Smiths*
Chart Performance: The single didn't chart, but the album reached
                    #150
Availability: CD, CS (Sire 25065)

Like many Smiths tunes, "This Charming Man" might be described musically as the melody of a Gregorian Chant placed overtop a ringing, shallow, guitar-dominated instrumental track. The lyrics, as always, give Morrissey an opportunity to expound his odd *weltanschauung*, which in this case is akin to *weltschmerz*, but even bleaker. In short, life is a tiresome ordeal in which, if anything good happens to you, it's either because it isn't really good at all but you're just deceiving yourself into thinking that it is, or because you're being set up to feel even more despair after the slippery rug of happiness is pulled out from under you.

In "This Charming Man," Morrissey's persona starts out in typical fashion. Fate does not deal good hands to this boy, who finds himself alone with a punctured bicycle tire on a desolate hillside. Not altogether sure what to do, he wonders, "Will nature make a man of me yet?" Droll, very droll. But along comes a potential rescuer, a "charming man" in a "charming car," apparently ready to give our antihero a ride. A strange exchange then takes place, in which the narrator complains about not having "a stitch to wear." In reply,

> This man said, "It's gruesome
> That someone so handsome should care"

I swear, it's like something out of *Brideshead Revisited*. Do the British really talk like that? Or do British writers of speculative sexual orientation merely insist that such garishly elegant language trip off their characters' tongues?

222

Not a lot more occurs in this song, actually—some stuff about a "jumped-up pantry boy" and a suggestion to "return the ring." Personally, I can't make heads or tails of it (no puns intended). But the gist of the song seems to be this: that when a charming man comes into your life and finds you attractive, complimenting you on your looks, be prepared for yet another of life's inevitable letdowns. This doesn't mean that you shouldn't necessarily hop right into his car, but rather that you shouldn't get too attached to it.

Poor Morrissey. Even when he's happy he's sad, too busy thinking about the sadness that will eventually come. Kind of like F. Scott Fitzgerald in his New York taxicab, starting to cry because he knows that he'll never again be so happy.

▪ SOFT CELL ▪ "TAINTED LOVE" ▪

Songwriter: Edward C. Cobb
Year of Release: 1982
Original Album: *Non-Stop Erotic Cabaret*
Chart Performance: The single reached #8 (blended into a remake of the classic Supremes hit "Where Did Our Love Go?")
Availability: Original album out of print; available on Marc Almond's *Memorabilia—The Singles*, CD (Mercury 314-510178)

The Gay Trivia Quiz Book states that "Tainted Love" is "a song about lost homosexual love." Well, all right, I don't dispute it. I've heard, read, and seen enough of vocalist Marc Almond of this now-defunct technopop duo to believe it wholeheartedly. But I just wish the *Trivia Book*'s pseudonymous authors had provided some information, maybe just a footnote, to tell the rest of us how they knew this for sure. Was it an interview somewhere? OK, OK, I suppose I shouldn't ask other people to do my homework for me. I do wonder, however, whether the love described in this song is "tainted" simply because it's lost or because of something else. Is it "tainted" because it's furtive? Because it's *gay*? I hope not. Gay love is *not* tainted love, at least not by virtue of that fact alone.

Great LP title, by the way.

Soft Cell, early 1980s: (l-r) Dave Ball and Marc Almond. (Photo: Courtesy Sire Records.)

▪ SOFT CELL ▪ "NUMBERS" ▪

Songwriters:	Marc Almond – Dave Ball
Year of Release:	1983
Original Album:	*The Art of Falling Apart*
Chart Performance:	Neither the single nor the album made the charts
Availability:	Out of print (Sire 25065)

Oh, the tiresomeness of it all. The endless stream of lovers one has to contend with. "Who's the person that you woke up next to today?" asks our friendly tour guide through this jerky, staccato land of electro-decadence. Why, if I didn't know better, I'd say a wee bit of bitchy self-righteousness was creeping into Marc Almond's voice as he counts off a promiscuous series of gay conquests. It seems that he has enjoyed sex with seven different people in the course of a 24-hour period, and he blithely observes that he doesn't know any of their names—

> *'Cause names make a person real*
> *And there's no real people in these games*

Ah, but he does have a point. When you're inclined to "throw 'em away like kleenex" (as Almond puts it in the song's best line), love is impossible. Besides, if all of your "lovers" are so disposable, what does that make you?

Equally disposable.

Soft Cell always did seem to show a strong streak of conscience even as they wallowed in the seamier states of *eros*. Maybe that's why they titled their final album *This Last Night in Sodom*. Too much of a thing, you know—good or bad, depending on how you look at it.

▪ JIMMY SOMERVILLE ▪ "READ MY LIPS" ▪

Songwriter:	Jimmy Somerville
Year of Release:	1989
Original Album:	*Read My Lips*
Chart Performance:	The single didn't chart, but the album reached #192
Availability:	CD, CS (London 828166)

As previously noted, Jimmy Somerville continued as a solo artist after his stints with Bronski Beat and the Communards. This track, "Read My Lips," is the pinnacle (to date) of his solo career.

It's hard to find a more vigorous, exciting track, at least within the genre of gay-oriented dance music. The undulating bass and synthesizers leave you no option but to *move*—if not in body, then in spirit. With his unmistakable falsetto, Somerville sings a lyric of open defiance. He takes the notorious George Bush (originally Clint Eastwood) cliché, combines it with a snippet of Donna Summer and Barbra Streisand's one-off disco confection, and turns this unlikely marriage of hyperboles to his own advantage:

> *Read my lips and I will tell you*
> *Enough is enough is enough is enough*

And just what is it that he's had enough of? All the shit that gay men, lesbians, and other sexual minorities have had to put up with, that's what. "We'll fight for love and pride," declares Somerville, "standing together for the right to live and love with dignity." But this isn't just political earnestness—it's supported by an overwhelming sense of confidence and joy. Chanting the refrain "The power within, we can use it to win," Somerville and his backup singers leave no room for doubt that, as serious as it is, social revolution can also be *fun*. It reminds me of certain sentiments held by the famous early twentieth-century reformer Emma Goldman, when she said of revolutions, "If there's no dancing, count me out," or something to that effect.

To summarize, "Read My Lips" is an amazing musical document of the Gay and Lesbian Rights Movement. Jimmy Somerville has every reason to be proud. If there's ever a Gay Rock Hall of Fame, he's on my short list of first nominees.

▪ DUSTY SPRINGFIELD ▪ "CLOSET MAN" ▪

Songwriters:	D. Foster – E. Mercury – D. Gerrard
Year of Release:	1978
Original Album:	*Living Without Your Love*
Chart Performance:	Not released as a single, and the album didn't chart
Availability:	Out of print (United Artists 936)

Had the smoky-voiced British singer Dusty Springfield never recorded anything but "Son of a Preacher Man," she would still be forever enshrined in the rock pantheon. The fact that she had an impressive string of sixties hits even before that blue-eyed soul classic (including "Wishin' and Hopin'," "I Only Want to Be with You," and "You Don't Have to Say You Love Me") only confirms that it was no fluke. By the time the seventies rolled around, however, the hits had dried up for her, though she continued somewhat sporadically to make music.

"Closet Man," one of these latter-day efforts, is one of the very few songs I'm aware of in which a heterosexual female narrator accepts and supports an ex-lover after learning that he's gay. No, Dusty never uses the G-word, but she doesn't have to with a refrain like "Your secret's safe with me," followed by a statement of moral support:

> *You know it's all right to go on and live your life*
> *So come out into the light, closet man*

Set to a sophisticated mid-tempo, gently rocking, even slightly jazzy backdrop, the lyrics are consistently positive. They sometimes assume a mildly comic tone, as in the loopy observation that her ex-boyfriend still wears the ring that she once gave him—but in his ear. And it's interesting to note that the song nods to the late-seventies *nouveau* stereotype of gay *machismo*, what with its passing references to tattoos and muscles. That, too, I believe is included for a vague comic effect. But I don't mind. I can certainly take a joke when the teller is this nice about it.

▪ JIM STAFFORD ▪ "MY GIRL BILL" ▪

Songwriter:	Jim Stafford
Year of Release:	1973
Original Album:	*Jim Stafford*
Chart Performance:	The single reached #12
Availability:	CS (Polydor 833073)

You might call this a "fake gay song." It derives its limited appeal from fooling first-time listeners (and dense second- or third-time listeners) into thinking that they may be hearing a song about a gay relationship when, in truth, they really aren't.

Jim Stafford had a short string of hits in the mid-1970s that were based on what a less jaded person than myself might describe as a "warped" sense of humor. This was several years before he wound up hosting a short-lived TV show called *Those Amazing Animals*. At any rate, the narrator of "My Girl Bill" describes a pleasant evening of dinner and conversation with Bill, who, in the chorus, is repeatedly referred to as "my girl"—or so it seems. By the final verse, it becomes apparent that, in actuality, the narrator and Bill are rivals for the attention of the same young woman, and this dinner and conversation is merely a civilized way of trying to hash the matter out. In the song's "punch line," so to speak, the narrator says: "She's *my* girl, Bill." And that's what all of those previous my-girl-Bills had been about, titter-titter. At this point, the average heterosexual listener is supposed to breathe a sigh of relief. "Golly, I guess those dudes ain't fags after all, huh-huh."

I imagine this was considered risqué in some circles back in 1974. But with David Bowie and Lou Reed already leaving heavy traces of mascara in their wake, "My Girl Bill" seems hopelessly bland in comparison. Besides, Bowie and Reed played queer *so* much better.

▪ STEELY DAN ▪
▪ "RIKKI DON'T LOSE THAT NUMBER" ▪

Songwriters: Walter Becker – Donald Fagen
Year of Release: 1974
Original Album: *Pretzel Logic*
Chart Performance: The single reached #4
Availability: CD, CS, LP (MCA 31165)

I was in college when this song appeared on the scene. Although *Pretzel Logic* was only the third album by Steely Dan, they had already made it into the upper echelon of really cool rock acts, at least in the crowd I hung out with. Steely Dan boasted superb musicianship, innovative yet catchy melodies and harmonic structures, and lyrics that were obtuse, referential, yet cynical as hell. Besides, Donald Fagen had a peculiar way of enunciating his lyrics that made everything he sang sound as if he were contemplating a criminal act. In short, Steely Dan possessed everything one needed to make it among the embryonic intelligentsia. And, despite the fact that my crowd distrusted Top Forty radio as the realm of the obvious and the mundane, we were extremely pleased to see the first single from *Pretzel Logic* succeed as a Top Forty hit—and a very big one at that. At last, somebody worthy of mass recognition was finally getting it!

But one thing bothered us: just *what* was this song about?

It seemed perfectly clear that the lyrics concerned a failed relationship as told from the perspective of someone who didn't want it to fail—who, in fact, was trying to talk the other person into giving it another chance, or at least to leave open that possibility. And since the singer was a man, the other person must be a woman, right?

So we told ourselves. But it bothered us that her name was Ricky. I mean, how many females are named Ricky? (This was years before Rickie Lee Jones became famous.) Oh, it's not spelled "Ricky"—it's spelled *"Rikki"*! Well, that's a little better. Like that Kipling mongoose. Maybe that odd spelling is actually Becker and Fagen's way of telling us that it really *is* a woman: *Rikki*, not Ricky.

Of course, it hadn't occurred to us that if Becker and Fagen were indeed concerned about how we might interpret Rikki's gender, then they would have chosen a name less subject to misinterpretation, such as Susie, or Sally, or Joanie. Why *Rikki*?

The reason, which we weren't willing to admit to ourselves back then, is that Rikki almost certainly isn't a woman at all. I submit the following pieces of evidence:

- The narrator's plea that Rikki not "lose that number." Remember, just a few entries back, Soft Cell's "Numbers"? The word "number" is virtually iconographic in the gay community, particularly among those persons who frequent bars, in which telephone numbers are exchanged with tremendous regularity. This is true to the extent that "number" has long been a cynical synonym for "man" or "trick." You just count them off.

- The name Rikki itself. Young gay men new to the big city (as Rikki seems to be) are notorious for changing the spelling of their first name to something more unusual and distinctive: *Tomm* instead of *Tom* or *Jaye* instead of *Jay*, for example. If it's a diminutive that normally ends with a *y* or *ie*, it often winds up ending with an *i* instead. This is not a universal experience by any means, but it's common enough to be something of a cliché.

- Most telling of all are certain lines from the song, especially in its melodic and emotional climax during the bridge before the final chorus—
    > *You tell yourself you're not my kind*
    > *But you don't even know your mind*
—which just about nips it in the bud, doesn't it? I mean, I suppose if the two persons involved, the narrator and Rikki, were of different races, religions, or socioeconomic backgrounds, the same could be said. But there's even less evidence of that being the case than there is for the gay interpretation.

That being said, here's a capsule summary of what the song seems to be about. Rikki is a young man, gay or bisexual, who's new in town. He's just had a fling with the narrator, an older, far more experienced man. The older man is clearly enamored of Rikki and wants the relationship to continue, but Rikki is now confused and wants to go "home," perhaps back to his mom and dad. So the narrator reluctantly lets Rikki go, giving him his telephone number and telling him to call if he changes his mind or needs help.

For all of this, the gay subtext of the song is subtle enough that most people didn't get it. Or, if they got it, they could easily brush it aside as my friends and I did, at least until we got older, wiser, and less fearful of homosexuality either in ourselves or in others. Otherwise, it probably wouldn't have been so big a hit.

Incidentally, "Rikki" was later covered by the openly gay singer Tom Robinson, who called it "the greatest gay love song ever written," or something to that effect. Well, I don't know about that, but I won't quibble.

Also incidentally, this would not be the last nor the most obvious gay-themed song Steely Dan would do. And one other thing: as has often been noted, the name "Steely Dan" comes from the novel *Naked Lunch*

by William Burroughs, in which it denotes a steam-powered dildo.
Say what?

▪ STEELY DAN ▪ "THROUGH WITH BUZZ" ▪

Songwriters: Walter Becker – Donald Fagen
Year of Release: 1974
Original Album: *Pretzel Logic*
Chart Performance: Not released as a single, but the album reached #8
Availability: CD, CS, LP (MCA 31165)

This little ditty—one of the shortest in the Steely Dan corpus—describes how the narrator is finished having anything to do with his former best friend, Buzz, because of all the awful things he's done. Among other things, Buzz has taken all of our hero's money and has stolen his girlfriend. So, as he ponders these betrayals, the narrator muses, "Maybe he's a fairy," over a brief backdrop of sweet, sugarplummish strings (one of only two times in which Steely Dan used violins, the other instance being "FM"). It's an idiotic insult, just the kind of thing a really stupid, insecure heterosexual might say about someone he doesn't like, regardless of evidence to the contrary. After all, Buzz did steal his girl, which makes the "fairy" speculation doubly moronic. And I suspect Becker and Fagen meant it to be taken that way.

▪ STEELY DAN ▪ "BLACK COW" ▪

Songwriters: Walter Becker – Donald Fagen
Year of Release: 1977
Original Album: *Aja*
Chart Performance: Not released as a single, but the album reached #3
Availability: CD, CS, LP (MCA 37214)

First things first: this song has nothing to do with the dairy industry. The "black cow" in the title refers to a non-alcoholic mixed drink, of which one of the central characters is quite fond.

Oh, but this one is subtle—so subtle that even those of us who understood "Rikki Don't Lose That Number" right away took a little longer to see it here. In fact, I may be totally mistaken; it may not be gay-related at all. Still, I'll make my case, and then you can decide for yourself.

The first verse of the song makes it clear that the narrator is involved in a relationship with someone who frequents bars behind his back. That could be either a man or a woman. But it's the second verse that reveals more:

> On the counter, by your keys
> Was a book of numbers and your remedies

There are those numbers again, suggesting a certain type of gay lifestyle. And juxtaposed with the book of numbers are keys, long used by some members of the gay community, especially when worn on the belt, to advertise their gayness and/or preferred "role" in sexual encounters. Personally, I don't know what to make of the "remedies."

Later in the song we learn a little more about the unfortunate habits of the narrator's lover, who likes to go "down to Green Street . . . lookin' so outrageous." Sounds like drag to me. So while I'll admit that this song could be about a man in love with a prostitute (female, that is), I'll do so only if everyone else admits that it could be about a gay relationship on the skids.

Oh, I can hear you now: "He sees gay stuff in everything!" But that's not true. There are quite a few other Steely Dan tunes, for instance, that are not obviously about heterosexual relationships but which I *don't* believe are gay-related. From the *Aja* album alone there are both the title song and "I Got the News," neither of which are unambiguously heterosexual, yet in which I don't see any evidence of gay themes. But whenever there's more evidence of a gay relationship in a song than of a heterosexual relationship, that's when I see it. And though I'm willing to say that I may be wrong, I *do* see it in "Black Cow."

■ STEELY DAN ■ "GAUCHO" ■

Songwriters:	Walter Becker – Donald Fagen
Year of Release:	1980
Original Album:	*Gaucho*
Chart Performance:	Not released as a single, but the album reached #9
Availability:	CD, CS, LP (MCA 37220)

If you push it, "Rikki Don't Lose That Number" may be debatable and "Black Cow" may be questionable, but the title song of Steely Dan's album *Gaucho* is indisputable. In fact, it's been widely recognized by mainstream music critics as a gay-related song from the moment it appeared. One reviewer, for example, described it as a song about "a gay spat." More precisely, "Gaucho" is one *side* of a gay spat.

It starts off with the narrator's expression of disappointment in his lover, whom he refers to as his "special friend." You see, he (the special friend) has just become infatuated with a cowboyish, possibly Latino third party. He's even brought him home to their luxury high-rise flat, where our protagonist sarcastically asks,

> Who is the gaucho, amigo?
> Why is he standing in your spangled leather poncho
> And your elevator shoes?

His lover is persistent, but our narrator holds his ground. Just in case there's still any doubt as to the gender of the people involved, the narrator chastises his partner, calling him "a nasty schoolboy" and ridiculing him for holding hands with "the man from Rio." Becker and Fagen don't make their protagonist out to be a particularly likable chap, but I suppose most of us would agree that he does have reason to be upset, suddenly seeing his "special friend" take up with somebody else in this way.

At any rate, we never do find out how this little domestic drama turns out, though the last we hear the narrator is still insisting that he'll never accept the "gaucho" in his home "high in the Custerdome." As Becker and Fagen themselves indicated in interviews shortly after the album's release, the fanciful "Custerdome" setting suggests an unhappy, perhaps even disastrous outcome to the whole story.

Not counting the passing reference in "Through with Buzz," we've seen three—OK, certainly one, probably two, and maybe three—Steely Dan songs with gay-related subject matter. What can we make of it? Does this mean that one or both of the songwriters are gay? Not that it matters one way or the other, but no, not necessarily. Over the course of their career as the nucleus of Steely Dan, Becker and Fagen wrote a large number of fascinating songs about all sorts of people, including Puerto Rican immigrants, African-American saxophone players, libidinous divorcees, jealous husbands, fetishists, obsessive introverts, drug dealers, mass murderers, members of religious cults, politicians, paranoids, prostitutes, johns, survivors of a thermonuclear holocaust, child molesters, gangsters (both earthly and extraterrestrial), gamblers, jewel thieves, and, of course, homosexuals. The songwriters certainly aren't most of these things, and, as far as I know, they aren't any of them. You obviously don't have to *be* something to write about it.

The one thing that most if not all of these personae have in common is that they serve as vehicles for cynical ruminations on the sociopathologies of the narrators and/or of society at large. Listening to a large number of Steely Dan songs in succession, you get the impression that you're playing witness to an audio rogues' gallery, as if the songwriters sat down on a regular basis and said, "So, what outcast, misfit, or otherwise really strange person can we choose as our spokesperson *this* time?" (Or as Becker and Fagen have put it, they wanted to write "funny" songs.) I mean, just look at the people in "Rikki," "Black Cow," and "Gaucho." Are they what you might call "well adjusted"? Are they fulfilled? Are they happy? No—

although you can make a strong case for most of these protagonists being at least better-adjusted than the people to whom they're speaking. When you get right down to it, Becker and Fagen paint a dreadful portrait of gay life. But, then again, they paint a dreadful portrait of *human* life in general. Why should the "gay" songs be any different? Steely Dan's heterosexuals are every bit as miserable as their homosexuals. In final consideration, most Dan songs are written so intelligently, constructed so artfully, and performed so skillfully—plus they're usually so much *fun*—that it's nearly impossible not to enjoy them in spite of their pervasive pessimism and exploitive grotesqueries.

■ ROD STEWART ■
■ "THE KILLING OF GEORGIE (PARTS 1 & 2)" ■

Songwriter:	Rod Stewart
Year of Release:	1977
Original Album:	*A Night on the Town*
Chart Performance:	The single reached #30
Availability:	CD, CS (Warner Brothers 3116)

Rod Stewart deserves a lot of credit for recording this, the first Top Forty song (and to this day, one of the precious few) to focus unambiguously on an openly gay character in a sympathetic manner. Rod (or his persona) tells the story of a friend, and he says forthrightly in the first verse—

> Georgie boy was gay, I guess
> Nothin' more or nothin' less

As Stewart goes on to tell us, Georgie's parents had thrown him out for being gay, so he settled in New York City. Things might have looked bleak for George at that point, but he was a survivor. Before long he became the toast of the town, beloved by everyone he met. He'd "cruise" down the boulevards, where "all the old queens blew a fuse." Hmm.

Stewart then says that the last time he saw his friend alive was in the summer of 1975, at which time George confided that he had fallen in love. Shortly thereafter, having attended the opening night of a Broadway show, George and his lover were attacked on their way home by a gang of toughs. George was killed by a switchblade-wielding punk who "did not intend to take a life." I find it interesting that, in a song that is so openly supportive of a gay man, the songwriter makes a point of coming dangerously close to excusing his murderer, a "kid" who allegedly never meant to kill anyone, despite his habit of carrying a switchblade around with him. Hmm, again.

The lyrics then turn somewhat philosophic as Stewart ponders the meaning of it all. After he quotes his dead friend—some platitudes about how short and tenuous life is—Stewart affirms once again, "Georgie was a friend of mine." The final portion of the song (Part 2) is an extended and repetitive bemoaning of Georgie's fate, clearly intended to be an expression of tragedy, angst, and grief.

The time was right for a song like this. In 1977, with the gay rights movement in full swing and gay-influenced disco music nearing its peak of popularity among young urban single heterosexuals who were discovering that they could cop a lesson from gay people and enjoy some freewheeling dancing and sex for themselves (this was, of course, before AIDS), the audience for such a message was probably as open as it ever was or ever would be in the entire rock era to date. Furthermore, gay-bashing was and continues to be a terrible problem that needs to be forcefully addressed in the media, and "The Killing of Georgie" was the first hit song to do so. Or was it? It's interesting to note that the murder is not unmistakably identified as a gay-bashing; the gang was out "to roll some innocent passerby" and, again, "did not intend to take a life." Nevertheless, make no mistake about it—this song was important.

Stewart's heart was certainly in the right place. "The Killing of Georgie" is so noble—a definite career risk for ol' Rod, you know—and full of good intentions that I now hesitate to pursue what I'm going to say next. But music-critic integrity (what little of it there may be) demands it. For all of its goodness, "The Killing of Georgie" suffers on several counts:

- It's all so horribly maudlin.
- The unfortunate references to "old queens" and the intentions of the murderer.
- The song's somewhat condescending attitude toward its gay hero, what with the diminutive name "Georgie" and his being referred to as "Georgie boy."
- The background vocals, which are transparent, unimaginative knock-offs of the infamous "colored girl" vocals on Lou Reed's "Walk on the Wild Side."
- The fact that Georgie is little more than a cipher, a quintessential gay-man-as-victim, and even by the 1970s the media had supplied us with more than enough of those. It would have been nice if George had lived —but maybe then we wouldn't have had a song, and certainly not one called "The Killing of Georgie." (By the way, is this a true story? I'd love to know. If I knew for sure that it were indeed a literal account of an actual incident, I might feel somewhat different about it.)
- All gay stuff aside, it's a second-rate song with a weak melody. Stewart has made some truly great music (his album *Every Picture Tells a Story* is a landmark), but "The Killing of Georgie" is definitely not one of his finest efforts, at least musically speaking.

Again, however, let me emphasize that its subject matter, dealt with frankly and bravely, makes it an extremely important record in the history of rock music, especially with regard to gay people. From this perspective, it's a pity that it wasn't a bigger hit than it was, and we'll never know whether it was its unabashedly gay-supportive theme or its aforementioned weaknesses that made it stall at #30 on the charts. On the other hand, the fact that it got that high is significant.

A sidenote: Around the time this song appeared, Stewart began to be plagued by persistent rumors that he had been rushed to a hospital one morning to have his stomach pumped after an all-night fellatio marathon. This rumor was *false*, mind you, but I wouldn't be surprised if it had been started by someone who either disapproved of "The Killing of Georgie" or read way too much into it.

▪ STING ▪ "ENGLISHMAN IN NEW YORK" ▪

Songwriter:	Sting
Year of Release:	1987
Original Album:	. . . *Nothing Like the Sun*
Chart Performance:	Not released as a single, but the album reached #9
Availability:	CD, CS, LP (A&M 6402)

In the album's liner notes, Sting writes that he wrote "Englishman in New York" for a friend who had moved to the states "in his early seventies to a small rented apartment in the Bowery." Although Sting doesn't identify his elderly friend by name, it's reportedly none other than Quentin Crisp of *The Naked Civil Servant* fame—a witty, charming, even admirable man despite some of his old-school attitudes about gay people, himself included. Of him it was once said, "England has two queens, and one of them is Quentin Crisp." Sting's full description in his liner notes seems to fit Crisp in every way. If the "Englishman in New York" is in fact Quentin Crisp, then this song is certainly quite a reversal from the touch of homophobia expressed in the earlier Police song "On Any Other Day." This is not altogether surprising since Sting has been outspokenly supportive of gay rights of late.

The music of "Englishman" is in Sting's jazz-lite vein, with a sprightly, skipping tempo. The early part of the song is sung from Crisp's perspective (we'll just go ahead and assume it's Crisp), snippets from one or more conversations that seem to dwell on nothing of importance. He notes how he prefers tea to coffee, how his toast has to be done just so, and how readily you can tell he's English from his accent. Later verses, however, are sung from the narrator's (that is, Sting's) own viewpoint as he sums up the significance of this individual, whom he declares to be a "hero":

It takes a man to suffer ignorance and smile
Be yourself no matter what they say

That's Quentin Crisp through and through. All in all, "Englishman in New York" is a delightful depiction of a gay man, and I'm grateful to Sting for such an uncommonly civilized, mature song as this.

Of course, if it should turn out that this song is *not* about Quentin Crisp, or any other gay person for that matter, won't I look ridiculous?

■ SYLVESTER ■ "YOU MAKE ME FEEL (MIGHTY REAL)" AND "DANCE (DISCO HEAT)" ■

Songwriters:	"You Make Me Feel (Mighty Real)": Sylvester – James "Tip" Wirrick "Dance (Disco Heat)": Eric Robinson – Victor Orsborn
Year of Release:	1978
Original Album:	*Step II*
Chart Performance:	"You Make Me Feel (Mighty Real)" reached #36; "Dance (Disco Heat)" hit #19
Availability:	Original album out of print; available on *Sylvester's Greatest Hits*, CD, CS (Fantasy 4519)

Thirty or forty years from now, when I'm old and gray and living at a pleasant gay retirement home, some nice young men will come up to me and say, "Tell us about disco." I'll pull out an old, long-obsolete disc of music by Sylvester and put it in my antique CD player. And as his gospel-tinged falsetto vocals waft overtop the pulsating dance beat, I'll say, "This, children—*this* was disco!"

Sylvester James Hurd, who succumbed to AIDS-related complications in 1988, was (if you don't count the backsliding Village People) the most successful of the forthrightly gay disco stars of the late seventies. A former drag performer and a self-proclaimed queen, he nonetheless managed to score several Top Forty hits, his two biggest being "You Make Me Feel (Mighty Real)" and "Dance (Disco Heat)" from his best-selling *Step II* album. While neither of these songs have unmistakably "gay" lyrics (unlike some later tunes), Sylvester's performance alone is gay enough. You can hear it in his voice, in his attitude. You can also read it between the lines, as in these words from "Dance (Disco Heat)": "Dancin', total freedom, be yourself and use your feelin'." It's essentially a gay message, but one from which everyone could learn. And, not insignificantly, to which everyone could dance.

A famous incident reported by Boze Hadleigh in *The Vinyl Closet*

The one and only Sylvester (1948–1988). (Photo: Courtesy Fantasy Records.)

summarizes what Sylvester was all about. When his somewhat nervous record company asked him to "butch it up a little" for an album cover, he responded by wearing a flaming red wig, a rhinestone jacket, and high heels to the photo session. The resulting shot appears on the sleeve of his album *Immortal*, where he's lying on his back, kicking up those heels, and laughing uproariously.

Long live the soul, spirit, and music of Sylvester.

▪ SYLVESTER AND PATRICK COWLEY ▪
▪ "MENERGY" ▪

Songwriters:	Patrick Cowley – Marty Blecman
Year of Release:	1981
Original Album:	*Immortal*
Chart Performance:	Neither the single nor the album made the charts
Availability:	Original album out of print; available on Patrick Cowley's *The Ultimate Collection*, CD, CS (Prelude 8023)

"Menergy" is the most memorable of Sylvester's numerous collaborations with gay producer-songwriter-keyboardist Patrick Cowley, who became an early casualty of AIDS in 1982. The supreme example of the high-tech, bass-heavy disco style that came to be known as the "Cowley Sound," "Menergy" originally served as a heady celebration of the communal eroticism of the circa-1980 gay dance-club scene. Now, after more than a decade of AIDS, hearing it again inspires a rush of mixed emotions: nostalgia, envy, joy, sorrow, regret, anger.

Cowley's music creates a virtual soundscape metaphor for sex—percussive thrusts, exploding orgasms, hissing ejaculations. The damn thing's almost obscene. Overtop this action, Sylvester's falsetto lays bare exactly what's going on:

> *The boys in the back room are all gettin' off*
> *Shootin' off energy*
> *We all know the feelin'* . . .
> *Talkin' 'bout menergy*

Menergy—what an ingenious coinage, a perfect summation-euphemism for the totally male sex-play of the notorious backrooms of certain bars in San Francisco, New York, and other gay meccas. And Sylvester's voice is the perfect vehicle for this menergetic message. Much has been made of his gospel roots. In "Menergy" he puts them to good use, confirming his status as the supreme evangelist of gay sexuality in music.

As for the abandon of the backroom—it seemed so vital, so life-affirm-

238

ing then. Now it seems so irresponsible, so deadly. Of course, hindsight is 20/20, and it would be hypocritical of us to judge it too harshly now. I'll grant the fundamentalists one thing and one thing only: amongst them the almost indiscriminate exchange of bodily fluids was never fashionable. We can, however, learn from the past. Play safe, people.

What a difference a decade makes.

▪ TEN YEARS AFTER ▪
▪ "I'D LOVE TO CHANGE THE WORLD" ▪

Songwriter:	Alvin Lee
Year of Release:	1971
Original Album:	*A Space in Time*
Chart Performance:	The single reached #40
Availability:	CD, CS (Chrysalis 21001)

This song, with its well-known, somnambulant, phase-shifted refrain about wanting to change the world but not knowing what to do about it, articulates one man's sense of helplessness and frustration with the state of the universe in which he finds himself. The opening stanza cites a few sources of this fellow's exasperation when he rails against "freaks and hairies, dykes and fairies" and asks, "Tell me, where is sanity?" I'll tell him where sanity is—it's in recognizing such a sentiment for the foul, bigoted screed that it is.

We can't be sure, however, that these words are intended to be taken at face value by vocalist-guitarist Alvin Lee and the other members of Ten Years After. They may not want their listeners to view the narrator as a model of logic and reason. After all, he complains about "freaks and hairies" as well as against gay people, and undoubtedly the long-haired members of Ten Years After would themselves have been considered freaks and hairies by many people back in 1971. And he does come across as an irresponsible, buck-passing wimp, what with the "I don't know what to do, so I'll leave it up to you" spiel. Not exactly a heroic figure.

So, unless I'm badly mistaken, "I'd Love to Change the World" may in fact be a surprisingly pro-gay song, if only in passing. Despite the sheer ugliness of its opening anti-gay slurs, it appears to satirize people who hold such opinions, just as it parodies the attitudes of those who sit around on their duffs and do nothing but complain about the miserable state of the world when they *could* be trying to do something constructive about it. I wonder how many people picked up on that in 1971? I certainly didn't. In fact, a satirical interpretation didn't occur to me until twenty years later. Maybe I'm just slow.

▪ TIMEX SOCIAL CLUB ▪ "RUMORS" ▪

Songwriters:	Marcus Thompson – Michael Marshall – Alex Hill
Year of Release:	1986
Original Album:	*Vicious Rumors*
Chart Performance:	The single reached #8
Availability:	CS, LP (Danya 9645)

It's one-hit wonder time, kiddies. Here's a flashbulb Top Ten single that preaches against the evils of gossip. The narrator bemoans the fact that rumors are constantly being spread by "wicked women." Among the ugly rumors he cites are tidbits about "loose" girls named Tina and Susan, and a hot little item about "Michael," whom people say "must be gay." When the narrator protests, they respond, "If he was straight he wouldn't move that way."

The suggestion that somebody might be gay is treated as though it were a put-down against which one must be defended. Not correct. But isn't it interesting that the song refers to "Michael" when the lead vocalist, who is also one of the authors, is named Michael Marshall? Or did they just *have* to use that name because they had some other, much, *much* more famous Michael in mind?

From a somewhat literary perspective, I also find a delightful extra layer of irony in this song: the narrator loudly professes his distaste for rumor-mongering, but while doing so he repeats a slew of alleged rumors himself—to a nationwide audience of record-buyers, no less. I trust the humor in this was intentional.

▪ TONE LÖC ▪ "FUNKY COLD MEDINA" ▪

Songwriters:	Marvin Young – Matt Dike – Michael Ross
Year of Release:	1989
Original Album:	*Löc-Ed After Dark*
Chart Performance:	The single reached #3
Availability:	CD, CS, LP (Delicious Vinyl 92197)

Maybe I've led a sheltered life, or perhaps I'm too old and/or white, but I have absolutely no idea what "Funky Cold Medina" is, or whether it's even real. Actually, I suspect it's imaginary. It's described as a drink that's "better than any aphrodisiac." But whatever it is, it became the focal point of one of the biggest rap hits of 1989. And it also included what you might call Aerosmith's "Dude (Looks Like a Lady)" revisited—from a rap perspective, of course.

It seems that the character portrayed by Tone Löc is having trouble making it with the girls—a rare admission in the world of rap. Tone Löc's laid-back L.A.-style persona might have something to do with it. At any rate, a much more successful acquaintance tells him his secret: Funky Cold Medina, a drink that apparently inflames the passions like nothing this side of a perpetual-motion vibrator. A little wary, the narrator first tries it out on his dog, who immediately "does the wild thing" on his leg and somehow attracts all the dogs in the neighborhood to his door. It does seem to work.

Emboldened by this display of potency, our hero decides to try it out at a local night spot. There he takes a fancy to a girl named Sheena. She asks him for a drink, and he gives her the mystic elixir. Sure enough, nature takes its course—albeit with a slight detour. They go back to his place, where the truth (which you've probably guessed by now) is revealed: "Sheena was a man!" It should come as no surprise that this revelation is unappreciated by our protagonist. He throws "Sheena" out, exclaiming that he doesn't "fool around with no Oscar Meyer wiener."

Fortunately, aside from Sheena's hasty expulsion itself, there's no suggestion of violence against him, for which I suppose we should be grateful. Rap music is not known for its enlightened attitudes about gay people. Again, maybe it's Tone Löc's casual style that precludes a physical or verbal gay-bashing. In fact, he may even hint, however slightly, that in another age ("this is the eighties") fooling around with Sheena might not have been so unthinkable. Perhaps back in the seventies, pre-AIDS, the incident would have turned out differently. If so, it's ignorant (since HIV can be transmitted by women as well as by men) but intriguing.

The incident with Sheena isn't the end of "Funky Cold Medina," for the narrator has one more adventure, this time with a real live female—one who's a little too eager for matrimony. But he's as unwilling to get married as he was to get it on with a drag queen. So much for Funky Cold Medina. Powerful stuff, but it fails to improve our hero's luck with the ladies.

What I ultimately like about "Funky Cold Medina" is that its rejection of gay sex doesn't come across as cruel, vicious, or self-righteous, as is too often the case in popular music. It's basically a straightforward (beg pardon) assertion that the narrator isn't interested in it, and little else. OK, so the "Oscar Meyer wiener" bit is crude. But I'd rather hear crude but nonviolent assertions of disinterest than bigoted tirades any day. Besides, Tone Löc's persona is so hapless that you can't help but feel for the guy even as you chuckle at his plight. In the final analysis, "Funky Cold Medina" may be a little unfortunate from a gay vantage point, but otherwise relatively harmless.

▪ PUSSY TOURETTE ▪
▪ "FRENCH BITCH" AND "I THINK HE'S GAY" ▪

Songwriter:	Pussy Tourette (both songs)
Year of Release:	1993
Original Album:	*Pussy Tourette in Hi-Fi!*
Chart Performance:	The "French Bitch" single didn't chart, and "I Think He's Gay" wasn't released as a single; the album also failed to chart
Availability:	CD (Feather Boa 93012)

A friend of mine whom I hadn't seen in two years was in town for a brief visit from San Mateo. He was all agog about my work on this book. "Wayne, it's *too* much! I can't *wait* to read it!" he emoted in that way of his, turning anything that offers even the slightest variation from the daily routine into hyperbole. "Oh, I simply *must* see what you have to say about Pussy Tourette!"

"About who?" I wondered aloud.

"Pussy Tourette!" he replied, incredulous that I should have to ask. He paused just long enough to see whether a glimmer of recognition had crept across my face, and seeing none, he continued. "She's *all* the rage back on the coast! She's a drag queen—tacky drag for *days*—who makes this really good music, but sings these *nasty* lyrics like you wouldn't *believe*! It's 'fuck my pussy' this and 'fuck my pussy' that—a *scream*!"

"Sounds interesting."

My friend gave me that look—you know, when somebody dips his chin down until it almost touches his chest and rolls his eyes up to glare at you as if you'd just wet the carpet. *"Interesting?"* He turned to my life's partner, George: "You've been keeping this boy *in* too much with his *books*!" Then back to me: *"Promise* me that you'll find Pussy Tourette!"

So I promised.

Pussy Tourette evokes a host of mixed emotions in me. On the positive side, he's an in-your-face queen with distinctive skills as a melodic, humorous, albeit vulgar singer-songwriter who successfully handles a variety of musical styles. On the negative side, his songs are contaminated by an apparent misogyny that manifests itself as a simultaneous identification with, disdain for, and competition against women in a world in which nearly every sex act has financial ramifications—all of which suggests internalized homophobia. (Hey, people, we've *all* got it to varying degrees, myself included.) The name "Pussy Tourette" as well as the sheer unattractiveness of the performer's chosen form of drag (as opposed to the far more appealing drag of, say, RuPaul) are themselves indicative.

One of the highlights of the album *Pussy Tourette in Hi-Fi!* is the would-be hit single "French Bitch," which appears in two versions: one uncensored and the other "*sans* bad words," in which the obscenities have been replaced with euphemisms. It's fabulously catchy, but it exhibits all of the aforementioned misogynistic tendencies—unless of course you assume that its references to women are actually references to other gay men, though even that doesn't obviate matters much. What a shame that a track of such quality should be marred in this way.

Funnier and far less disturbing is the ultra-high-camp "I Think He's Gay," featuring guest vocalist Deb del Mastro. In this brief "operatic" tune set to pizzicato strings, the soprano singer spends her time bewailing the fact that the man for whom she carries a torch would "rather swim to France than have to kiss a girl." The incongruity of such a "tasteful" singer using less-than-tasteful language ("I hope he's not a fag," she sings in a voice worthy of the Met) provides a marvelous comic edge. The pervasive sense of competition with women remains, though it doesn't carry the unpleasant overtones that it does elsewhere on the album.

One additional caveat: an African-American artist like RuPaul could have gotten away with recording Andy Razaf's classic feast of sexual double-entendres, "If I Can't Sell It." And the European-American Tourette might have, too, if he hadn't felt the need to affect a stereotypical "black" dialect. But in so doing, he maneuvers this otherwise delightful song dangerously close to a parody of black womanhood.

Tell you what—I'll gladly forgive Pussy Tourette all these things if he moves beyond the anti-woman stuff on any subsequent recordings he can manage. He's got a lot of talent and tremendous potential, but I would hate to see it wasted on things that I could never play for my closest female friends.

So in a telephone conversation with my other friend—the one who recommended Pussy Tourette in the first place—I tell him how I feel about the album. You could hear him shaking his head on the other end of the line. "Lighten *up*, girl! Where *is* your sense of humor?"

I haven't the nerve to tell him that I think he's using the word "girl" in a sexist manner.

▪ PETE TOWNSHEND ▪ "ROUGH BOYS" ▪

Songwriter:	Pete Townshend
Year of Release:	1980
Original Album:	*Empty Glass*
Chart Performance:	The single reached #89
Availability:	CD, CS (Atco 32100)

As anybody who loves rock music knows, Pete Townshend is both the avatar of the Who and one of the most insightful, articulate rock musicians ever to tread a stage. It has been through the Who—as on the absolutely seminal album *Who's Next*—that he has found the most powerful expression of his muse. But that hasn't stopped him from pursuing a solo career, both before and after the demise, for all intents and purposes, of his group. And *Empty Glass* is the most successful and satisfying of his solo albums to date. For one thing, it contains his biggest solo hit, the nifty Beach Boys knockoff-with-a-twist, "Let My Love Open the Door."

Far more interesting from our viewpoint, however, is the album's opening number, "Rough Boys." In the liner notes, Townshend dedicates this song to his children, Emma and Minta, and to the Sex Pistols—the latter largely because of the new, fresh, albeit controversial vitality that they were bringing to rock music at the time. But there's more to it than that. As Townshend indicated in a well-publicized and revealing 1991 interview, "Rough Boys" was at least partly inspired by the homosexual aspect of his previously well-hidden bisexuality. The lyrics make it perfectly plain where at least some of his interests lie:

> *Come a little closer*
> *Rough toys under the sheets*

A moment later, Townshend even dares to sing, "I wanna bite and kiss you."

For all of its rapid, explosive musicality (Townshend practically invented power-chord rock), an alcoholic haze permeates the track. Perhaps it's no more than a recognition of the role that booze plays in the song's apparent barroom setting. Or it could be an expression of Townshend's own admitted past problems with drink—which itself may have been linked to his sexual repression. Remember the old cliché: "Gosh, I was really drunk last night. I can't remember a thing."

Townshend's narrator repeatedly begs the rough boys not to abandon him. Instead, he suggests that one of them go home with him, where he hopes to get to know him better: "Gonna get inside you, gonna get inside your bitter mind." What emerges is an intriguing application of physical, sexual imagery to intent that is both physical and psychological. Here's Townshend, the aging rock star, for whom the implications of middle age for a rock musician have supplied a major theme in his music ever since the

Who's superb, underrated *By Numbers* album from 1975. He's smarting after recent criticisms by punk rockers, and he's torn between his defensive disdain and his aggressive fascination for these toughs. He wants to know them, to get inside of them, psychologically and otherwise.

In a remarkable act of honesty, Townshend wears his middle-agedness on his sleeve, rendering himself almost pitiful. He calls himself "pale and weedy," sarcastically making note of the "Hush Puppy shoes" he wears—symbols of safe, secure, complacent comfort that they are. He wants to absorb youth from these rough boys, to revitalize himself with their energy and sexuality, to understand himself by understanding them. And he wants to make love to them, not only to satisfy his lust, not even merely to satisfy his curiosity, but as a way of staving off death. "I very nearly missed you," he sings. Townshend's comrade from the Who, drummer Keith Moon, did indeed miss the height of the punk rock movement, dying before his and Townshend's musical children, the punkers—who had drawn inspiration from the Who but, like typical children, rebelled against their elders—had come into their own.

The promotional video for "Rough Boys" places Townshend in a bar, playing his guitar while shoving up against and being shoved around by the pool-playing young toughs he's singing to. It's a virtual ballet of aggression, figuratively dancing around the homoerotic roots of the song and translating it into horsing around, like football players wrestling with each other in the locker room. Before Townshend talked about his bisexuality, I always wondered about what was going on in that video. I don't wonder about it anymore.

▪ PETE TOWNSHEND ▪ "AND I MOVED" ▪

Songwriter:	Pete Townshend
Year of Release:	1980
Original Album:	*Empty Glass*
Chart Performance:	Not released as a single, but the album reached #5
Availability:	CD, CS (Atco 32100)

In a mid-eighties interview with Bill Flanagan, Pete Townshend said that he wrote "And I Moved" for a woman—Bette Midler, to be specific—but decided to keep the song for himself. He also decided not to change the pronouns. As a result, "And I Moved" comes across as a decidedly gay song. Townshend discounted that impression at the time, stating that it "wasn't entirely sexual," but in light of his more recent coming out as a bisexual, a homosexual interpretation seems more or less undeniable.

In essence, "And I Moved" is about the narrator's discovery of a male voyeur at his window. The voyeur quickly becomes an intruder, silently entering the home. And by the sound of it, that's not all he enters. The movement alluded to in the title is the narrator's movement *toward* the intruder, not *away* from him as one might expect under such circumstances. A seduction scene ensues. "His hands felt like ice exciting," sings Townshend, "as he laid me back just like an empty dress."

Townshend told Flanagan that "And I Moved" was about surrendering oneself to another and the prerequisite trust between people in order for that to occur. While some may argue that this still doesn't necessarily mean that the song is "gay," I would contend that it certainly isn't necessarily *not* gay, either. And of the various possibilities—gay, non-gay, or asexual—which is the least contrived?

What it all boils down to is the fact that, when it's sung by a man in this way, you'd have to try awfully hard to read anything *other* than a homoerotic encounter into "And I Moved."

▪ 2 LIVE CREW ▪ "S&M" ▪

Songwriters:	The 2 Live Crew
Year of Release:	1989
Original Album:	*Move Somethin'*
Chart Performance:	Not released as a single, the album didn't chart
Availability:	CD, CS, LP (Luke 101)

From the rap group that would soon ignite a national censorship debate and inspire the arrests of record store personnel, we have a track ostensibly about sadomasochism, but actually about the solipsism of the narrator. "S&M" is unbelievably pornographic for a pop song, a virtual catalog of sexual vulgarity. It invites "bull daggers," "fags," "sissies," and "asshole fuckers" as well as a wide assortment of other more heterosexually oriented persons (described in equally prurient terms) to join together in an orgiastic free-for-all garnished by whips, the sole purpose of which is to satisfy the narrator's seemingly insatiable lust. "Bring your cock-suckin' friends!" he cries in the refrain.

Undoubtedly the chief goal here is to shock and titillate the audience out of its disposable income. And like the "whores" that they constantly put down (even as they make use of them, at least lyrically), the main product being sold is sex. Exploitation of this sort may be a running theme in "gay images" in popular music, but nowhere else does that exploitation take on a more palpable quality than it does here. This isn't mere libertinism. It's unbridled disdain, frightening in its intensity, for the basic humanity of other people.

▪ U2 ▪ "ONE" ▪

Songwriters:	Bono – U2
Year of Release:	1992
Original Album:	*Achtung Baby*
Chart Performance:	The single reached #10
Availability:	CD, CS (Island 314-510347)

U2's "One" provides a dramatic contrast to Elton John's "The Last Song." Both lyrics are written from the perspective of a young gay man with AIDS talking to his father. But whereas "The Last Song" is conciliatory and comforting, "One" is angry and confrontational. Nevertheless, both songs arrive at soberly optimistic conclusions.

Lead vocalist and chief lyricist Bono designated that the profits from the sales of the "One" single should benefit AMFAR (the American Foundation for AIDS Research). And the song itself, with its dark, brooding melody, is one of the most moving ruminations on troubled family relationships I've ever heard. When the AIDS-stricken narrator growls to his father in Bono's harsh tenor, "Did I leave a bad taste in your mouth?" and adds one of several scathing accusations,

> You act like you never had love
> And you want me to go without

it's not hard to visualize the kind of highly charged, emotional turmoil that AIDS can inspire. But "One" is by no means a work of despair. Rather, it evolves into an affirmation of love as Bono proclaims that "we get to carry each other." (Note the "get"; it's a *privilege* to help another person.) By song's end, he's literally shrieking about "one love" in a simultaneous cry of anguish and joy, a celebration of the oneness of humanity in the face of love and death. Not bad for a bunch of apparently straight young Irishmen—though perhaps not so surprising when you consider that throughout their career they've always been outspoken about their activist-oriented, socially conscious brand of liberal Christianity.

Moreover, the video for "One" makes for a fascinating study in the ways in which marvelous good intentions can become sullied by reality. The stark black-and-white video that was originally filmed featured the four members of U2 dressed alternately in "regular" clothes and in various degrees of drag, brazenly mixing stereotypically "male" and "female" looks. But when the band, their management, and executives at their record company viewed the completed video, they asked the video's director, Anton Corbijn, to "tone down" the drag imagery. Ultimately, it was eliminated altogether. With little left of the original, they decided to shoot two new videos, one of which was dominated by the image of Bono singing directly to the camera while seated at a table in a smoky New York nightspot. This was the video that was shown on MTV during the single's chart run.

It would appear that the reasons for the suppression of the original "drag video" were two-fold. From Bono's point of view (as related to Adam Block of *The Advocate*), there was the fear that the drag would perpetuate stereotypes about gay men in general and people with AIDS in particular, maybe even hurting the cause of AIDS-awareness. But, no doubt, there was also the fear that such a video would do irreparable harm to U2's career—in much the same way, perhaps, that the drag video for "I Want to Break Free" may have put the kibosh on Queen in the United States for the better part of a decade, alienating many of their fans. Still, Bono seems to feel some regret at what occurred. "It's a powerful video," Block quotes him as saying. "It's amazing. And we suppressed it."

Interestingly, months after "One" had ceased selling as a single and the *Achtung Baby* album no longer floated near the top of the charts, the original video finally made occasional appearances on MTV—probably since hurting record sales was no longer a major consideration. But even if those images had never surfaced, U2's "One" would still stand as *the* most powerful, evocative song yet to appear in the nineties.

▪ VALENTINO ▪ "I WAS BORN THIS WAY" ▪

Songwriters:	Bunny Jones – Phil Spierer
Year of Release:	1975
Original Album:	Not released on any album
Chart Performance:	The single didn't chart
Availability:	Out of print (Motown/Gaiee single 90001)

With this obscure disco single, Valentino (whose real name was Charles Harris) became one of the first singers to come out as a gay man on record —that is, to say without equivocation the words "I'm gay." The lyrics, written by a woman, independent producer Bunny Jones, are about as direct as you can ask for:

> Yes, I'm gay
> 'Tain't a fault, 'tis a fact
> I was born this way

Reportedly intended as a gay anthem—albeit a highly danceable one—its distribution rights were picked up by Motown. One might have thought that the support of such a record-industry powerhouse would have guaranteed the single a real shot at commercial success. Perhaps it *would* have if Motown had truly supported it. Instead, Motown did next to nothing to promote the record, even within the large gay disco audience, and it quickly faded into near-oblivion.

Two years later, in 1977, a singer named Carl Bean released a slick

Philadelphia-style cover of the song, again on Motown. It proved a bigger hit in gay discos, but suffered the same fate as the original in the mainstream media. Bean's version is especially noteworthy, however, as Sylvester's professed inspiration for entering show business as an openly gay performer. And anything that can claim even *remote* responsibility for the career of Sylvester can claim a high honor indeed.

But when I said that "I Was Born This Way" faded into near-oblivion, I meant it. Just *try* to find a copy of either version in your local used record stores. Maybe even go so far as to contact businesses that sell hard-to-find discs to avid collectors. Lotsa luck.

▪ VELVET UNDERGROUND ▪ "SISTER RAY" ▪

Songwriters: Lou Reed – Sterling Morrison – John Cale – Maureen Tucker
Year of Release: 1968
Original Album: *White Light/White Heat*
Chart Performance: Not released as a single, but the album reached #199
Availability: CD, CS (Verve 825119)

Perhaps the less I say about this the better. Two generations of rock critics have gone ga-ga over the Velvet Underground for their daring forays into uncharted lyrical territory (drug addiction, unconventional sex, etc.) as well as their pioneering exploration of the musical potential of out-and-out noise. The group did spawn Lou Reed and John Cale—as things would turn out, two important rock artists—and proved highly influential. But as far as I'm concerned, their work seems as vacuous and transparent as the self-conscious pop imagery favored by their champion and mentor, Andy Warhol. A panel full of multiple images of Marilyn Monroe may be interesting the first time you see it, but after that it has nothing more than decorative value. And decorative value is something that the Velvet Underground certainly *didn't* have.

"Sister Ray" is reportedly about a gay and/or transvestite heroin dealer, which is why it merits inclusion in this book. Its garbled lyrics include a much-repeated drug reference about "searchin' for my mainline," and an almost as frequently repeated reference to oral sex, "Too busy suckin' on a ding-dong." (You heard right.) Again and again Reed sings, "Aw, just like Sister Ray said," but I can't tell what it is that Sister Ray is supposed to have said.

The song's "plot," if you can call it that, seems to have something to do with a sailor who's just been screwed or shot—perhaps both. In the one truly inspired moment of the song, Reed's persona expresses his concern about this, worrying that it might "stain the carpet." That's *dark* camp, baby. But, since most of the lyrics are unintelligible, I can't make out much more than that.

Then there's the music. The *White Light/White Heat* album is said to have been recorded in a single day, and I don't doubt it. Like the rest of the album, "Sister Ray" sounds muddy, distorted, and unfocused. It rambles on in its abrasive way for approximately seventeen agonizing, interminable minutes. That explains why some critics call it an "epic," as if seventeen minutes of redundant, poorly played three-chord rock qualifies as anything but an epic *bore*.

When all of the noise has passed, you finally realize that the Velvet Underground wasn't half as pretentious as all of the critics who continue to swallow this stuff whole, mistaking amateurishness for honesty, confusing the novel with the valuable, misinterpreting the facile as the profound.

▪ VILLAGE PEOPLE ▪
▪ "SAN FRANCISCO (YOU'VE GOT ME)" ▪

Songwriters:	Jacques Morali–Henri Belolo–Peter Whitehead–Phil Hurtt
Year of Release:	1977
Original Album:	*Village People*
Chart Performance:	The single didn't chart, and the album reached #54
Availability:	Original album out of print; available on *Village People's Greatest Hits*, CD, CS, LP (Rhino 70167)

Looking back on it after more than a decade, it's hard to believe that the Village People even happened. For a short while, during the height of the disco craze, they were almost too good to be true (sociologically, not necessarily aesthetically). The late producer Jacques Morali (who succumbed to AIDS in 1991) wanted to produce dance music specifically emerging from and designed for gay audiences. He assembled a group of male singers and dancers (the ad that he placed to attract auditions specified that applicants should ideally have moustaches, which at the time were all but *de rigueur* in the gay community), dressed them in hypermasculine-iconographic-fetishistic regalia (biker, cop, cowboy, American Indian, soldier, construction worker), and had them record a batch of songs that he had written in collaboration with his business associates Henri Belolo, Phil Hurtt, and Peter Whitehead. The New York-based Morali named his group the "Village People," after Greenwich Village, the center of the Big

The Village People at the peak of their popularity, 1978: (clockwise from top center) Victor
Willis, Alexander Briley, Glenn Hughes, Felipe Rose, David Hodo, Randy Jones. (Photo:
Casablanca Records. Michael Ochs Archives.)

Apple's gay subculture. The result: for about a year, the Village People reigned as the king-queens (reportedly all but one of them were indeed gay) of the disco phenomenon, a brief but blazing worldwide success virtually ubiquitous on radio and television. You figure it out.

"San Francisco," the People's first big dance club hit, was a disco hymn to the city that during the 1970s had become synonymous with gay liberation. A less popular but no less indicative song from the same album was "Fire Island." This came before mainstream success, so everybody who heard these songs knew *exactly* what they were about. But how could anybody have predicted what followed?

▪ VILLAGE PEOPLE ▪ "MACHO MAN" ▪

Songwriters:	Jacques Morali – Henri Belolo – Victor Willis – Peter Whitehead
Year of Release:	1978
Original Album:	*Macho Man*
Chart Performance:	The single reached #25
Availability:	Original album out of print; available on *Village People's Greatest Hits*, CD, CS, LP (Rhino 70167)

Everybody got the joke; it's just that some people got the joke a little better than others. Here are these six cartoonish caricatures of maleness (portrayed by Alexander Briley, Glenn Hughes, Randy Jones, David Hodo, Felipe Rose, and lead singer Victor Willis) singing and dancing around on a stage to this paean to masculinity:

> *Macho, macho man*
> *I've got to be a macho man*

It was like a drag show from the anti-matter universe, complete with proud, narcissistic references to moustaches, muscles, and chest hair. And it came with a powerful element of sexuality to boot, what with the song's earnestly repeated, celebratory declaration, "Body, my body, it's so hot, my body!" A cartoon, to be sure, but an overtly sexy cartoon.

Everyone who heard and saw it knew it was a put-on, an absolute scream. Everybody likes a good laugh—and, in the disco era, especially a good laugh that you could dance, dance, dance to. So, with this single, the Village People began to take off as a mainstream act. But most non-gay people weren't fully conscious of just what was going on. Those who read some of the magazine articles about the group discovered their gay origins and learned about the symbolic significance of the particular costumes they wore. But the word "gay" was rarely mentioned on radio or television in connection with the Village People. So, while most people understood

252

that it was a joke, they didn't understand *the* joke. Much of the United States and the rest of the Western world began to go on a gay roller-coaster ride, and they didn't even know it. As Village People "construction worker" David Hodo once put it in a *Rolling Stone* interview, "We're sticking our tongues in society's cheek."

If only more of society had bought the album or, having bought it, paid more attention to the words tripping off those tongues.

▪ VILLAGE PEOPLE ▪ "I AM WHAT I AM" ▪

Songwriters:	Jacques Morali – Henri Belolo – Victor Willis – Peter Whitehead
Year of Release:	1978
Original Album:	*Macho Man*
Chart Performance:	Not released as a single, but the album reached #24
Availability:	Out of print (Casablanca 7096)

The *Macho Man* album contained a number of songs that must have tipped off a sizable portion of those "straight" people who bothered to buy it instead of the single. The track "Macho Man" segued, in typical disco fashion, directly into the most unambiguous of the lot, "I Am What I Am." This isn't the big number from Jerry Herman's musical *La Cage Aux Folles*, which came several years later, but rather a somewhat defensive assertion of technically unspoken (they didn't say "gay") but otherwise forthright gayness:

> *I did not choose the way I am*
> *I am what I am*

A veritable catalog of assertive, gay-positive truisms ensued, such as "No one has the right to choose my love for me" and "To love is not a sin!" Anyone who has decried the Village People as a phenomenon of the closet —as, remarkably enough, some gay journalists have—has forgotten songs like this. Yes, as we shall see, the closet came later in the brief story of their success, but when they recorded "I Am What I Am," their only closet was the one in which they hung up their macho costumes after the last encore.

Songs titled "Key West" and, of all things, "Sodom and Gomorrah" also appeared on the *Macho Man* album. And it contained a medley of the old pop classics "Just a Gigolo" and "I Ain't Got Nobody." This was seven years before heavy-metal bad boy David Lee Roth had a hit record with the exact same medley. Does this mean that Roth is a closet Village People fan?

▪ VILLAGE PEOPLE ▪ "Y.M.C.A." ▪

Songwriters: Jacques Morali – Henri Belolo – Victor Willis
Year of Release: 1978
Original Album: *Cruisin'*
Chart Performance: The single reached #2
Availability: Original album out of print; available on *Village People's Greatest Hits*, CD, CS, LP (Rhino 70167)

Although it came after "Macho Man," this was the song that immortalized the Village People. How could *anybody* not have grasped the double meaning of the chorus?

> *Y.M.C.A., it's fun to stay at the Y.M.C.A.*
> *They have everything for young men to enjoy*
> *You can hang out with all the boys*

And there was much more in the same double-entendre-laden vein. Admittedly, most people probably didn't know that urban Y.M.C.A.'s have long been notorious in the gay community as dens of man-to-man sex. But did people really think that this song merely extolled the innocent virtues of the Y.M.C.A., and that's all? Maybe not. Perhaps large numbers of record-buyers were fully cognizant of the song's gay connotations and didn't give a damn—in fact, they got the joke and liked it. In that case, were they laughing *with* gay people or *at* them? I'm sure it varied from one case to another. One thing to keep in mind, however: most strongly homophobic people didn't care for disco music, period, so the "gayness" of this song either slipped right past them or served to strengthen their dislike of an already hated musical genre. (Remember the "Disco Sucks" motto? Never for an instant have I thought that the choice of verb was an accident. I cringe whenever I hear a woman or gay man say that such-and-such "sucks." Don't they realize how sexist and homophobic that insult is?)

By the way, legend has it that certain Y.M.C.A. officials liked this song so much that they wanted to arrange for its use in their promotions—that is, until certain other officials who were a little more knowledgeable about such things pointed out the gay aspects of the song and of the Village People in general. I have no idea whether this story is true, but it's too good to let pass without a mention.

And an update: In the summer of 1993, I had dinner at the Hard Rock Cafe in Orlando, Florida. For those of you unfamiliar with the ambiance of the Hard Rock Cafe chain, suffice it to say that delicious meals are served to you accompanied by rock music blaring nonstop at deafening levels. On this particular occasion, most of the songs came and went with little notice from the crowd. But when the deejay played "Y.M.C.A." the whole place erupted into a laughing, clapping sing-a-long, with diners ritualistically spelling out the letters of the title with their arms above their heads. This scene astonished me, suggesting nostalgia, campiness, and the sheer joy of dance, all rolled into one.

Gay culture strikes again.

▪ VILLAGE PEOPLE ▪ "IN THE NAVY" ▪

Songwriters:	Jacques Morali – Henri Belolo – Victor Willis
Year of Release:	1979
Original Album:	*Go West!*
Chart Performance:	The single reached #3
Availability:	Original album out of print; available on *Village People's Greatest Hits*, CD, CS, LP (Rhino 70167)

I promise this is the last Village People song I'll talk about.

By the time our boys in butch released what would become their third and final Top Forty hit, "In the Navy," they were well on their way to being totally compromised by success in the broader (read "heterosexual") marketplace. "In the Navy" boasted far fewer gay double-entendres than "Y.M.C.A.," after which it was in every other way closely (too closely) modeled. There was a recurring chant—

> *They want you!*
> *They want you!*
> *They want you as a new recruit!*

—which sounds like an ironic twist on the frequent accusation of homophobes that gay people try to "recruit" young people. And one line of the chorus—the one about how you can "join your fellow man" in the Navy —is mildly ambiguous. (OK, *more* than mildly.) But, by and large, "In the Navy" took a clear step in the direction that would culminate in the dreadful 1980 film *Can't Stop the Music*, in which the Village People would be bowdlerized of all gay connections aside from a few teasing shots of naked male flesh during the film's rendition of "Y.M.C.A." The movie represents one of the most insipid, disgusting sell-outs in the history of gayness in popular music.

Incidentally, history (or historical rumor) is said to have repeated itself with "In the Navy." This time it was apparently some U.S. Navy officials who seriously considered using this song in their recruiting campaigns until someone pointed out what the Village People were (or at least had been) all about. Again, I can find no absolute verification as to the veracity of this story. But I do vaguely remember some television show in which the Village People lip-synched (I always want to say "lip-*sank*") "In the Navy" on the deck of an actual aircraft carrier or some other large naval vessel. Presumably the U.S. Navy agreed to this TV appearance before—or in spite of—any knowledge of "gay readings" into the song.

▪ THE WHO ▪ "FIDDLE ABOUT" ▪

Songwriter:	John Entwistle
Year of Release:	1969
Original Album:	*Tommy*
Chart Performance:	Not released as a single, but the album reached #4
Availability:	CD, CS, LP (MCA 10005)

Forgive the turn of phrase, but let's get one thing perfectly straight. The character of Uncle Ernie in the rock opera (and now Broadway musical) *Tommy* is a child molester—not your basic, guy-next-door homosexual, despite the fact that the object of his sexual interest happens in this case to be of the same sex. Any respectable psychologist will tell you that the majority of forced sexual activity occurs with children of the opposite sex from that of their molesters and that girls are far more frequent victims than boys. "Fiddle About" was written by the Who's bassist, John Entwistle, who's always had a knack for turning out the occasional perverse song about spiders, homicidal wives, and the like. It fits right in—a regrettable, possibly gratuitous, but understandable part of *Tommy*'s plot.

When the film version was made, its creators made matters even worse by showing Uncle Ernie (portrayed by the late Who drummer Keith Moon) drooling over *Gay News*, Great Britain's only major gay publication at the time, apparently just to illustrate how truly sick and disgusting he really is. This is nothing but vicious heterosexist propaganda, and the Who's leader, Pete Townshend, should be ashamed of himself for allowing such an image to appear in the movie (presuming he had any say in the matter).

Of course, there are some other tracks in the rock corpus that deal with child molestation, too, such as Steely Dan's sickly amusing "Everyone's Gone to the Movies" from *Katy Lied*. But these should not be confused with songs dealing with gay people. I just mention them here to keep everybody on their toes about what is and isn't "gay."

▪ THE WHO ▪ "HELPLESS DANCER" ▪

Songwriter: Pete Townshend
Year of Release: 1973
Original Album: *Quadrophenia*
Chart Performance: Not released as a single, but the album reached #2
Availability: CD, CS, LP (MCA 6895)

In *Quadrophenia*, the Who's second "rock opera" ("rock oratorio" would probably be more accurate), songwriter-guitarist Pete Townshend tells a rather confused story about a rather confused young man, who apparently possesses four distinct personalities modeled after the four members of the Who. Each member-personality has his own musical theme. Lead vocalist Roger Daltry's theme, "Helpless Dancer," describes someone who is being emotionally overwhelmed by the multitude of problems that surround him, especially rampant poverty. It includes the following lines, spit out by Daltry right in the middle of this list of troubles:

> *If you complain you disappear*
> *Just like the lesbians and queers*

I'm not sure how to interpret this. It may be an acknowledgment of how lesbians and gay men (unfortunately called "queers" here—definitely uncool in 1973—but the demands of rhyme must be met, you know) are among the oppressed, any of whom may suddenly disappear at the hands of a hostile society or government. On the other hand, Townshend might have been suggesting that homosexuals themselves are among the problems he cites.

A clue may lie just a few lines later, when Daltry sings about being "beaten up by blacks, who . . . got the sack." Here "blacks" are clearly described as both victims and oppressors. Perhaps a similarly ambiguous role is meant for the "lesbians and queers." In light of the fact that Townshend admitted his bisexuality to an interviewer in 1991—nearly two decades after this song was written—these lines may simply express his confusion and internal struggle over his own sexual identity at the time. At least I hope that's what they are.

■ TOM WILSON WEINBERG ■ "GAY NAME GAME" ■

Songwriter:	Tom Wilson Weinberg
Year of Release:	1979
Original Album:	*Gay Name Game*
Chart Performance:	Not released as a single, and the album didn't chart
Availability:	CD, CS, LP (Aboveground 101)

Though he's probably too modest to do so, Tom Wilson Weinberg can rightly claim status as one of America's premier openly gay singer-songwriters. His first two albums, *Gay Name Game* and *All-American Boy*, were recorded when he went simply by the name Tom Wilson. And they marvelously exemplify the way in which he carved a niche for himself as something of the gay answer to another Tom—Lehrer, to be specific. (And if you're not sure who Tom Lehrer is, do the titles "Vatican Rag," "Poisoning Pigeons in the Park," or "Masochism Tango" ring a bell? If not, you poor, satirically deprived thing, you!) Like Lehrer, Wilson Weinberg often displays a flair for combining neo-vaudevillian melodies and arrangements with outlandishly clever rhymes to create spicy and frequently hilarious social commentary.

Take the title song of the *Gay Name Game* album, where Wilson Weinberg educates his listeners as to the many lesbians and gay men (ranging from the obvious—Gertrude Stein and Oscar Wilde—to the indisputable yet unexpected—"some of the troops at Valley Forge") who have played and continue to play important roles in our history and culture. At the same time, he satirizes the almost obsessive need (inspired by social repression) that gay people have shown through the years to engage in precisely this kind of name-dropping. Affecting a nasal voice that heightens the almost carnival-like atmosphere of the song, Wilson Weinberg regales us with such inspired rhymes as "Radclyffe Hall" and "Gore Vidal." Utterly irresistible.

Gay Name Game boasts a number of other outstanding songs, most notably "The Love That Dare Not Speak Its Name" (with more delightfully flawed rhymes, such as "pubescence"-"lessons" and "discovered"-"mother'd"), the Anita Bryant-dishing "Second Runner-Up," and the truly quirky yet emotionally stirring "Lesbian Seagull." Together, these and other tracks make *Gay Name Game* an incontestable landmark in the field of "gay music." If you can find it, buy it. An auspicious debut, to say the least.

Tom Wilson Weinberg, the dean of American "gay music." (Photo: Bill Addison. Courtesy Aboveground Records.)

▪ TOM WILSON WEINBERG ▪ "TONS OF VINYL" ▪

Songwriter: Tom Wilson Weinberg
Year of Release: 1982
Original Album: *All-American Boy*
Chart Performance: Not released as a single, and the album didn't
                     chart
Availability: CD, CS, LP (Aboveground 102)

Since in this book I've repeatedly invoked the questionable term "gay music"—questionable because, to paraphrase a gay comedian I heard years ago, is "gay music" music that's attracted to music of the same sex?—I feel it's only right to also call your attention to "Tons of Vinyl," Tom Wilson Weinberg's testimonial about what it's like to be a sub-genre artist with a specialized audience. The narrative finds him searching, without luck, for his albums in a well-known nationwide "chain" record store. Meanwhile, he's becoming increasingly annoyed at the music playing over the store's system—music that he seems to consider inferior.

With unintentional irony, Wilson Weinberg mentions the B-52's as one of the acts whose music is being played in the store and quotes a line from one of their most popular early songs, "Planet Claire." Little did he or anyone else know that, only a few years later, the guitarist and original guiding light of the B-52's, Ricky Wilson, would die of complications from AIDS. Compounding the tragedy, it was only shortly thereafter that the B-52's finally broke through their "cult band" status and became a big-time success with their *Cosmic Thing* LP. And not too long after that, in 1992, the surviving male members of the group publicly came out as gay in the pages of *QW* magazine.

Getting back to Wilson Weinberg, it's unfortunate that the music for "Tons of Vinyl" and most of the remainder of *All-American Boy* fails to match the high standards set by his debut album. (Hey, the sophomore slump happens to the best of 'em. Just ask Wilson Phillips.) For one thing, Wilson Weinberg and his cohorts tried to make the instrumentation and arrangements of the songs more sophisticated, but generally succeeded only in making them sound somewhat cheesy. They should have remembered one of the cardinal rules of pop music:

A synthesizer in the wrong hands is a deadly weapon.
Deadly to the music, that is.

But all was not lost. *All-American Boy* did have a few good tracks, most notably "He Likes Me." And Wilson Weinberg went on to write, produce, and often perform in highly acclaimed musicals (well, they've been highly acclaimed in the gay community), *The Ten Percent Revue* and, more recently, *Get Used to It!*, which are available on CD and cassette from Aboveground Records—though perhaps not in most nationwide chain stores. And, of course, you can always go back and listen to *Gay Name Game*.

Remember: if you go looking for Tom Wilson Weinberg's music, the first two albums were by Tom Wilson, without the Weinberg. Gee, how such a simple name-change complicates matters!

▪ FRANK ZAPPA ▪ "BOBBY BROWN" ▪

Songwriter: Frank Zappa
Year of Release: 1979
Original Album: *Sheik Yerbouti*
Chart Performance: Not released as a single, but album reached #21
Availability: CD, CS, LP (Rykodisc 40162)

I can take a joke. It's just that some jokes are so nasty that they're not funny anymore.

Sometimes it seems as though hardly anything in this world—ranging from hippies to "straight" (that is, "non-hip") culture, from fifties rock and roll to the Beatles, from "Jewish princesses" to Catholics—escaped the late Frank Zappa's consistently controversial, startlingly prolific satirical sights. So no one should be surprised that gay people also came under his unscrupulous scrutiny. "Bobby Brown" (retitled "Bobby Brown Goes Down" on recent reissues) is one of several Zappa pokes in our direction. The only trouble is, this song distinguishes itself as one of the most ignorant, repulsive songs mentioned in this book—and considering the competition, that's saying a lot.

The title character is a handsome, egotistical bisexual (despite the fact that he refers to himself as a "homo") who's looking forward to his upcoming date with a pretty cheerleader (of the female variety) whom he's contemplating raping. (Yes, *raping.*) He also tells of having had sex once with "a dyke named Freddie" who is herself a vicious caricature of the clichéd "castrating bitch." Bobby describes sex with her as like having his balls in a vice. Meanwhile, he disdains "women's liberation," enjoys S&M and "golden showers," and leads a thoroughly hedonistic lifestyle in which he cares nothing for anyone or anything other than himself. Repeated at the end of the track is the assertion that "Bobby Brown goes down"—that is, he's a cocksucker and/or muffdiver—used, as you might expect, as an expression of contempt.

In short, "Bobby Brown" is a wretched, abhorrent portrayal of a stereotypical bisexual, or perhaps even an out-and-out gay man who simply doesn't mind screwing women now and again.

For more about Frank Zappa's apparent attitude problems, read on.

▪ FRANK ZAPPA ▪ "HE'S SO GAY" ▪

Songwriter:	Frank Zappa
Year of Release:	1984
Original Album:	*Thing-Fish*
Chart Performance:	Neither the single nor the album made the charts
Availability:	CD, CS, LP (Rykodisc 10020)

Another of Zappa's sarcastic, heavy-handed attempts at humor, though thankfully not quite so vile as the last.

Musically, "He's So Gay" is a devastatingly acute parody of the Village People, only that it's about five years too late. (The last V.P. hit was in 1979.) The choral vocals (probably Zappa multi-tracked) are deep and self-consciously "masculine," set to a purposefully hackneyed synthesizer-generated disco backdrop (augmented by hand-claps), with Bee-Gees-as-screaming-queens falsetto background punctuations thrown in for good measure. As for the lyrics, they start out like this:

> *He's so gay, he's very, very gay*
> *He's so gay, and he likes to be that way*

Nothing you can argue with so far. As the song continues, you realize that Zappa must have had an awful lot of gay friends—either that or he did a great deal of specialized research—to be so well acquainted with so many aspects of certain gay subcultures. But, then again, I guess anyone who paid much attention to the Village People might have picked up on a lot of this. For example, he goes all-out on the matter of role-playing, noting "rubber every night" and the desire to be "a cowboy for a day." On it goes with assorted references to roller-skating, S&M ("Maybe he wants a little spankie"), "daddy" roles, fetishistic shaving, and "water sports." It's all somewhat stereotypical, but nothing to get upset about. It really doesn't seem homophobic—yet.

The most unpleasant lines come near the end, when Zappa allows himself to indulge in some heterosexist paranoia. He worries about the way gay people seem to "rule the city," which seems thoroughly dominated by them both politically and stylistically. We're told that "every leather boy's a prince," and we're warned that perhaps with time everyone will become gay—an assertion as ignorant as it is revolting.

But then you wonder. Zappa probably knew that most of this song is repellent, so to what extent did he *want* his listeners to consider it repellent as well? Can anybody really be so stupid to think that they might "become gay" because of gay social influence? In a word, yes. Could Zappa therefore have been satirizing his own satire? Was he merely making fun of gay people or was he also making fun of people who make fun of gay people? Or am I giving him way too much credit? Is "He's So Gay" facile, bigoted crap and nothing more? *I'm so confused! Aaargh!*

Ah, but there's one last line in the song, sung oddly enough in a doo-wop style: "Do you really want to hurt me?" So, if the Village People schtick was five years passé, at least Zappa could be up-to-date through his reference to Culture Club. After all, Boy George was just about the biggest—and gayest—pop culture phenomenon on earth in 1984, when "He's So Gay" was released. A final, unsubtle dig.

Like so much of Zappa's work, "He's So Gay" is quite accomplished for what is essentially a one-joke parody. I'm sure his legion of cult-followers appreciated it tremendously, many of them considering it a right-on put-down of faggots. That I sorely regret.

■ FRANK AND MOON ZAPPA ■ "VALLEY GIRL" ■

Songwriters: Frank Zappa – Moon Zappa
Year of Release: 1982
Original Album: *Ship Arriving Too Late to Save a Drowning Witch*
Chart Performance: The single reached #32
Availability: CD, CS (Barking Pumpkin 74235)

There aren't many comedy or novelty tunes that can still make me smile after the first several listenings, but this—which raised Valley Girl consciousness beyond its point of origin in Southern California—is one of them. This record earns its place here because Moon Zappa's Valley Girl character mentions an English teacher who "like plays with all his rings" and "like flirts with all the guys." She also says of him—

> He's like Mr. Bu-Fu
> We're talking Lord God King Bu-Fu

—which she considers to be "like so gross." (For the benefit of the less worldly among us, "Bu-Fu" is short for "butt fuck" and, as such, is a common term of contempt in some circles.) This may appear to be terribly homophobic—and it is—but this Valley Girl clearly serves as an exemplar of San Fernando Valley provincialism. We can safely assume that her attitudes were less than ideal in the minds of father and daughter Zappa, who were, after all, ridiculing her and her ilk. Of course, Frank Zappa never showed reticence about ridiculing anybody, including gay people, so we can at least take comfort in being the equal-opportunity butts (so to speak) of his sometimes brilliant, sometimes sophomoric jokes.

But, then again, there's the heritage of "Bobby Brown" to look back on. If it weren't for that deeply offensive track from 1979, neither "He's So Gay" nor "Valley Girl" would bother me in the least. Taken together, however, they paint a very suggestive and disturbing portrait of Zappa's possible feelings about gay people.

263

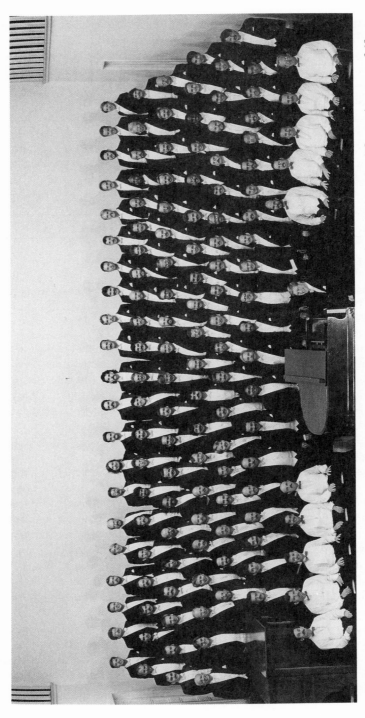

The San Francisco Gay Men's Chorus, 1993. (Photo: Courtesy Golden Gate Performing Arts, Inc.) See review on p. 269.

▪ SOME ADDITIONAL SONGS AND PERFORMERS ▪

Ambrosia — "Dance with Me, George (Chopin's Plea)"
This exploits the public's dual fear and fascination regarding homosexuality without actually delivering. The George in question is George Sand, female author and Frederic Chopin's paramour. A virtual pun-fest, the humor of which lies in its pretending to be something it's not.

Angry Samoans — "Homo-sexual"
They're angry all right. But since these guys are often regarded as satirists—the subject of their satire being the inflated nihilism and chip-on-their-shoulder attitudes of certain branches of the punk movement—I'm a wee bit perplexed by a track like this, which seems to carry a streak of uncertainty within its anger. "I'm like you," they sing. OK, but if you hate yourself, that's no compliment.

Army of Lovers — "Crucified"
If there were no such word as "camp," they would've had to invent it for this product of Sweden—especially for the over-the-top video with its relentless parody of neoclassical imagery. And you *do* know the significance of the group's name, don't you? If not, check your Greek history. Whoever said that the Swedes were dull?

Bananarama — "I Heard a Rumour"
A tribute to heterosexual high-camp sensibilities, which would be unthinkable if it weren't for the gay influence. I mean, what *else* can you make of that chorus line of hunky, shirtless, glisteningly sweaty numbers in baseball caps and shorts? Besides, this song gives us proof positive that disco never died; it simply adopted a lower profile in the face of a homophobic onslaught.

Buju Banton — "Boom Bye Bye"
A reggae dance track which earned its allotted fifteen minutes of notoriety by advocating that gay men be shot in the head, execution-style. "Boom Bye Bye"—get it? I wish a plague of gout on everyone who enjoyed dancing to this one.

Ben Gay and the Silly Savages — "The Ballad of Ben Gay"
Right up Dr. Demento's alley. The only trouble with novelty songs is that once you've heard them, they're not novelties anymore. That's when what had previously sounded funny starts to sound insulting.

B-52's

Nearly everything that's ever been recorded by these people has been permeated with an ironic-silly ambiance probably stemming from the gayness of the group's male members—"officially" announced in 1992, but an open secret to those in the know long before then. The early "Private Idaho," which coined an ingenious metaphor that later inspired the title of a gayish movie, deserves special mention here. And did you catch Fred Schneider's makeup in the "Deadbeat Club" video?

Black Sabbath — "Fairies Wear Boots"

Among other things. But seriously, folks, this proto-headbanger titillator ("fairies" = elves or homos?) was an early example of just how dumb heavy metal can get.

Blondie — "Little Caesar"

A negligible but indisputable passing reference. "Back in the days of funny funny, they called me queer." But what the heck is "days of funny funny" supposed to mean?

David Bromberg — "Will Not Be Your Fool"

A long, overwrought, stultifying harangue against the narrator's ex-lover (a woman), which includes the line "I'll see that faggot dead" in reference to some primordial proto-lover in her background. Simply hideous.

Miquel Brown — "So Many Men, So Little Time"

An intoxicating period piece from the late-seventies height of disco. Back then it seemed half credo, half satire, all fun. Now, in the wake of the AIDS crisis, it seems to take on an air of tragic foreboding. As good a lesson as any in how historical context can change how we feel about a song.

Buffalo Springfield — "I Am a Child"

A Neil Young rumination on father-son relationships, which some people insist on interpreting homosexually. To each his or her own.

Clovers — "Love Potion No. 9"

A classic single from 1959, remade in 1964 into an even bigger hit by the Searchers. The mysterious title elixir is so potent that it makes the male narrator kiss everything in sight—including a policeman, who promptly smashes the bottle. We can't have that, now can we?

Alice Cooper

Son of a preacher man, the former Vincent Furnier made a name for himself by blending feigned gender ambiguity with gruesomely comical theatrics (straightjackets, hangings, decapitations, and the like), thus confirming in his gullible public's mind a false equation between "queerness" and morbidity. No wonder Philip Core called him "the Dracula of Drag." Yet most likely the only thing gay about it all was the mood of this ex-habitué of *The Hollywood Squares* back when he was accustomed to cashing huge royalty checks.

David Crosby with Phil Collins — "Hero"
Some gay men got all excited when this single came out during the summer of 1993 because it features one man professing his love for another man, even if that other man seems only a fictional character. But the fact that someone can't say that he or she loves another of the same sex without people automatically interpreting it as "gay"—either approvingly or disapprovingly—just shows how screwed up our culture is.

Dead or Alive — "Come Home with Me, Baby"
Banned by the BBC for alleged "homosexual content," though it's largely in the eye of the beholder. But coming from the scandalously androgynous Pete Burns, there's a lot to behold. This song isn't nearly as much fun, however, as their biggest hits—the infectious "You Spin Me Round (Like a Record)" and its peevish follow-up, "Brand New Lover."

Deee-Lite — "Groove Is in the Heart"
Groovy people meet in the back of Bootsy Collins' retro-psychedelic van (the one with the fuzzy bucket seats) to party and discuss the meaning of life with Lady Miss Kier, the finest real-female drag queen since the Divine Miss M herself. She's so good at it that I still sometimes have my suspicions. It may be pantomime gayness, but when it's this much fun, who can complain?

John Denver and Placido Domingo — "Perhaps Love"
Perhaps not. I wanna slap the queen who first suggested this one.

Disco-Tex and the Sex-o-lettes — "Get Dancin'"
Nothing explicitly gay about this—except the way it was performed. I was still in the closet when I saw Sir Monti Rock III and gang do camp with a capital K on *American Bandstand*. I think it helped nudge me out. Feather boas to *die* for. If it was just an act, it was a convincing one.

Double Exposure — "Ten Percent"
It's not what you think—in spite of the multiple connotations of this black disco vocal group's name and the fact that they posed for the back cover of a later album, *Locker Room*, wearing nothing but jockstraps. Though the lyrics have nothing to do with gayness, it's possible that the title "Ten Percent" was purposefully chosen to lure gay consumers. And

don't pretend that somebody didn't have that in mind when they shot that *Locker Room* photo.

Bob Dylan — "Just Like a Woman"

It's been suggested that this *Blonde on Blonde* song concerns a transvestite or transsexual. I wouldn't bet on it, but I suppose you can't dismiss out of hand any lyric that has so many ambiguous "just like a woman" lines, makes all of those references to clothes, jewelry, and drugs, and includes the words "Queen Mary, she's my friend."

Leroy Dysart

It's hard to find this fellow's 1982 album *We Are Everywhere*, released on a small independent label with limited distribution. But for such songs as "I Love a Man" and "A New Gay Dawning," it's worth trying.

Eagles — "Hotel California"

"Pretty, pretty boys" who spend all their time dancing serve as faceless figures of depravity in a thinly veiled extended metaphor about modern-day decadence. Yawn.

Esquerita

According to some sources, this little-known but nonetheless legendary figure in early rock 'n' roll history was barely more than a Little Richard clone. But other reliable sources—including the testimony of Little Richard himself—suggest that he strongly influenced the young Mr. Penniman. Most likely the two influenced each other. And it would seem that Esquerita was every bit as flamboyant as Richard, reportedly as openly gay as the fifties music scene would allow. Esquerita's trailblazing career ended in 1986 with his untimely AIDS-related death.

Diamanda Galás

A relatively little-known performer, though among the most controversial of our time (the Italian government has officially labeled her "blasphemous"), the Greek-American singer-composer Diamanda Galás has been etching her angry mark across the artistic landscape for several years now. She has also participated in ACT-UP protests against the Catholic Church's stand on gay issues. Inspired by the AIDS-related deaths of her brother and a number of friends, as well as assorted cases of the world's injustice and hypocrisy, she has created such serious works as *Plague Mass*, *Vena Cava*, and *Masque of the Red Death*, using and abusing her classically trained voice, augmented by aural and visual effects (such as dousing herself with blood), to shock and move her audiences to heightened awareness. Don't listen to this music unless you're fully prepared to be challenged and disturbed by it.

Gay Choruses

This is in recognition of the numerous gay and lesbian choruses across the country—around 120 of them at last count—which contribute so much to our lives. Knowing that their bread is buttered on both sides, they're usually careful to include both "serious" and popular selections in their repertoires. Several of these groups have recorded albums, including Chicago's Windy City Gay Chorus, the New York City Gay Men's Chorus, the Gay Men's Chorus of Los Angeles, the Twin Cities Gay Men's Chorus, and the San Francisco Gay Men's Chorus. Extra-special kudos to the latter not only for being one of the first, best, biggest, and most prolific of these choruses but also for their unrelenting playfulness in reinterpreting music that often walks a thin line between the worlds of classical and pop. Take, for instance, their rendering of the Sigmund Romberg oldie "Stouthearted Men," found on the album *The San Francisco Gay Men's Chorus Tours America '81*. Somewhat predictable, perhaps (I mean, what gay chorus *hasn't* done it?), but irresistible nonetheless. Best of all, there's the Leonard Bernstein medley on their 1993 album *Brahms, Bernstein, & The Boys*. "Christopher Street" (from the musical *On the Town*) is a real eye-opener, while the *Candide* treasure "Glitter and Be Gay" just *begged* for the embrace of a gay ensemble—although, to be honest, I would have preferred to hear a new transcription employing a male vocal instead of the original female part, sung here by a guest soprano. But it matters little. This stuff is so good, you don't even have to be gay to like it. Of course, it doesn't hurt.

Gloria Gaynor — "I Will Survive"

It's no accident that this Number One smash—a *bona fide* pop classic as well as one of the biggest hits of the disco era—became an anthem for the gay community in 1979 and remained so for several years thereafter. Given all that's happened since then, it resonates more than ever.

Go — "Fear of a Gay Planet"

Pro-gay rap meets nineties-style punk. I've never found the record, but I've heard it on daring alternative radio stations. If you can tolerate all the busy-noise, you'll receive some blunt but healthy messages, such as "What the fuck's wrong with lovin' my own sex?" Maybe Public Enemy (who inspired the title) can learn something from this.

Hair (original cast) — "Sodomy"

A shallow song from a homophobic show whose characters disdain real gayness even as they contemplate fake faggotry as a means of avoiding the draft. "Sodomy" itself is little more than a brief catalog of alleged sexual naughtiness, the musical equivalent of children who delight in shocking their elders via the gratuitous use of no-no words. And spare me that character who claims that Mick Jagger is so fabulous that he'd even "go gay" for him.

Emmylou Harris — "Mister Sandman"

When the Chordettes recorded this near-masterpiece during the pre-dawn of the rock era—1954 to be precise—Liberace was a genuine heart-throb for countless women. By the time Emmylou Harris revived it in 1981, the line about the singer's dream man having "wavy hair like Liber-ace" had acquired a devastating level of irony virtually unrivaled in the body of Western popular music. Hence this song's status as a perennial favorite with gay audiences, for whom irony is a life-sustaining force.

Murray Head — "One Night in Bangkok" (from *Chess*)

The homophobic jabs in this big hit ("The queens we use would not excite you") are among the subtler ones found in the musical *Chess*. Some of those nasty remarks may be designed to illustrate the vile personal-ities of the characters who utter them, but is it only accidental that such cheap humor should come at the expense of gay people?

George Hearn — "I Am What I Am"

The great gay pride song of the American musical theatre, as if there were a lot to choose from. Who would've thought that the big hit tune from *La Cage Aux Folles* would be an anthem of self-assertiveness sung by a drag queen? And what *did* the Broadway tourists from Pocatello think? Inci-dentally, if you don't care for musicals, get Gloria Gaynor's disco remake. Crass but cool.

Heart — "Bébé Le Strange" and "Strange Night"

First the Wilson sisters offer us a lyrical puzzle: it's either a female groupie coming on to a female rock star or a male groupie coming on to a male rock star. Anything else and it wouldn't be so *strange*. Then there's the "Strange Night" in which a young lady tries to persuade a friend—and it sounds like a *male* friend—to dress in drag for a wild night on the town.

The Homosexuals

A little-known British punk-rock band whose 1984 album, *The Homo-sexuals' Record*, demonstrates how gay or gayish sensibilities can come wrapped in even the unlikeliest of guises.

Ice Cube — "Horny Lil' Devil" and "No Vaseline"

Rap vitriol peppered with gay-baiting insults directed at assorted people on Ice Cube's shit-list, including the members of his former group, N.W.A.

Impotent Sea Snakes — "I Wanna Fuck Your Dad"

Unfortunately, I've only read about this one in other sources. It seems the narrator has the hots for his girlfriend's pop. It may be a legend in its own time, but it's a dickens to find.

Michael Jackson — "In the Closet"

A bit of linguistic imperialism in which one of the best-known metaphors from the gay experience is itself made into a metaphor for a secretive heterosexual affair. Nothing more than a tease, and a pretty lame one at that.

Joe Jackson — "Jamie G." and "The Other Me"

Both of these songs come from Jackson's superb, grossly underrated *Laughter and Lust* album. In "Jamie G." the gender of the title character—the object of the narrator's desire—is ambiguous, but Jackson's persona expresses a willingness to "risk all diseases." And then there's "The Other Me," one of the most profoundly sad songs I know. To be sure, being torn between a wife and a lover is not necessarily a bisexual's dilemma, but once again there's nary a clue as to the gender of the third party. And don't you think one would have to put some *effort* into such neutrality?

Mick Jagger — "Memo from Turner"

A collection of condescending insults directed at a group of gayish figures who belong "in the circus" where the narrator (who sounds as though he's had sex with at least some of them) can laugh at them. This is yet another transparent device for fostering Jagger's cultivated image of depravity as he provides his listeners with vicarious thrills, bragging about his supposed adventures among the "low life."

The Jam — "Strange Town"

Which tries to answer the musical question, "What does a confused young man do when he finds himself alone in an unfamiliar city?"

Billy Joel — "Piano Man"

Amidst the other regulars, we find two images of repressed homosexuality—a frustrated bachelor writer and a career sailor—having a conversation over their drinks. Billy Joel may not have *meant* them to be gay, but they sound that way to me.

Elton John — "The Bitch Is Back"

Was he ever gone?

Grace Jones — "I Need a Man"

I could hardly approach the conclusion of this book without mentioning the archly androgynous Grace Jones, whose entire career has been founded on queer sensibilities. "I Need a Man," an early dance-floor hit, provides one of many examples of how her work is predicated on a knowing identification with gay men. And what about that infamous 1980 magazine spread of her kissing another woman, both naked except for shoes, socks, and boxing gloves? That kind of thing transcends mere camp, inhabiting a weird netherworld between sexist self-exploitation and queer revolution. If only it hadn't been in *Hustler*.

Rickie Lee Jones — "Easy Money"

In this sordid and amusing narrative about street hookers, pimps, and johns, where everybody's out to scam everybody else, there's that bit about the "cat" who proposes to a boy, "Come up to my room and play with my toy." More obtuse than it sounds ("toy" could refer to a prostitute of the female persuasion), but it sounds intriguing nonetheless.

Jose and Luis — "The Queen's English"

Hot, hot house music—perfect for voguing if that weren't so passé now —by a couple of Latino fellas who sing and rap (with very *knowing* voices) lyrics that consist primarily of the repeated question "Do you know the Queen's English?" Somehow I suspect that most of the people who'll hear this record would answer in the affirmative.

Kitchens of Distinction — "Hammer"

A brutal, feedback-laden assault on your senses that evokes the spectre of death hovering over sex in the age of AIDS. The metaphor couldn't be simpler: if you're not careful, you could get crushed.

Cyndi Lauper — "He's So Unusual"

Witness the anxiety of a Betty Boop clone. She's terribly worried about her boyfriend, who doesn't seem the least bit interested in making love to her. It must have been a hoot even in 1929, when it was written. I just want to know how Lauper *found* this thing in the first place.

LL Cool J — "Rock the Bells"

This one includes some mighty dissin' of various rock stars, including a clever but homophobic pun involving the word "mince" in reference to Michael Jackson and Prince.

Madonna

Never before has a performer so shrewdly courted the gay audience and so successfully mined its sensibilities for fun and profit. Having early on realized that the core of her initial dance-club constituency consisted of gay men, she set about expanding on that base by transforming herself into a sieve through which quasi-gayness could be made palatable to youth culture at large.

The evidence is staggering. She publicly outed her own brother and played coy is-she-or-isn't-she lesbian guessing games on nationwide television, with Sandra Bernhard as witting and David Letterman as unwitting co-conspirators. In her "Open Your Heart" video, a woman in male drag appears among the customers who watch Madonna perform in a sleazy Italian peep-show. (And aren't those cheek-to-cheek identical twins dressed in naval uniforms a bizarre touch?) In "Vogue" she took a dance style invented by gay African-Americans and, aptly enough, turned it into one of the gayest things ever seen on MTV. Her *Truth or Dare* movie merely made it official. The "Justify My Love" video was banned by MTV largely because of brief but blatantly bisexual scenes, which naturally guaranteed mondo sales of the uncut video. (Whatever else you may think of Madonna, you have to admire her business acumen.) More recently, "This Used to Be My Playground" may be precisely what some gay commentators have said it is: an elegy grown out of the AIDS crisis. And she's even reported to have stated that she hopes her first child is gay.

Unfortunately, Madonna's stock seems to be in decline of late—largely, I suspect, as a reaction to her notorious 1992 *Sex* picture-book. She will, however, remain a gay icon forever, or at least as long as forever lasts in pop culture, or at least as long as she doesn't do as Donna Summer was alleged to have done and stab her gay fans in the back. (More about that shortly.)

Barry Manilow — "I Made It Through the Rain" and "One Voice"
If you can poo-poo these two, you're even more cynical than I am.

Marilyn
For a while there it looked as if a very androgynous British singer named Marilyn would follow Boy George as the next big gender-twisting thing in popular music. (Rumor had it that the two were former lovers.) It didn't happen, at least not in the States, though Marilyn did manage to turn out four U.K. hits in the early eighties before vanishing as suddenly as he had appeared. You can catch a glimpse of him, however, as a guest star in the Eurythmics' brilliant "Who's That Girl?" video, in which Annie Lennox, playing both male and female roles, kisses herself via the miracle of modern videography. Essential viewing.

Marky Mark and the Funky Bunch — "Wildside"
For his tasteless, unimaginative sampling of Lou Reed's classic—plus his transformation of the line "Take a walk on the wild side" into a synonym

for murderous criminality—Marky Mark Dahlberg deserves at least a mild reproach from right-thinking people everywhere. And don't let him sway you with that tacky dropping-the-pants act of his, either. This guy's over-exposed in more ways than one.

Daniel Martin & Michael Biello — "Clones in Love"

A funny technopop dance track from 1985 that both glorifies and parodies the sexy, hedonistic pleasures of the narcissistic "clone mentality." The narrator enthuses about how great it is to have a well-muscled mirror-image man with whom one can work out at Nautilus, discuss diets and poodles, and go disco dancing in sweaty Izod shirts. Brilliant in a sardonic sort of way. Also look for their cassette *Homo Love Songs*.

Paul McCartney and Wings — "Jet"

From the immeasurably talented man who gave us "Ob-La-Di, Ob-La-Da," another meaningless excuse for would-be snickering. Even considering the basic triviality of this astoundingly catchy bit of fluff, what's with the repeated "I thought that the major was a little lady suffragette?" My guess is that it means absolutely nothing aside from a lame effort to make listeners *think* it means something naughty. Roughly on a par with fart jokes, though considerably more enjoyable to listen to.

Paul McCrane — "Is It Okay If I Call You Mine?" (from *Fame*)

A dour song by a dour character. More than one commentator has noted the ludicrousness of *Fame*'s depiction of a lone (and lonely) gay student at New York's High School of the Performing Arts, which surely in real life has a much higher percentage of gay people than your average school. Yet they had the gall to title the climactic number after a Walt Whitman poem.

George Michael — "Freedom"

This catchy, insistently danceable track (also known as "Freedom '90" to distinguish it from an earlier Wham! hit of the same name) is widely recognized as one of Michael's first salvos in his battle to overcome the sex-symbol image he had developed for himself, which proved at best to be a mixed blessing. Michael confesses that it's time to convert lies into truths, that there's something "deep inside" of him yearning to get out, and that there's someone that he "forgot to be." I'm not saying that this necessarily means anything in particular, but you're free to draw your own conclusions.

Miracles — "Ain't Nobody Straight in L.A."

Again, it's *not* what you think. "Straight" does *not* necessarily mean "heterosexual." (*Re* also Ian Dury's "I Want to Be Straight.")

Morrissey — "Lucky Lisp" and "Hairdresser on Fire"

As I said before, the driest wit in rock. But the prevarications can get damn annoying.

New York Dolls

An extremely influential but commercially unsuccessful glitter-rock band of the mid-seventies. With their heavy makeup and propensity toward fishnet, they took the gender-bending aspect of glam about as far as it could go without breaking the law onstage. Yet from all indications it was just another instance of "it's only an act," with little or nothing gay beneath the surface. Years later, former Doll David Johansen would record the popular novelty tune, "Hot, Hot, Hot" in the guise of Buster Poindexter, a nightmare incarnation of a tasteless, talentless lounge singer. In other words, Johansen simply switched from one form of camp to another.

Olivia Newton-John — "Physical"

The video for one of the biggest hit singles of all time has a punch line in which gorgeous muscle-boys are far more interested in each other than in Olivia.

The Nylons — "Rise Up"

"We want the freedom to love who we please." Any questions? Extra credit for anyone who can propound in fifty words or less the full implications of this *a cappella* vocal group's name in terms of both gay culture and pop music history.

Paul Parker — "Right on Target"

I remember dancing my fool head off to this one. With the essential assistance of Patrick Cowley, the very handsome Mr. Parker—slightly flat singing and all—created one of *the* immortal gay disco seduction stomps.

Pogues — "The Old Main Drag," "Transmetropolitan," and "Fairytale of New York"

Gritty but poetic tales from the underside of modern life, as relentlessly bleak as they are Irish. What a shame that the "gay" figures here are "poofs," "queers," and "faggots" who are invariably lumped together with "drunks," "whores," and "lechers."

Eric Presland

Especially popular with gay audiences in Britain, Presland is known for his satirical songs. His 1984 live album *File Under Gay* boasts such key numbers as "Invisible People," "What Do You Do in Bed?" and the historically oriented "We Were in There."

Robert Preston — "Gay Paree" (from *Victor Victoria*)
You didn't think I'd forget this, did you?

Procol Harum — "Simple Sister"
A truly warped tune in which Gary Brooker sings of locking up his sister so that he can "wear her clothes" and "steal her beaus." His persona could well be female, but it's genderfuck nonetheless. Moreover, it shows Procol at their most majestically stupid. I love it.

The Queers
These spiritual grandchildren of the Ramones repeatedly refer to themselves as "Queer" (with a capital Q), but I can't tell whether that's a profession of gayness or an appropriation by "straights" who somehow fancy an identification with real homos. If they really are queer, then the album *Love Songs for the Retarded* demonstrates that the gay generation gap may be even wider than we feared.

Shabba Ranks
A reggae star who stated on British television that gay people should be "crucified." 'Nuff said.

R.E.M. — "Losing My Religion"
Some people read gay interpretations into the lyrics of this wonderful song, but I prefer to look at the video, with its wealth of gay iconography (most notably Saint Sebastian). Of course, most viewers just wonder what the hell is going on.

Replacements — "Androgynous"
"Something meets boy, something meets girl." *Huh?*

Revolting Cocks — "Beers, Steers, and Queers"
Cacophonous industrial white-boy art-rap in which the title cliché, a notorious intended put-down of Texas, is used to—what else?—put down Texas. Either that or it's a perverse tribute to the Lone Star State. It even opens with a passing reference to the Village People. I can't decide whether it's nifty or despicable. Maybe both.

Smokey Robinson — "Cruisin'"
No, this gorgeous song had nothing to do whatsoever with that dreadful film of almost the same name. (The movie's title was *Cruising*, with the *g*.)

Tom Robinson — "The Wedding"

An expression of anger at seeing one's ex-boyfriend get married. And the line "It isn't the bride that I want to kiss" may be more than a dig at matrimonial tradition; a few years earlier Elton John had scored a major hit with a song whose chief recurring line was "I wanna kiss the bride," which the activist Robinson may have found galling coming from the then-ambivalent Elton.

Rolling Stones — "(I Can't Get No) Satisfaction"

Many believe that women in general are the chief source of the narrator's lack of satisfaction. But from where I'm sitting, it's only wishful thinking to read gayness into it. Misogyny, to be sure, but not gayness.

Rolling Stones — "When the Whip Comes Down" and "Rocks Off"

I've read that "When the Whip Comes Down" contains references to homosexual S&M, but damn if I can tell. The vocals are so far down in the mix that the only clause I can make out is the title. Meanwhile, in "Rocks Off" Jagger asks, "What's the matter with the boy?" If you ask me it just sounds like more posturing from rock's perennial king of fashionable decadence. Don't waste your time with penny-ante teases like this. If you *really* want the dirt, read Christopher Andersen's unauthorized biography, which depicts Jagger as something of a bisexual Casanova.

Diana Ross — "Muscles"

So what if Michael Jackson wrote this lusty ode to male muscularity? Just because Gerry Goffin wrote the words to then-wife Carole King's "(You Make Me Feel Like) A Natural Woman" certainly doesn't mean that he's a transsexual. If I had a dollar for every song written by a male from a female viewpoint for a female singer, I could retire quite comfortably to Key West right now.

Todd Rundgren — "Is It My Name?"

"My voice goes so high, you would think I was gay." Only if you believe in stereotypes. But since Todd's *A Wizard, A True Star* album is awash in comedy, much of it self-effacing, it would be humorless to take offense.

Schoolly D — "Signifying Rapper" and "No More Rock 'n' Roll"

The first is a classic rap narrative that liberally uses such words as "faggot," "dyke," and "whore" in portraying life on the mean streets of urban America. The second demonstrates how homophobia can be conveniently enlisted in the service of other prejudices: rock and roll is "a thing of the past," so "all you long-haired faggots can kiss my ass."

Screeching Weasel with Bruce La Bruce — "I Wanna Be a Homosexual"
I'm cheating on this one. I've never heard it (very hard to find), but I've read good things about it in the gay press. And I just *had* to include it for the group name, if for no other reason.

Neil Sedaka — "Stephen"
About as close to a male-to-male love song as you can get without coming right out, in a manner of speaking, and saying so.

Sister Double Happiness — "On the Beach" and "Freight Train"
According to lead singer Gary Floyd, these songs (from the band's eponymous debut album) are "screams of agony" that arose from his anxiety over waiting for the results of his HIV test. That's something an increasingly large number of people, gay and otherwise, can identify with.

Frank Sinatra — "Strangers in the Night"
Pre-Stonewall gay audiences eagerly adopted this intensely romantic play-by-play account of that mating ritual known as "cruising." The Chairman of the Board may not like it, but he has no say in the matter.

Skyhooks — "Straight in a Gay Gay World"
Awkward heterosexist paranoia from a deservedly obscure band. I think this is meant to be a satire, but of *what* I'm not sure.

The Smiths — "Vicar in a Tutu"
"He's *not* strange!" While it would be tempting to say, "Methinks he doth protest too much," I actually suspect there's great truth at work here. But as far as lessons in open-mindedness go, I've heard more convincing ones.

Stories — "Another Love"
This group specialized in songs with a "forbidden love" theme. Their only big hit, 1973's "Brother Louie," told of a white guy who dismays his family and friends by falling in love with a black woman. "Another Love," an obscure single from the following year, flopped, possibly because the subject this time was bisexuality.

Barbra Streisand — "Somewhere"
The famous "there's a place for us" song composed by Bernstein and Sondheim for *West Side Story*. Streisand donated half of the proceeds from her *Broadway Album* rendition to AIDS-related charities. Truly admirable, but I'm not the first to say that it would have been even nicer had the video included at least one gay couple along with all of those other folks who were apparently there to symbolize what the song is all about.

Donna Summer

Summer became the Queen of Disco—and, in the year 1979, the undisputed Queen of Pop overall—by working with producer Giorgio Moroder to generate a body of high-quality Europop that focused almost exclusively on the twin obsessions of late seventies gay male culture: dance and sex. In so doing she made herself a gay icon, her hit singles intensely camp exercises in musical sexploitation.

To cite the best examples, we have "Love to Love You Baby" (simulated multiple-orgasmic sex), "I Feel Love" (robotic, mechanized sex), "Last Dance" (the last chance for a night of sex), "Hot Stuff" (extremely horny demands for sex), and "Bad Girls" (sympathy for practitioners of illegal professional sex). Gay men formed the heart of her audience, and when they abandoned her—in the wake of stories, now disputed by Summer, of her preaching against gayness following a well-publicized "born again" experience—her commercial appeal fell dramatically. Her career has yet to rebound fully. Which just goes to show how risky it is to bite the gay hand that feeds you, even if the biting may only be apocryphal.

10,000 Maniacs — "Hey, Jack Kerouac"

This tribute to the Beat Generation includes a matter-of-fact nod to the homosexuality of poet Allen Ginsberg: "Allen, baby, why so jaded? Have the boys all grown up and their beauty faded?"

Thompson Twins — "Queer"

Can avowed heterosexuals rightly lay claim to the word "queer"? Yes, they can, and in so doing make a statement about the evil of turning labels into weapons.

Traffic — "Low Spark of High-Heeled Boys"

If only for the title. You know, I've surely heard this song a hundred times or more through the years, and I *still* don't know what it means.

T-Rex — "Rip Off"

One of the definitive works of glam rock. When the late Marc Bolan (reportedly a bisexual) sang, "I'm the King of the highway, I'm the Queen of the hop," everyone knew what he was implying—if not confessing.

Village People — "Hot Cop" and "My Roommate"

Need I say more?

Voice Farm

Purveyors of the wackiest dance pop since the prime years of the B-52's. This San Francisco trio samples liberally from television and sundry other sources, punctuating the beat with some of the most off-the-wall commentary you're likely to hear this side of a gay gossip-columnists' convention. Speaking of gay, lead singer Charly Brown is openly so, and his vocals are as out of the closet as he is. If you like non-hardcore techno with a goofy sense of humor, check out Voice Farm's 1991 album *Bigger Cooler Weirder*. The first time I heard "Free Love" I couldn't help but smile, "Thank You" made me laugh out loud, and the recited "Ode to Buffy," with its speculation about deviant practices on the sets of *Family Affair* and *Gilligan's Island*, convinced me once and for all that it has indeed been a long, strange ride since the coda to "Nights in White Satin."

Wall of Voodoo — "Can't Make Love"
A cry of bisexual angst. The narrator is so torn between his attraction for both males and females that he can't seem to get it on with anyone. What was it that Alvin Toffler said about "overchoice"?

Weather Girls — "It's Raining Men"
Two former backup singers for Sylvester deliver a disco fantasy spectacular complete with pseudo-gospel embellishments. An incomparable drag number—except, of course, it's performed by real, live women.

Wham! — "Young Guns (Go for It)" and "Bad Boys"
I don't know about you, but I never doubted Andrew Ridgely's valuable contributions to his brief but profitable partnership with George Michael. Catch the videos, if you can find them.

Wild Fantasy — "Jungle Drums"
The capitalistic apotheosis of the music industry's awareness of the purchasing power of gay people. The nondescript disco music is instantly forgettable. But who can forget the album cover, the front of which shows two women, naked save for loincloths, a drum sandwiched between them, obviously kissing, though the lips are just barely cut off from view? And the back cover repeats the scene, but this time with two men. (I can hear it now: "Make damn sure you put the more offensive perversion—the one less appealing to voyeuristic heterosexual males—on the back.") I wonder how many people bought this on the basis of the cover alone. You did? See, it worked.

. . . plus everything by Tom Robinson, Sylvester, Jimmy Somerville, and every other artist who's been openly gay from Day One.
Now, what have I left out?

▪ S E L E C T E D   B I B L I O G R A P H Y ▪

Aaron, James (pseudonym). *The Gay Trivia Quiz Book.* New York: Arbor House Publishing Company, 1985.

The Alyson Almanac: A Treasury of Information for the Gay and Lesbian Community. Expanded new edition. Compiled by the staff of Alyson Publications. Boston: Alyson Publications, Inc., 1990.

Avicolli, Tommi. "Images of Gays in Rock Music." *Lavender Culture.* Jay, Karla and Allen Young, editors. New York: Jove/HBJ Books, 1978, pages 182–194.

Bonanno, Massimo. *The Rolling Stones Chronicle: The First Thirty Years.* New York: Henry Holt and Company, 1990.

Braindrop, Lily, *et al.* "Queer Music." *The Advocate,* 587 (October 8, 1991), pp. 37–44.

Bronson, Fred. *The Billboard Book of Number One Hits.* Revised and enlarged edition. New York: Billboard Publications, Inc. 1988.

Chambers, Ian. *Urban Rhythms: Pop Music and Popular Culture.* New York: St. Martin's Press, 1985.

Coleman, Ray. *Lennon.* New York: McGraw-Hill Book Company, 1984.

Core, Philip. *Camp: The Lie That Tells the Truth.* New York: Delilah Books, 1984.

Costello, Mark and David Foster Wallace. *Signifying Rappers.* New York: Ecco Press, 1990.

Denselow, Robin, *When the Music's Over: The Story of Political Pop.* London: Faber and Faber, 1989.

Dowlding, William J. *Beatlesongs.* New York: Fireside, 1989.

Dynes, Wayne R., editor. *The Encyclopedia of Homosexuality.* Two volumes. New York: Garland Publishing, Inc., 1990.

Fletcher, Lynne Yamaguchi and Adrien Saks. *Lavender Lists: New Lists About Lesbian and Gay Culture, History, and Personalities.* Boston: Alyson Publications, Inc., 1990.

Gammond, Peter. *The Oxford Companion to Popular Music.* Oxford: Oxford University Press, 1991.

Goldstein, Richard, editor. *The Poetry of Rock.* New York: Bantam Books, Inc., 1969.

Green, Jonathon, compiler. *The Book of Rock Quotes.* New York: Delilah/Putnam, 1982.

Hadleigh, Boze. *The Vinyl Closet: Gays in the Music World.* San Diego: Los Hombres Press, 1990.

Hardy, Phil and Dave Laing. *The Faber Companion to 20th-Century Popular Music.* London: Faber and Faber, 1990.

Hill, Dave. *Designer Boys and Material Girls: Manufacturing the '80s Pop Dream.* New York: Sterling Publishing Company, 1986.

Huston, John. "All My Friends Are Girls Wrapped in Boys: Gender in Pop." *Christopher Street,* 144 (February 1989), pp. 16–23.

Jacobs, Dick. *Who Wrote That Song?* White Hall, Virginia: Betterway Publications, Inc., 1988.

Jay, Karla and Allen Young, editors. *Lavender Culture*. New York: Jove/HBJ Books, 1978.

Macken, Bob, Peter Fornatale, and Bill Ayers. *The Rock Music Sourcebook*. Garden City, N.Y.: Anchor Books, 1980.

Marsh, Dave. *The Heart of Rock & Soul: The 1001 Greatest Singles Ever Made*. New York: New American Library, 1989.

Marsh, Dave and Kevin Stein. *The Book of Rock Lists*. New York: Dell/Rolling Stone Press, 1981.

Nelson, Havelock and Michael Gonzales. *Bring the Noise: A Guide to Rap Music and Hip-Hop Culture*. New York: Harmony Books, 1991.

Pareles, Jon and Patricia Romanowski, editors. *The Rolling Stone Encyclopedia of Rock & Roll*. New York: Rolling Stone Press/Summit Books, 1983.

Peters, Dan and Steve Peters, with Cher Merrill. *Why Knock Rock?* Minneapolis: Bethany House Publishers, 1984.

Preston, John, editor. *The Big Gay Book: A Man's Survival Guide for the 90's*. New York: Plume, 1991.

Russell, J.P. *The Beatles on Record*. New York: Charles Scribner's Sons, 1982.

Russo, Vito. *The Celluloid Closet: Homosexuality in the Movies*. New York: Harper and Row, 1981.

Rutledge, Leigh W. *The Gay Book of Lists*. Boston: Alyson Publications, Inc., 1987.

Rutledge, Leigh W. *The Gay Decades*. New York: Plume, 1992.

Rutledge, Leigh W. *The Gay Fireside Companion*. Boston: Alyson Publications, Inc., 1989.

Savage, Jon. *The Kinks: The Official Biography*. London: Faber and Faber, 1984.

Shannon, Bob and John Javna. *Behind the Hits*. New York: Warner Books, Inc., 1986.

Stambler, Irwin. *The Encyclopedia of Pop, Rock, and Soul*. Revised edition. New York: St. Martin's Press, 1989.

Whitburn, Joel, editor. *The Billboard Book of Top 40 Albums*. Revised and enlarged second edition. New York: Billboard Books, 1991.

Whitburn, Joel, editor. *The Billboard Book of Top 40 Hits*. Fifth edition. New York: Billboard Books, 1992.

Whitburn, Joel, editor. *Top Pop Albums, 1955–1992*. Menomonee Falls, Wisconsin: Record Research, Inc., 1993.

Whitburn, Joel, editor. *Top Pop Singles, 1955–1990*. Menomonee Falls, Wisconsin: Record Research, Inc., 1991.

White, Charles. *The Life and Times of Little Richard*. New York: Pocket Books, 1984.

Williams, Paul. *Rock and Roll: The 100 Best Singles*. New York: Carroll & Graf Publishers, Inc., 1993.

The following index lists the songs that are discussed or at least mentioned with regard to the topic of "gayness" in popular music. Other songs that are mentioned in passing only for the purpose of providing background information about an artist or to make some other point not directly related to this book's central topic are not listed.

BOOKS FROM LEYLAND PUBLICATIONS / G.S PRESS